MOUNTAIN BIKE
ALASKA

49 Trails in the 49th State

Published by Glacier House Publications
P.O. Box 201901 Anchorage, Alaska 99520

Produced and printed in Alaska

Printed by A T Publishing & Printing, Inc.
1041 E 76th Ave., Suite C Anchorage, Alaska 99518-3215

First printing, Fall 1991

Edited by Mitch Lipka
Design and layout by the author
Illustrations and photos by the author

Cover Photo:
Stephan Mitchell of Borealis Backcountry Cycling
stands victorious after completing a 90-mile ride that crossed
4 mountain passes and traversed Denali National Park.
In the background, the Alaska Range and mighty Mt. McKinley (20,320 ft.).

ISBN 0-944780-05-9

This book is dedicated to my father, Jack R. Larson, who guided me to the mountains and valleys beyond the big cities. This one is for you dad.

49 Trails in the 49th State

THANKS TO....

An enormous amount of time and energy has gone into the making of this trail guide. Without the support and encouragement from friends, or the cooperation of government agencies, this project would not have been finished. I thank everyone who helped.

Special bell ringing thanks to the following:

Kathy Larson
Scott 'n Suzi Nissenson
Alan Colter, Cycles North
Sage Cohen, proofreading
Relo Alaska, vehicle support
Marc Bravo, off-road support
Mike Dinneen, photo assistance
Doug Van Reeth, photo assistance
Bob Honda for topo map assistance
Arctic Bicycle Club/Mountain Bikers
Larry Kajdan, BLM Glennallen District
Chuck and Fran Morton of Bicycle R & R
Dave Thorp at Glacier House Publications
Steve and Teresa of Borealis Backcountry Cycling
Dohnn Wood with the Bicycle Department of the Motorcycle Shop
Every lodge owner, gas station attendant, bartender, waitress, hotel manager, miner, hunter, ranger and local resident that offered information or assistance.
thank you

This book is funded in part by Dan Bull and the Bull family. Dan, in the mid 1980s, founded Mountain Bikers of Alaska, an organization that sponsored races and professional mountain bike tours in southcentral Alaska. Dan's enthusiasm for the sport has given us several long-distance biking events, such as the famous 200-mile Iditabike (now called IditaSport), the 1,100-mile Nome Odyssey, a 358-mile winter road race from Anchorage to Fairbanks on New Years day and the 60-mile Chitina to McCarthy Fat Tire Festival.

Some of the information used in this book was gathered from the numerous printed flyers and handouts that city, borough, state and federal agencies have printed for public use. My thanks to them all.

It is interesting to note that most of the trails listed in this guide book were originally established through the labor of hard working miners. Because of their endeavors, a multitude of user groups enjoy access to backcountry Alaska.

INTRODUCTION

This book was written to provide the growing number of mountain bike owners with a simple trail guide to many of the established trails in southcentral Alaska. This selection offers a diverse trail menu for all skill levels in a variety of settings. An invitation to ride somewhere new and exciting, to experience the Alaska countryside on a mountain bike. Enjoy the wooded waterways, alpine uplands and coastal valleys that are home to a wide variety of flora and fauna.

The mountain bike owner will find within these pages 49 trails ranging from family picnic rides to strenuous mountain treks. A few of the author's personal favorites include: trail 6 (Powerline Pass), trail 15 (Russian Lakes), trail 17 (Eklutna Glacier), trail 28 (Syncline Mt. Loop), trail 45 (Nugget Creek) and the Mt. McKinley triad consisting of trail 31 (Petersville Rd.), trail 32 (Denali Park Rd.) and trail 34 (Ferry Trail). This triad offers wonderful views of the south peak, the north peak and both peaks, respectively.

Enjoy the rides, the countryside and the exercise. And remember, share the trail.

WARNING

Most of the trails described in this book take the rider into remote Alaska, where numerous hazards exist. To participate in backcountry rides, a cyclist must be able to surmount numerous hills, cross streams and rivers, handle changing weather, tolerate rough trail conditions, deal with hordes of mosquitoes and travel into country that is home to bear, moose and other wild animals. Erosion and other factors may alter trail conditions. Negotiating swift rivers, steep hills, large rocks, long distances and other obstacles can be dangerous.

This is not a handbook on backcountry riding techniques. Prepare yourself before heading onto a trail. Take classes, read books, do workshops and practice before venturing onto backcountry trails. The decision to do a mountain bike ride lies with the rider. Each rider is responsible for learning the skills needed to participate in that ride.

Just because a trail is listed in this book does not mean that it is safe. The backcountry cyclist should use common sense. Not every trail is for every rider. If a trail looks unsafe to you, don't ride on it. Don't take a trail that is beyond your ability. It's better to walk away so you can ride another day.

Land ownership and or the rules governing land management can change. A private landowner may prevent, at a future date, access across their land, thus blocking access to a backcountry trail. Always check with controlling officials about land status before doing a backcountry ride.

The author and publisher are not responsible for your safety and assume no liability in the event of accident, injury, death or property damage on any of the trails listed in this book.

49 Trails in the 49th State

SOUTHCENTRAL

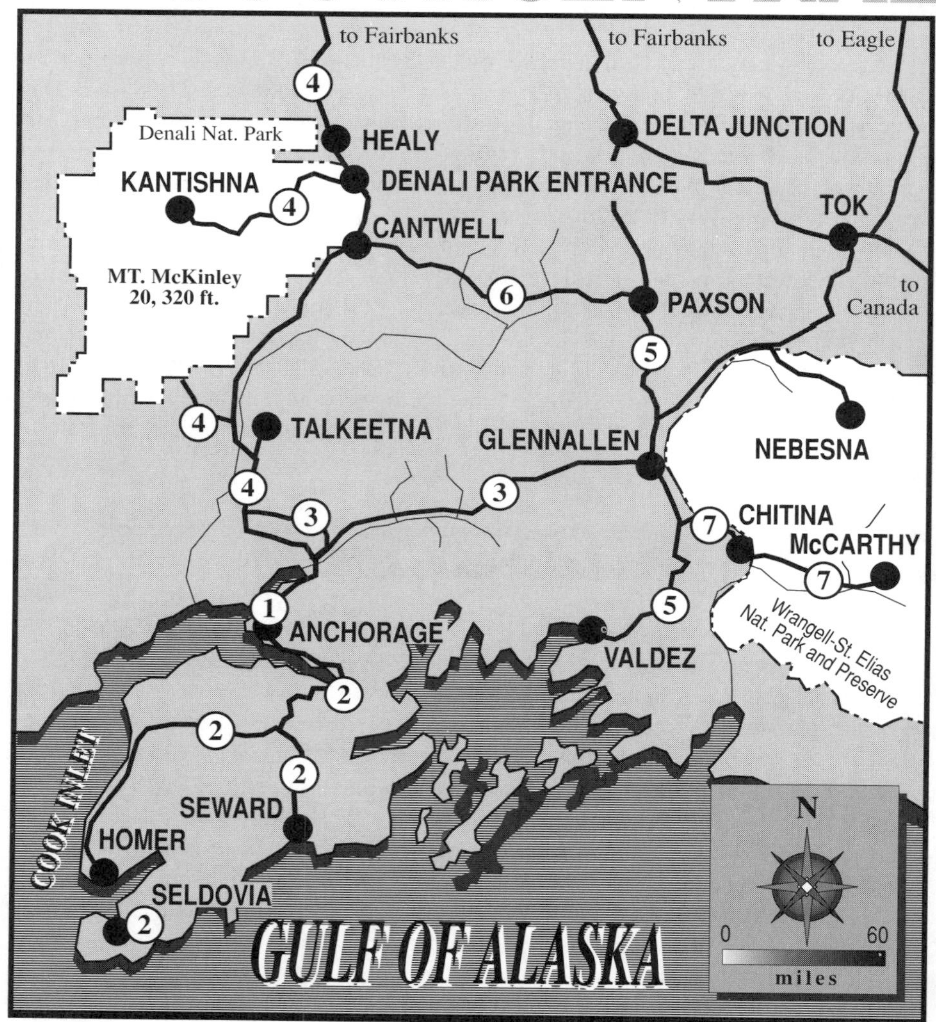

area	chapter
ANCHORAGE	1
KENAI PENINSULA	2
GLENN HIGHWAY	3
PARKS HIGHWAY	4
RICHARDSON HIGHWAY	5
DENALI HIGHWAY	6
EDGERTON HIGHWAY	7
WINTER TRAILS	8

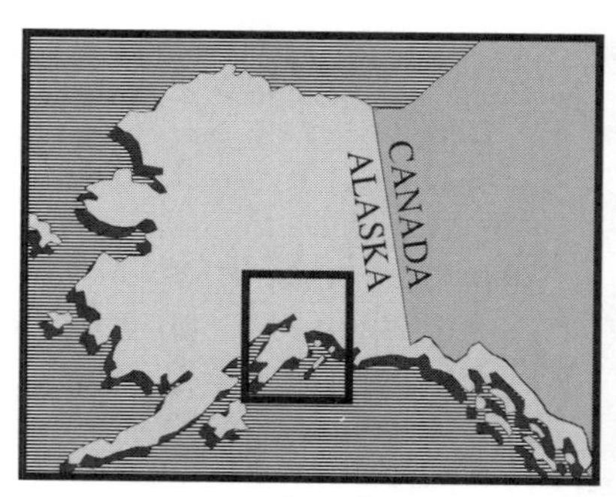

map location

49 Trails in the 49th State

TRAIL MENU

49 Trails in the 49th State

USING this GUIDE

The trails in this guide are grouped into 8 chapters, according to where individual trails are accessed from. Each chapter is introduced with two pages. The first page is an overview map, showing the general area and where each trail lies in that specific area. The second page gives a general description of the area, a brief summary of the trails and a blank area for personal trail notes. Use it to keep records of who rode with you on what day, weather information, favorite spots, trail conditions, how far you went, how long it took, etc.

Each trail has two pages. The first is a U.S.G.S. topographical map with the trail highlighted. The second page has a descriptive trail narrative, an information box called "AT A GLANCE" and a black bar at the bottom which indicates what mountain range this trail rides into.

The first paragraph of the trail narrative describes the general area. The second paragraph gives general trail information. The third paragraph gives specific trail and camping information. The "AT A GLANCE" box provides quick information that is useful in selecting a new trail.

TRAILHEAD: tells what mile and what road the trail head is located at. Only one given, see text for others.

FROM ANCHORAGE: tells the distance from Anchorage to trailhead.

LENGTH OF TRAIL: tells how many miles each trail is. Miles given are always approximate. "Round trip," indicates a trail that goes in and comes out on the same trail. "One-way," indicates a trail with multiple trailheads.

RIDING TIME: tells approximately how long it takes to complete this ride. It includes short breaks, lunch and stopping for photos.

DIFFICULTY: trails are rated on a sliding scale of 1 to 5, with 5 being most difficult. Overall trail conditions dictate the rating, even though a section or two may warrant a higher or lower rating. Multiple ratings reflect a trail that exhibits characteristics from both ratings. The ratings are:

1 a flat, easy trail.
2 a dirt surface and a few hills.
3 a rough surface, numerous hills, mudholes and stream crossings.
4 a long trail with a rough surface, large rocks, big hills and lots of water crossings.
5 indicates a long hill climb with possible pushing. Rocks, potholes and stream crossings may be encountered.

LOW POINT: tells the lowest point according to U.S.G.S. topographic maps.

HIGH POINT: tells the highest point according to U.S.G.S. topographic maps.

ELEVATION GAIN: simple subtraction of low point and high point. Does not include actual cumulative gain.

U.S.G.S. MAPS: tells what topographical maps you should bring for each ride.

Use the provided check-off boxes on the Trail Menu to keep track of your trail rides.

Several different bicycle computers were used to do this guide and each gave a little different reading. All distances and times should be used as rough guides only.

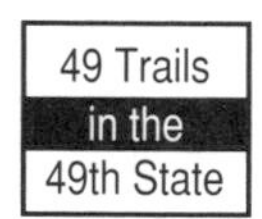

RULES of the TRAIL

Although mountain bikes have been around for a number of years, our impact on the environment and on other trail users is still being determined. We will be judged by how we act. Ride in control, with a friendly disposition, and respect the environment you are cycling into.

RIDE ON OPEN TRAILS ONLY - Respect trail and road closures (ask, if not sure), avoid possible trespass on private land.

LEAVE NO TRACE - Even on open trails, you should not ride under conditions where you will leave evidence of you passing. Practice low-impact cycling. Brake in a controlled manner: refrain from skidding the rear tire. Pack out a little more than you brought in. Clean trails are for everyone! If you must have a camp fire, use an existing fire pit or fire ring.

SHARE THE TRAIL - Give advanced warning when approaching anyone on the trails. Remember, a speeding bicycle in not only threatening but dangerous. In passing horses, use special care, ride slowly and ask the equestrian for special instructions. Pass everyone in a friendly manner. Smiles and a polite exchange will promote better feeling towards bikers.

ANIMALS - All animals are startled by an unannounced approach. Harassing wild animals is a serious offense. Treat bears with respect. Make noise by singing songs, talking out loud and wearing bear bells. Several brands of bear repellant are on the market.

PLAN AHEAD - Know your equipment, your ability and the area in which you are riding and prepare accordingly. Be self-sufficient at all times. Carry and know how to use a first aid kit and a tool kit.

WEAR YOUR HELMET - modern materials and designs are providing the cyclist with a variety of lightweight helmets with good ventilation. Most head injuries can be avoided by wearing a helmet.

DRINKING WATER - Water is very plentiful in the back country and usually can be found every couple of miles.

TREAT YOUR DRINKING WATER - *Giardia lamblia* is ("beaver fever"), a water borne microorganism, causes intestinal problems. Boil all water for 5 minutes, or use an iodine water purifier or a water filter pump that removes giardia.

RIVERS & STREAMS - Before crossing any moving water, check its depth. Using a long stick as a probe, carefully cross the moving water without your bike. Do not enter water that is too deep or too swift. Keep your bicycle on the downriver side of you to prevent being trapped by it in the event of a fall.

chapter 1

ANCHORAGE

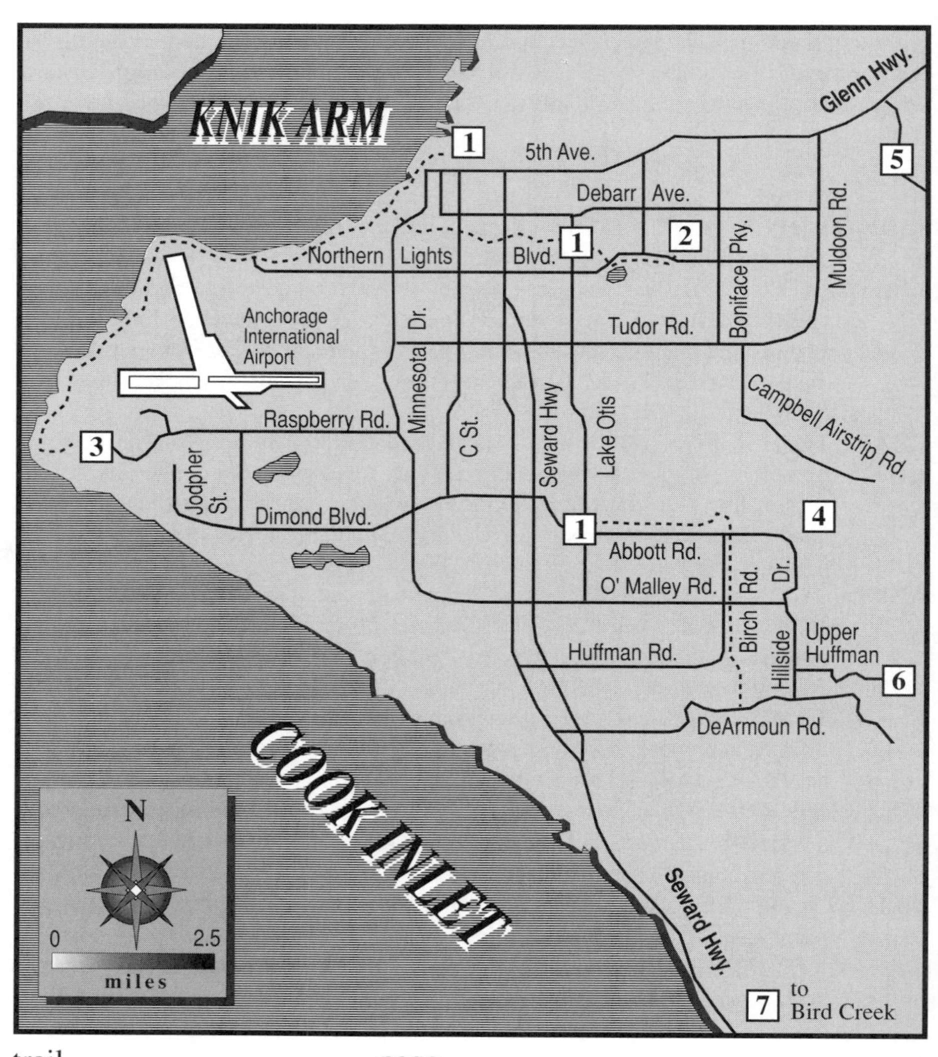

Anchorage is Alaska's largest city, an urban center that is home to more than a half dozen bike shops to meet your cycling needs. The Arctic Bicycle Club, a local organization, welcomes new members and sponsors an impressive racing and touring schedule for road bikes and mountain bikes. Also located within the city limits are many of the state, federal and city offices that regulate the lands we ride on (see Agency Information for additional information).

The Anchorage Bowl harbors countless trails which crisscross residential and urban areas. Described in this chapter are 7 established trails that are very popular with the biking community. The most popular is the scenic Tony Knowles Coastal Trail. This, must-do bike path is paved and a delight to ride. Trails 2, 3, and 4, are on maintained cross country ski trails which provide endless hours of fun riding for all skill levels. Powerline Pass, trail 6, is less than an hour from downtown and offers mud holes, rocky hills and stream crossings in a mountain setting, like most of the back country trails in this guide.

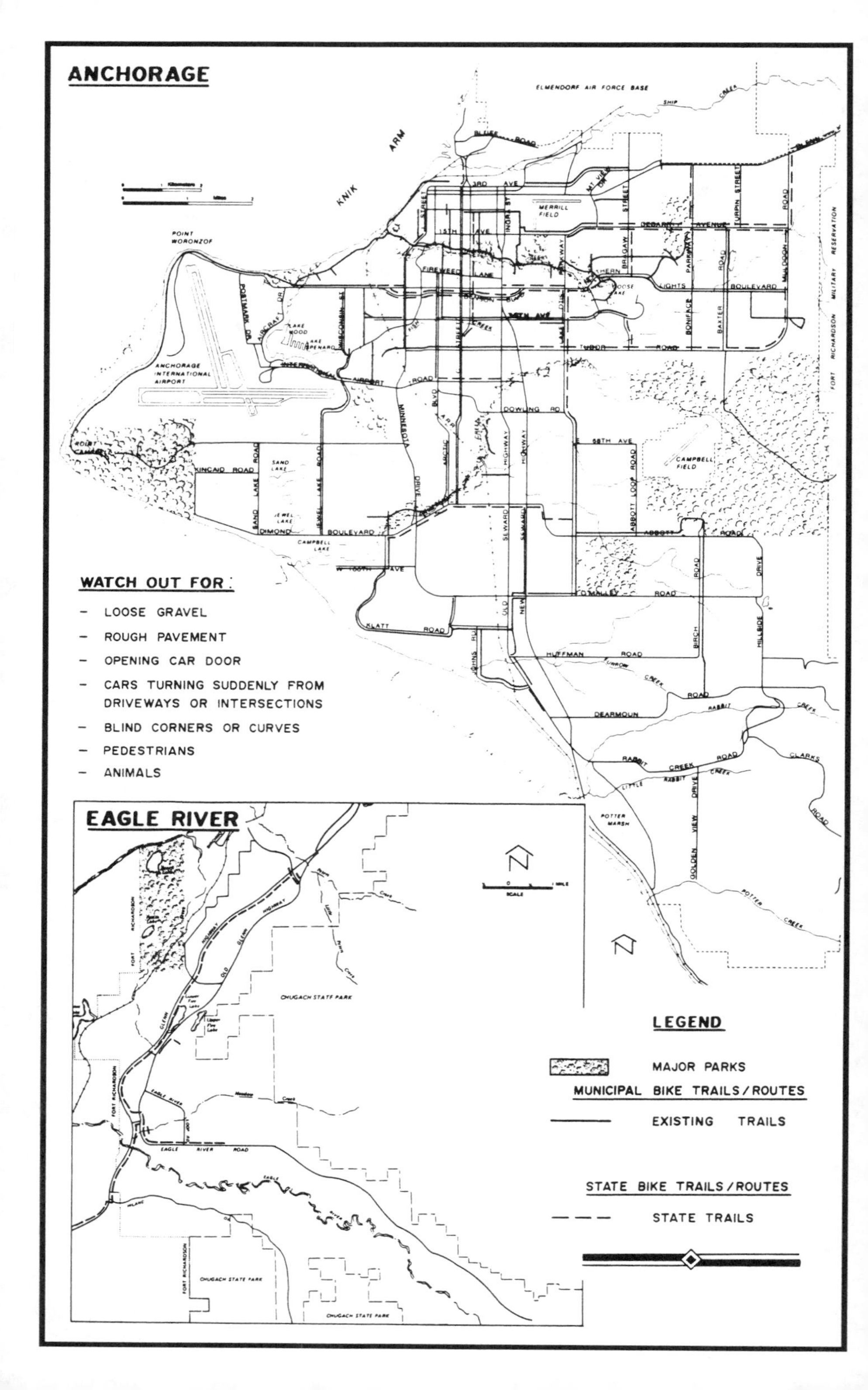
ANCHORAGE
ELMENDORF AIR FORCE BASE
KNIK ARM
POINT WORONZOF
MERRILL FIELD
3RD AVE
15TH AVE
FIREWEED LANE
NORTHERN LIGHTS BOULEVARD
TUDOR ROAD
AIRPORT ROAD
DOWLING RD
ANCHORAGE INTERNATIONAL AIRPORT
LAKE HOOD
LAKE SPENARD
SAND LAKE
JEWEL LAKE
KINCAID ROAD
DIMOND BOULEVARD
CAMPBELL LAKE
W 100TH AVE
KLATT ROAD
MINNESOTA DRIVE
SEWARD HIGHWAY
OLD SEWARD
NEW SEWARD
O'MALLEY ROAD
ABBOTT ROAD
ABBOTT LOOP ROAD
CAMPBELL FIELD
HUFFMAN ROAD
DEARMOUN
RABBIT CREEK ROAD
GOLDEN VIEW DRIVE
POTTER MARSH
POTTER CREEK
CLARKS ROAD
HILLSIDE DRIVE
BIRCH ROAD
BONIFACE
BAXTER ROAD
MULDOON ROAD
TURPIN STREET
DEBARR AVENUE
FORT RICHARDSON MILITARY RESERVATION
WATCH OUT FOR:
- LOOSE GRAVEL
- ROUGH PAVEMENT
- OPENING CAR DOOR
- CARS TURNING SUDDENLY FROM DRIVEWAYS OR INTERSECTIONS
- BLIND CORNERS OR CURVES
- PEDESTRIANS
- ANIMALS
EAGLE RIVER
GLENN HIGHWAY
OLD GLENN HIGHWAY
EAGLE RIVER ROAD
FORT RICHARDSON
CHUGACH STATE PARK
LEGEND
MAJOR PARKS
MUNICIPAL BIKE TRAILS / ROUTES
EXISTING TRAILS
STATE BIKE TRAILS / ROUTES
STATE TRAILS

trail 1

CITY BIKE PATHS

AT - A - GLANCE

TRAILHEAD: ....several, see text

FROM ANCHORAGE: ......within the city

LENGTH OF TRAIL: ..over 100 miles (total)

RIDING TIME: ....1 hour to all day

DIFFICULTY: ....1 to 2

LOW POINT: ....sea level

HIGH POINT: ....800 ft.

ELEVATION GAIN: ....800 ft.

U.S.G.S. MAPS: ....Anchorage A-8, Municipality of Anchorage trails map

Glide upon a smooth ribbon of asphalt through city parks and winding greenbelts as you traverse Anchorage almost unaware of the sprawling city. This was the dream turned reality for a group of visionaries in 1971. Led by Lanie Fleischer, they rallied support for the first bike path, which in turn led to others being built. Today you can discover many of the beautiful places in this city as you cycle 15 uninterrupted miles from Russian Jack Springs to Kincaid Park (see Russian Jack Springs). These corridors of lush greenery pass by lakes and creeks to the enjoyment of a diverse group of users that include joggers, in-line skaters, walkers and bikers. Expect high use on sunny days. Always cycle with care and respect the space of others on this shared trail.

The trail surface is generally smooth asphalt although several rough sections may be encountered where tree roots and cracks have damaged the path. Bridges and tunnels allow cyclists to cross much of the city without intersecting a roadway. Approach and travel through any tunnel with caution. They are narrow and have blind entries and exits.

Three of the many bike paths that crisscross the city have routes with minimal contact with roadways and traffic. Chester Creek Trail, the flattest path, travels 4 miles along a greenbelt from Goose Lake to Westchester Lagoon, where it intersects with the Tony Knowles Coastal Trail. The Coastal Trail, possibly the most popular route, begins at 3rd Avenue and H Street downtown and extends 11 miles to Kincaid Park. It dips to the tidal flats following Cook Inlet and then climbs to high cliffs. When trees part, fantastic views of the city center, with the Chugach Mountains in the background, are revealed. Save some energy for the big hill which ends at Kincaid Chalet. The hilly Abbott/Birch Road Trail begins at the intersection of Abbott and Lake Otis Parkway. Climb Abbott, traveling briefly through Service High School's parking lot before crossing the road on a high bridge. This bike path now follows Birch Road, climbing three hills before crossing O'Malley Road and continuing uphill to DeArmoun Road.

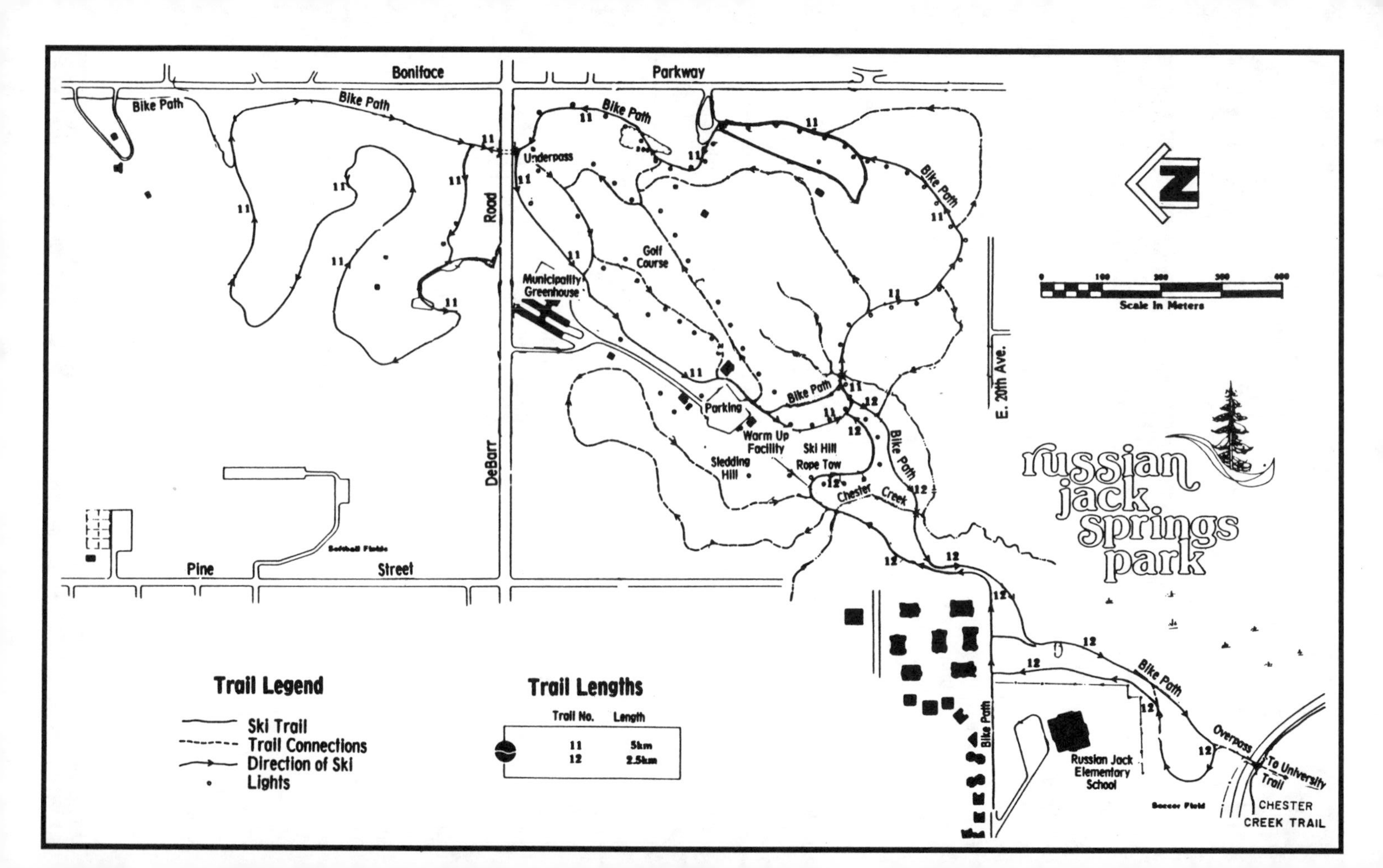

russian jack springs park
Boniface
Parkway
Bike Path
Underpass
Road
DeBarr
Municipality Greenhouse
Golf Course
Parking
Warm Up Facility
Ski Hill
Rope Tow
Sledding Hill
Chester Creek
E. 20th Ave.
Scale In Meters
0 100 200 300 400
Pine
Street
Softball Fields
Russian Jack Elementary School
Soccer Field
Overpass
To University Trail
CHESTER CREEK TRAIL
Trail Legend
Ski Trail
Trail Connections
Direction of Ski
Lights
Trail Lengths
Trail No. Length
11 5km
12 2.5km

RUSSIAN JACK SPRINGS

Russian Jack Springs Park has something for everyone. Bike trails, ski trails, tennis courts, softball fields, a 9-hole golf course and the municipal greenhouses provide enjoyment for many. Consider taking a tour of the greenhouses, it will reveal a solarium, tropical house, an aviary as well as a native plant and wildflower garden. It is an enjoyable side trip that shouldn't be missed.

AT - A - GLANCE

TRAILHEAD: ......between Boniface and Pine on DeBarr Rd.

FROM ANCHORAGE: ....in the city

LENGTH OF TRAIL: ....5 paved miles

RIDING TIME: ....1 hour to all day

DIFFICULTY: ....1 to 2

LOW POINT: ....200 ft.

HIGH POINT: ....250 ft.

ELEVATION GAIN: ....50 ft.

U.S.G.S. MAPS: ....Anchorage A-8, Municipality of Anchorage ski trails map

A short, paved bike path takes the cyclist through 38 tree covered acres. Here, 2 bridges and a tunnel allow the rider to bike uninterrupted past creeks or busy streets. Follow Russian Jack trail 11 for a combination of paved and dirt riding on a fun trail with a few small hills. A multitude of dirt trails crisscross these woodlands offering fun, but challenging riding. Moose, ducks and diving birds are frequently seen along the waterways.

Although there are several ways to enter this trail system, the main entrance takes the visitor to a chalet in the center of the park. The chalet, open from 7:30 a.m. to 9 p.m. in the summer, is staffed, has rest rooms and a snack bar. Find this trailhead by driving north on DeBarr Rd. Cross Pine St. and take a right at the municipal greenhouses. Pass by the greenhouses and park at the chalet. From the chalet, cycle down a hill on a paved path that "Y's" at the bottom. To the right is the Russian Jack Spurr, which travels 1.5 miles to Goose Lake, a trailhead for the Chester Creek Trail (see City Bike Paths). Stay right at the next "Y" and cross a bridge. Go right at a building complex and cross Northern Lights Blvd. on a high overpass. Go right and continue a short distance to Goose Lake. To do the enjoyable trail 11 loop, go left after dropping down from the Russian Jack Springs chalet and immediately cross a bridge. Cycle up a short, steep hill and wind through the woods before crossing a car access road. Ride through a tunnel before turning left and climbing trail 11, which loops back to the chalet, for a total of 3 miles. Numerous short side paths depart from the main trail, providing access to city streets. Bicycles are not permitted on the fairways or maintained greens of the golf course.

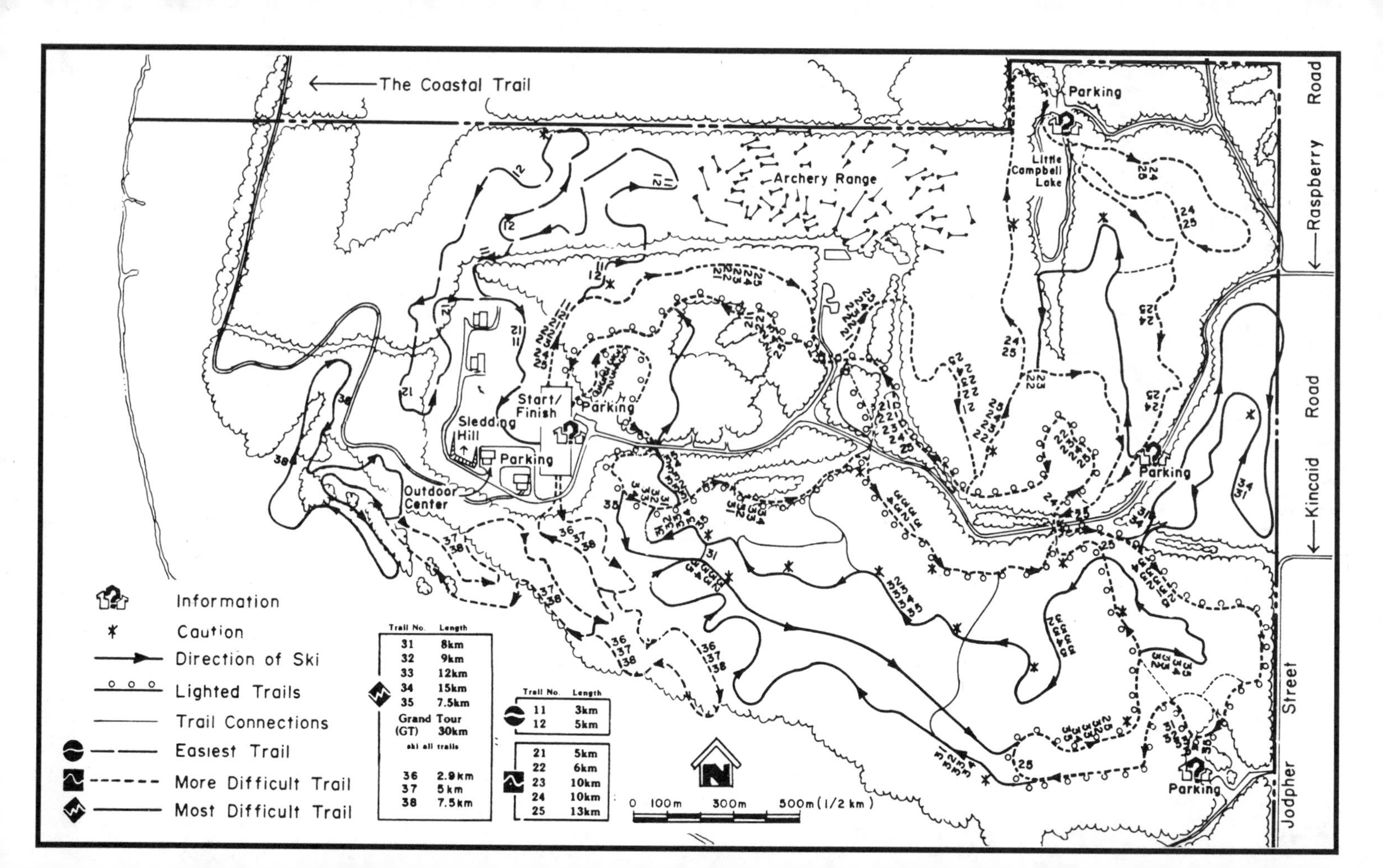
The Coastal Trail
Archery Range
Parking
Little Campbell Lake
Raspberry Road
Kincaid Road
Jodpher Street
Start/ Finish
Parking
Sledding Hill
Parking
Outdoor Center
Information
Caution
Direction of Ski
Lighted Trails
Trail Connections
Easiest Trail
More Difficult Trail
Most Difficult Trail
Trail No. Length
31 8km
32 9km
33 12km
34 15km
35 7.5km
Grand Tour (GT) 30km
ski all trails
36 2.9km
37 5km
38 7.5km
Trail No. Length
11 3km
12 5km
21 5km
22 6km
23 10km
24 10km
25 13km
0 100m 300m 500m (1/2 km)

trail 3

KINCAID PARK

AT - A - GLANCE

TRAILHEAD: ....the end of Raspberry Rd.

FROM ANCHORAGE: ....in the city

LENGTH OF TRAIL: ....over 25 miles

RIDING TIME: ....1 hour to all day

DIFFICULTY: ....2 to 3

LOW POINT: ....50 ft.

HIGH POINT: ....200 ft.

ELEVATION GAIN: ....150 ft.

U.S.G.S. MAPS: ....Tyonek A-1, Municipality of Anchorage ski trail map

Nothing beats an invigorating romp through the woods on short, rolling uphills and fiery downhills. This cross-country ski trail system by winter becomes an excellent mountain biking location during summer. It offers a wonderful collection of dirt trails and roller coaster riding that is enjoyable for most experience levels. Over 25 miles of trails wind and twist through thick woodlands in this coastal playground.

Soft, earthen trails give excellent traction for uphill climbs, swift descents and hard cornering. Expect an occasional rutted or sandy section and minor erosion on these grassy paths, which are a delight to ride on. Watch out for moose that frequent the area. It is necessary that everyone travels in the same direction to avoid head-on collisions. Always follow the directional arrows. It also is recommended that you bring mosquito repellant. Many riders (and skiers in winter) are intimidated by the maze of trails. Pick one trail, learn it and then slowly add others as you become more familiar with the system. In general, the lower the number, the easier the trail. Before long, you will have a grasp of the layout and will be enjoying an array of fun trails.

Four entrances allow riders to choose where they wish to begin their ride. Reach the Jodpher entrance by driving/cycling down Dimond Boulevard to its western end. A sweeping right turn places you on Jodpher Road. Travel a short distance and look for a Kincaid Park sign on the left. A large parking lot and trail map designates this as the trailhead. The remaining trailheads are reached by traveling down Raspberry Road and entering Kincaid Park (a large wood sign indicates this). Turn right at the sign and then left to find the Little Campbell Lake entrance. A left at the sign will take the cyclist past another entrance (indicated by a large trail map) and onto the main trailhead at Kincaid Park Chalet. Drinking water, rest rooms, an information board and an employee provide services to the visitor. Normal summer hours for the chalet are 1 p.m. to 9 p.m. A large gate crossing the road leading to Kincaid Chalet is locked each evening at 9 p.m.

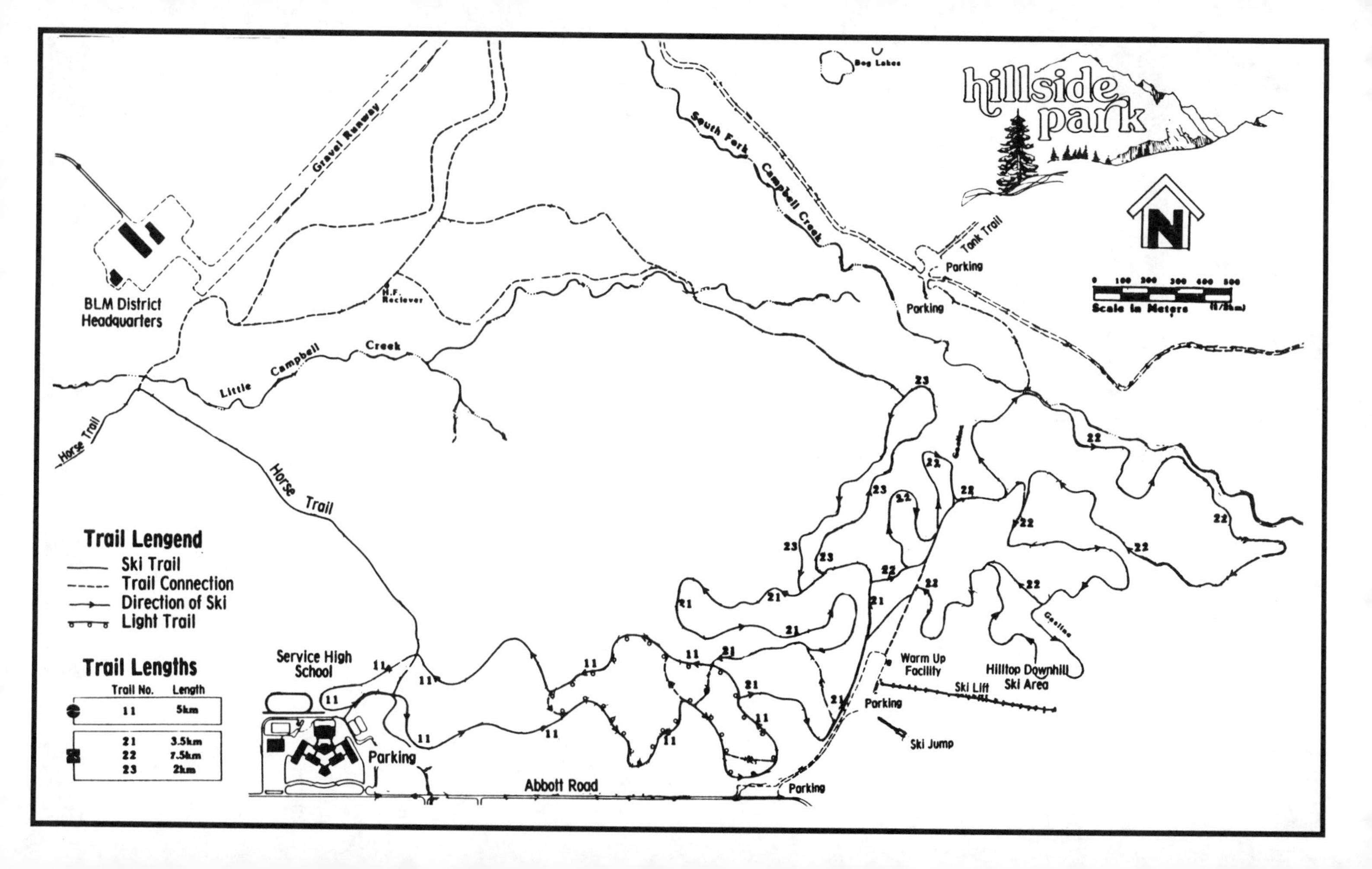

hillside park
Bog Lakes
Gravel Runway
BLM District
Headquarters
H.F. Reciever
Little Campbell Creek
South Fork Campbell Creek
Tank Trail
Parking
Parking
Scale in Meters
0 100 200 300 400 500
Horse Trail
Horse Trail
Trail Lengend
Ski Trail
Trail Connection
Direction of Ski
Light Trail
Trail Lengths
Trail No. Length
11 5km
21 3.5km
22 7.5km
23 2km
Service High School
Parking
Abbott Road
Parking
Warm Up Facility
Parking
Ski Lift
Ski Jump
Hilltop Downhill Ski Area
Gasline

trail 4

HILLSIDE PARK

AT - A - GLANCE

TRAILHEAD: ....top of Abbott Rd.

FROM ANCHORAGE: ....5 miles

LENGTH OF TRAIL: ....over 12 miles

RIDING TIME: ....1 hour to all day

DIFFICULTY: ....2.5 to 3.5

LOW POINT: ....400 ft.

HIGH POINT: ....800 ft.

ELEVATION GAIN: ....400 ft.

U.S.G.S. MAPS: ....Anchorage A-8, Municipality of Anchorage ski trail map

Hillside Park is a perfect place to improve skills, build endurance or just have fun. Four ski trails, linked together, wind and twist over and around an assortment of hills at the base of the Chugach Mountains. The world-class Spencer Loop (trail 22) is both scenic and demanding. It parallels the South Fork Campbell Creek and climbs a high ridge with a city view before descending in a flurry of invigorating turns. In the fall, a blanket of leaves covers these trails like a rainbow quilt. This is an enjoyable trail system for many. In general, the lower the number of the trail, the easier it is.

Under wheel, the surface is hard-pack dirt, allowing for swift descents, hard cornering and superior traction on uphill climbs. Erosion is minimal on these maintained ski trails. The greatest hazards are the ruts left by individuals who foolishly use the trail when it is too wet (especially during breakup). Damage left by cyclists, joggers, equestrians and moose often remain throughout the year. It is important that everyone follows the directional arrows to avoid head-on collisions. Moose often are seen in the old burn area along trail 11 and although they are typically docile, exercise caution around them. They are unpredictable.

Four entrances provide access to this trail system. Take Campbell Airstrip Road 2.4 miles to a large parking lot on the left with a sign indicating South Fork Campbell Creek Trail Head. A well-defined access trail drops before crossing the South Fork Campbell Creek and intersecting with the Spencer Loop. (Go left, cycling clockwise.) The remaining trailheads are located near the top of Abbott Road. The first is behind Service High School at the east end of the oval running track. Stay on the dirt trails and cycle counterclockwise. A paved bike path also leaves from here. It crosses Abbott Road and parallels Birch Road (see City Bike Paths). Just east of the high school is the main parking lot for Hillside Park (a large wood sign indicates this). Cycle in a counterclockwise direction. The remaining trailhead is the northern parking lot of the Hilltop Downhill Ski Area. To enter the Spencer Loop, cycle down a dirt road and take the second trail to the right.

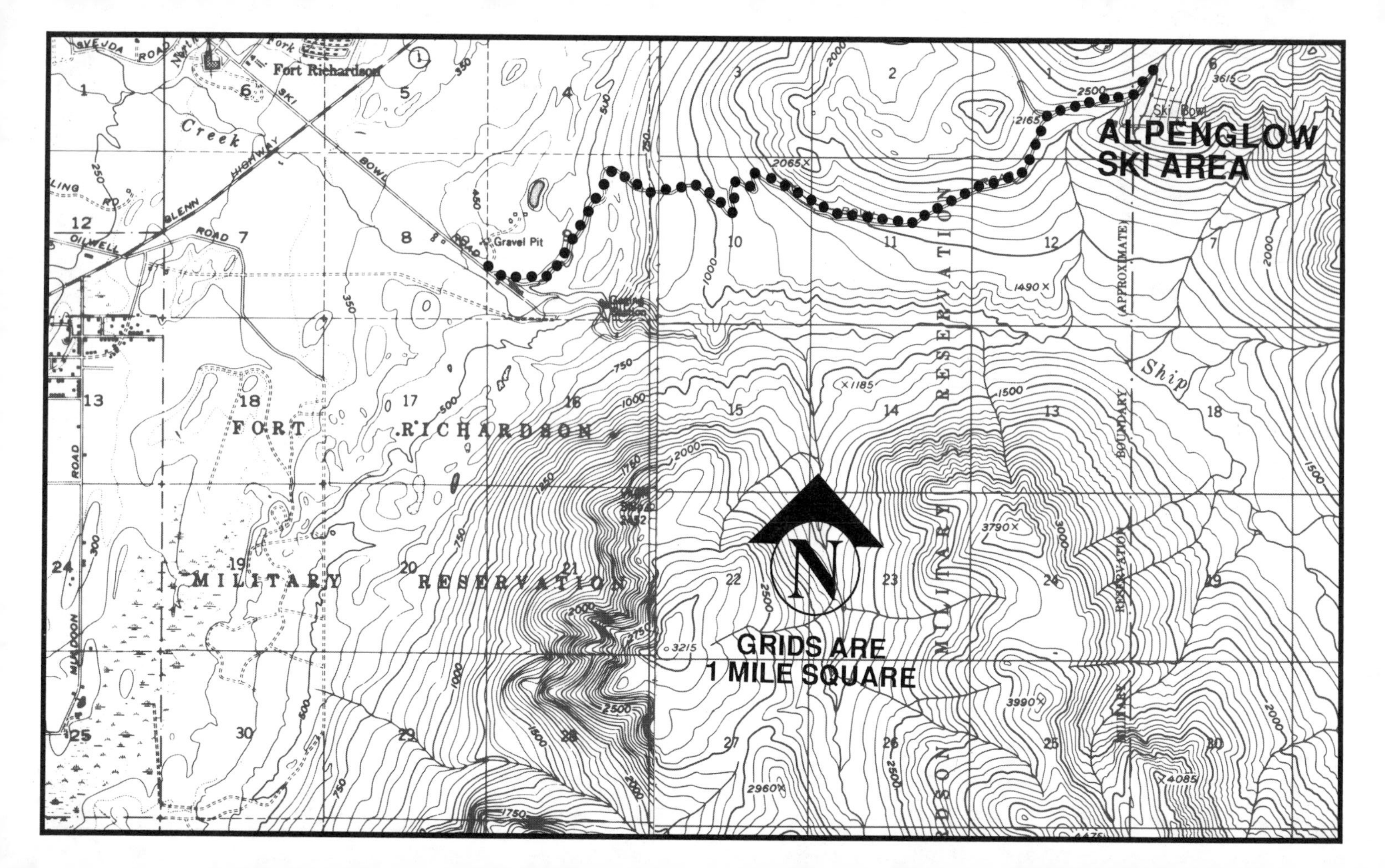

ALPENGLOW SKI AREA
Ski Bowl
Fort Richardson
Creek
GLENN HIGHWAY
SKI BOWL ROAD
Gravel Pit
FORT RICHARDSON MILITARY RESERVATION
MILITARY RESERVATION BOUNDARY (APPROXIMATE)
Ship
OILWELL
MULDOON ROAD
GRIDS ARE 1 MILE SQUARE
N

trail 5

ARCTIC VALLEY RD.

Start the year training on this 6.4 mile uphill and you'll be ready for a fun-filled season of riding. While the high country is still snowbound, use this road to build stronger legs and lungs. Alpenglow Ski Area, at the top of Arctic Valley Road, has slopes covered with blueberries and wildflowers. Leave your bike behind and walk upon a smooth, earthen foot path that follows a small stream around the base of the ski area and climbs to a pass providing a view of the South Fork Eagle River. The dry tundra in the pass allows for easy hiking to any number of nearby peaks.

AT - A - GLANCE

TRAILHEAD: . . . .mile 1 Arctic Valley Road

FROM ANCHORAGE: . . . . .2.5 miles

LENGTH OF TRAIL: . .12.8 miles round trip

RIDING TIME: . . . . .1 to 3 hours

DIFFICULTY: . . . . .5 (hillclimb)

LOW POINT: . . . . .500 ft.

HIGH POINT: . . . . .2,550 ft.

ELEVATION GAIN: . . . . .2,050 ft.

U.S.G.S. MAPS: . . . . .Anchorage A-7, A-8, Anchorage 1 : 250,000

A maintained dirt road leads the rider through several switchbacks as you slowly climb above tree line. Loose gravel, potholes, washboard and dust are the only hazards other than vehicle traffic. Many cyclists keep track of their time to the top in order to judge how much progress has been made throughout the season. Highly tuned local racers hammer up the mountain in just over 37 minutes. Regardless of how long it takes to reach the top, the main reason for doing this ride is to strengthen the body and build stamina.

On the Glenn Highway, drive 1.5 miles east of Muldoon Road and take the Arctic Valley Road exit. Drive 1 mile down this road and park opposite an old military guard shack. Begin your ride here. Soon the pavement turns to gravel and the uphill begins. Climb steadily, rounding switchbacks as you gain elevation on the valley below. Enjoy the panorama (mile 3.5) of the Anchorage bowl. Sleeping Lady (Mt. Susitna) lies just across Cook Inlet with snow-covered Mt. McKinley and Mt. Foraker to her right. Continue climbing, building stronger, healthier legs and lungs as you ascend this steep mountain road. Keep left near the top. A final push on the steepest grade places the rider in the upper most parking lot of Alpenglow Ski Area and within Chugach State Park. This is the turn-around. High speeds can be reached quickly on this bumpy downhill return. Wear a helmet and be sure your brakes are functioning properly. Consider bringing along a wind suit for an often chilly descent.

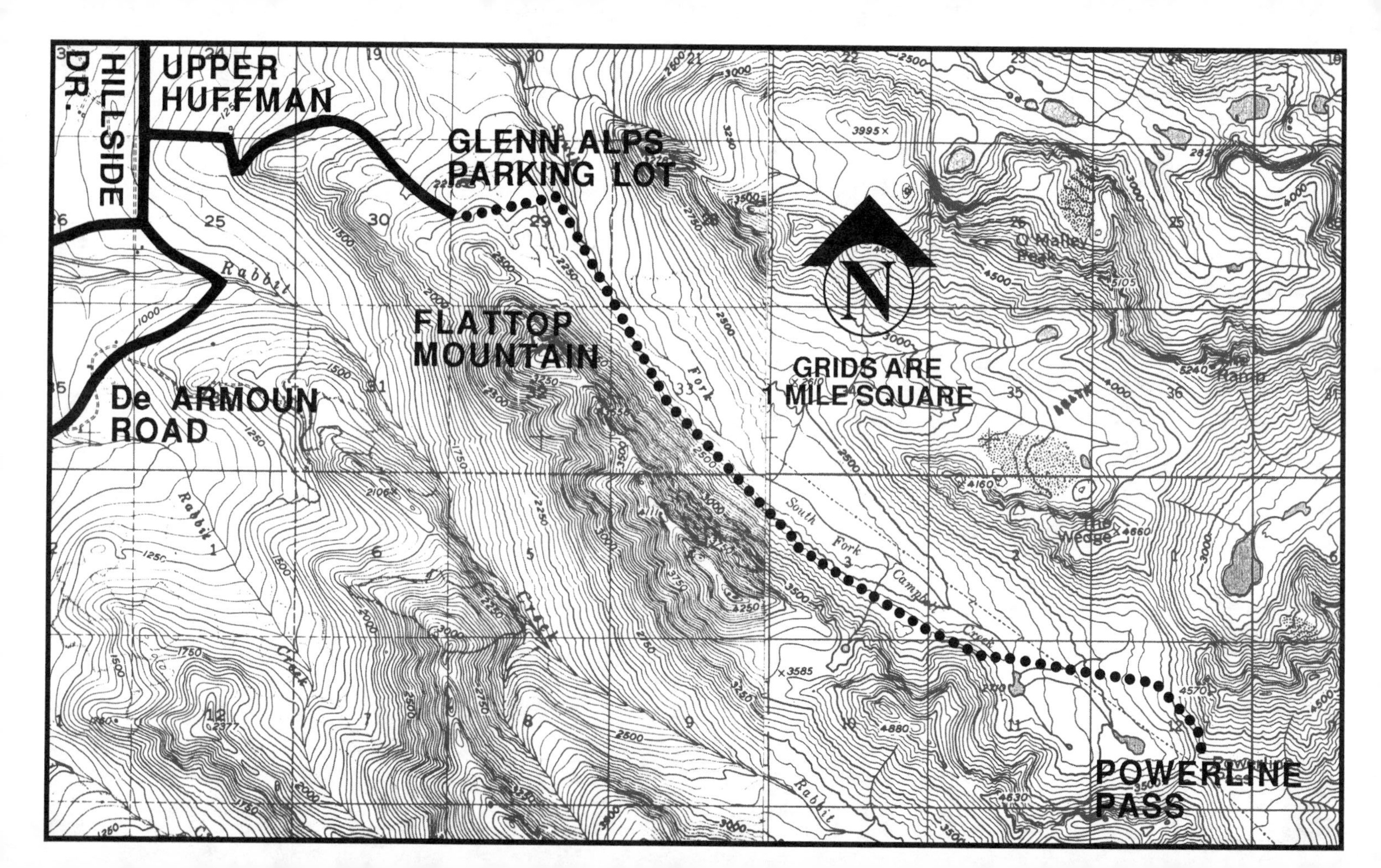
HILLSIDE DR.
UPPER HUFFMAN
GLENN ALPS PARKING LOT
FLATTOP MOUNTAIN
De ARMOUN ROAD
N
GRIDS ARE 1 MILE SQUARE
O'Malley Peak
The Wedge
South Fork Campbell Creek
Rabbit Creek
POWERLINE PASS

trail 6

POWERLINE PASS

Ride into the Chugach Mountains, where towering mountain peaks, alpine lakes and grassy meadows dotted with wildflowers surround you. Less than 1 hour drive from downtown Anchorage lies this challenging trail that is very popular and well-used by most skill levels. A number of animals use this valley including moose, bear, eagles, Dall sheep and ptarmigan, the Alaska state bird.

Gravel and hard-pack dirt (mud when wet) give way to rock as the rider heads up the valley. Your riding skills and strength will be tested at several sections. Always use good judgment. If unsure of your skills, dismount and walk until comfortable.

AT - A - GLANCE

TRAILHEAD: ....2 miles Toilsome Rd.

FROM ANCHORAGE: ....12.7 miles

LENGTH OF TRAIL: ....11 miles round trip

RIDING TIME: ....3 to 5 hours

DIFFICULTY: ....2.5 to 3.5

LOW POINT: ....1,450 ft.

HIGH POINT: ....3,500 ft.

ELEVATION GAIN: ....2,050 ft.

U.S.G.S. MAPS: ....Anchorage A-7, A-8, Anchorage 1 : 250,000

The most popular trailhead, Glen Alps, has plenty of parking, rest rooms and direct trail access. From the Seward Highway drive 4 miles up O' Malley and take a right onto Hillside Drive. Go 1 mile and turn left onto Upper Huffman. Drive .7 of a mile and take a right onto Toilsome Road, which winds its way for 2 miles to the Chugach State Park parking lot and trail head. A short access trail at the end of the parking lot takes the rider to the power line. Two trails travel the length of this upland valley, one staying under the power line (and is usually wet and slow), while the other hugs the right mountain wall and is the more favored route. Toward the end of the valley, the trail climbs up and then drops before it crosses the knee-deep South Fork Little Campbell Creek. This is a great place to leave the bike and walk a short distance up the creek to an alpine lake at the base of towering mountains to have lunch or take photos. The trail then steepens before it traverses, placing the rider onto the pass. From here you can drop down the backside of the pass into the small town of Indian on Turnagain Arm or return the way you came. The Indian side is quite steep, very rocky, and often off-camber, making for a difficult descent. This back trail should be negotiated by advanced riders who are comfortable with steep, rocky terrain. Arrange for a vehicle pick-up in Indian. The strong-legged can cycle back to the Glen Alps parking lot.

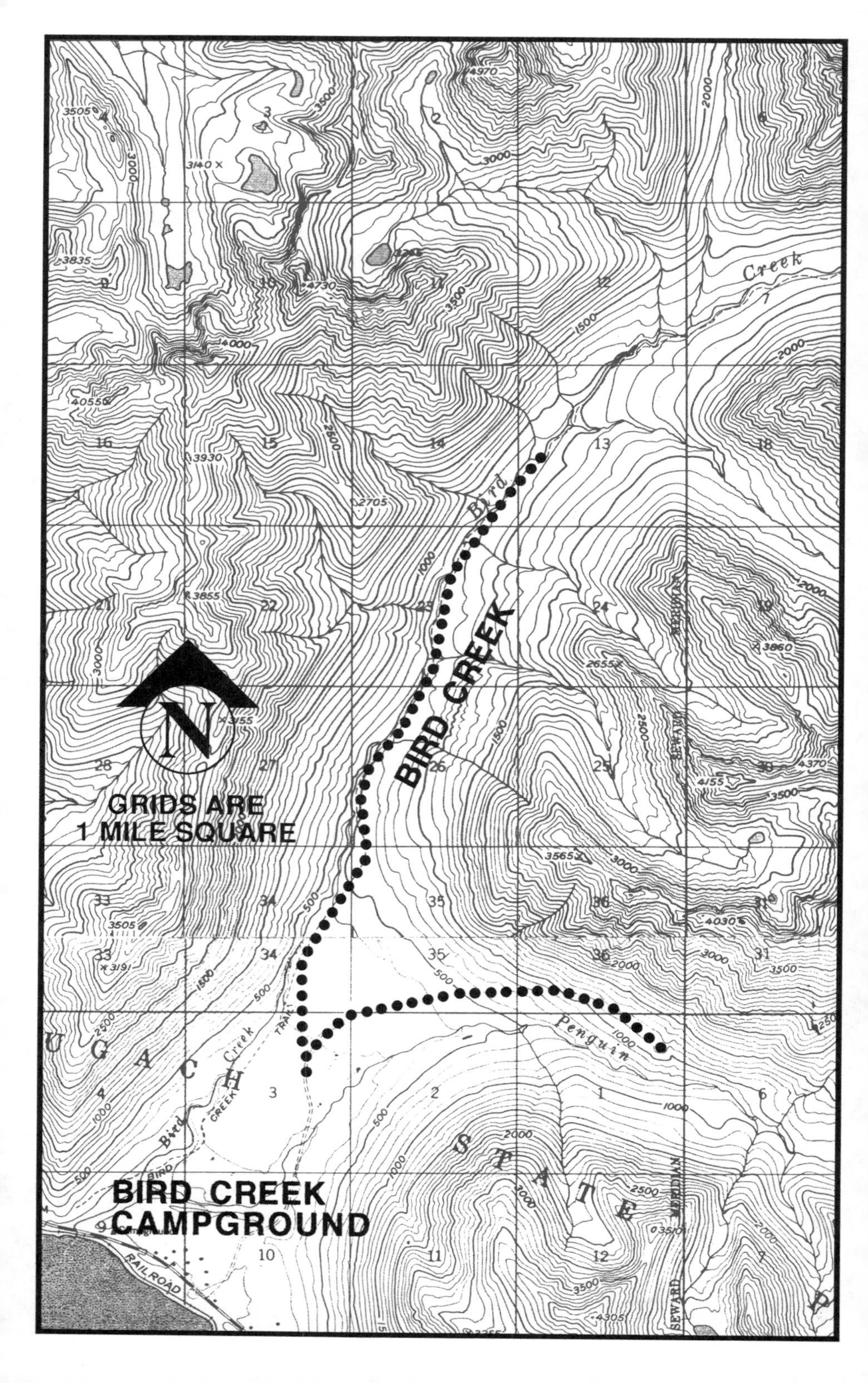
GRIDS ARE
1 MILE SQUARE
BIRD CREEK
BIRD CREEK
CAMPGROUND
Bird
Creek
Penguin
SEWARD MERIDIAN
RAILROAD
BIRD CREEK TRAIL

trail 7

BIRD CREEK

AT - A - GLANCE	
TRAILHEAD:	mile 100.5 Seward Hwy.
FROM ANCHORAGE:	26.5 miles
LENGTH OF TRAIL:	11 miles
RIDING TIME:	1 hour to all day
DIFFICULTY:	3
LOW POINT:	50 ft.
HIGH POINT:	1,000 ft.
ELEVATION GAIN:	950 ft.
U.S.G.S. MAPS:	Anchorage A-7, Seward A-8, Anchorage and Seward 1 : 250,000

A labyrinth of trails set in a dense forest await the cyclist in this playground for mountain bikes. This wooded valley adjacent to Turnagain Arm, originally a site for commercial timber harvest, is now a recreation area for multiple user groups. Old logging roads still crisscross the valley, intersecting with the main trail as it loosely parallels Bird Creek. Look for moose, brown bear, black bear, arctic hare and eagles in this section of Chugach State Park. Also, Dall sheep and Beluga whales are often sighted along Turnagain Arm while driving to this trailhead from Anchorage.

Soft, earthen trails radiate in all directions from the main gravel trail. Some loop back to the main trail while others end high on a hillside. A fun combination of short, steep uphills, winding downhills, mud holes and creek crossings keep the aggressive mountain bike enthusiast coming back for more. Numerous lower trails with few hazards offer the beginning and intermediate cyclist an enjoyable forested ride without having to climb long, steep hills. Consider biking with a picnic lunch and finding an open field to soak in the sights and sounds of these coastal mountains.

Drive south of Anchorage to mile 100.4 of the Seward Highway. Turn left at the Bird House Bar and travel down a gravel road for .7 mile, passing several private homes before reaching the trail head. Because of the maze of trails at hand it is recommended that you cycle the main trail first, getting the feel of the layout before exploring the side trails. Observe and orient yourself with the valley. It is a classic "V" shape, with Bird Creek flowing down the middle to the highway. The main trail loosely follows the creek up the valley with side trails heading away from the creek and up the mountain slope. To get to the main trail, follow an obvious path a short distance to a "Y" in the trail and go left. You are now on the main trail. Nearby state-maintained Bird Creek Campground offers camp sites, water, tables and toilets for a small fee. Cycling anglers may wish to try their luck in Bird Creek, where returning salmon draw large crowds.

chapter 2

KENAI PENINSULA

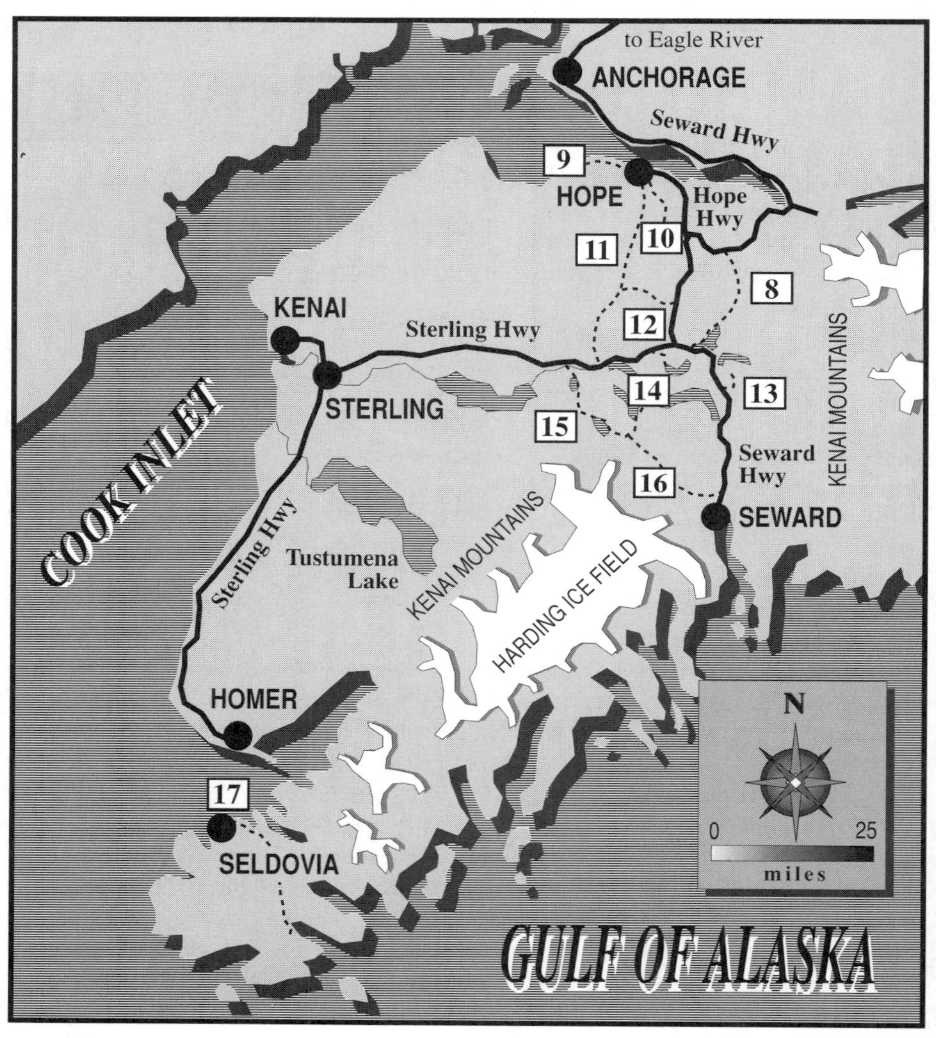

The three main roads used to access the trails in this chapter are the Seward Highway, Hope Highway and the Sterling Highway. Exercise caution if you cycle any of these roadways. Many sections are narrow and have no shoulders. Traffic on weekends, particularly during fishing season, can be bumper to bumper.

The Kenai Peninsula is a rugged land with glaciated fiords and towering mountains. A multitude of trails traverse these mountains, giving us some of Alaska's best single-track riding (a trail wide enough for one bike). Expect tall grasses, thick woodlands and long hills on these challenging but fun trails. The easiest rides are trails 10 and 14. The most difficult are 11,13 and 16.

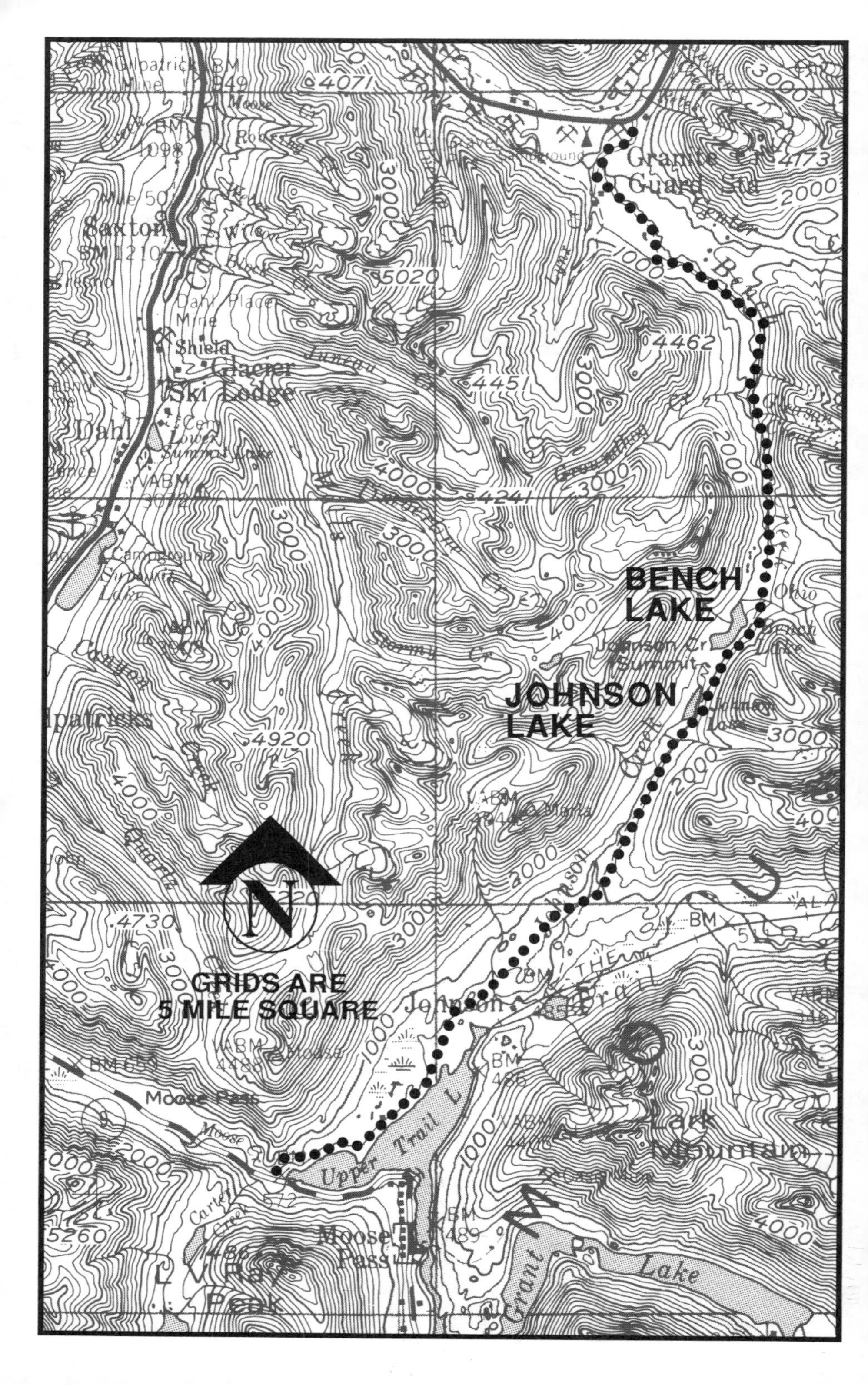
BENCH LAKE
JOHNSON LAKE
N
GRIDS ARE
5 MILE SQUARE
Moose Pass
Upper Trail L
Grant
Lake
Saxton
Glacier
Ski Lodge
Dahl Placer
Mine
Shield
Stormy
Quartz
Creek
Johnson
Mountain

trail 8

JOHNSON PASS

AT - A - GLANCE

TRAILHEAD:	mile 63.8 Seward Hwy
FROM ANCHORAGE:	63.2 miles
LENGTH OF TRAIL:	21 miles one way
RIDING TIME:	7 to 10 hours
DIFFICULTY:	3 to 3.5
LOW POINT:	500 ft.
HIGH POINT:	1,500 ft.
ELEVATION GAIN:	1,000 ft.
U.S.G.S. MAPS:	Seward C-6, C-7, Seward 1 : 250,000

Mountain bike among the lofty peaks and alpine lakes of the Kenai Mountains as you follow portions of the original Iditarod Trail of 1890 that went from Seward to Nome. Ruins from the past, including cabins and old wagon parts, can still be found.

This single-track adventurous ride is challenging but not overly difficult. Bridges over most water crossings on this well-kept trail will keep the feet dry on this mountainous trek. Hazards include large rocks, water erosion ditches, one steep and rocky incline and Cow Parsnip. Cow Parsnip is a tall, hollow-stemmed plant with large palmate leaves and white flowers. The hairy leaves and stems inflict on some people a photo-sensitive sunburn which blisters and is slow to heal. Wash contacted areas with water. This trail is shared by many user groups including bikers, family hikers and pack llamas.

This 21-mile trail has two trailheads, Granite Creek (mile 63.8 Seward Hwy.) and Upper Trail Lake (mile 32.7 Seward Hwy.). Coordinate a car drop at each end of the trail, allowing the rider to cycle the entire route. Or choose the most convenient trailhead, cycle in as far as you like, and cycle back out on the same course. Drive south from Anchorage on the Seward Highway to mile 63.8 where a Chugach Forest sign and a short access road direct you to the Granite Creek trailhead. Cross several bridges as you cycle through forest and mountain pasture on a single-track trail that steadily gains in elevation. At the top of a particularly steep and rocky hill (mile 4) is a pull-off with a beautiful waterfall cascading over tall cliffs. This is a wonderful place to take a break and admire Alaska's mountain wilderness. You're soon cycling along the shores of Bench Lake as you make your way to Johnson Pass (mile 10), the highest point on the trail at 1,500 feet. From the pass, descend to Johnson Lake and parallel Johnson Creek on a roller coaster downhill that is quite enjoyable. The trail is smoother and wider on this side of the pass all the way to the shores of Upper Trail Lake (mile 19), where loose rocks are encountered.

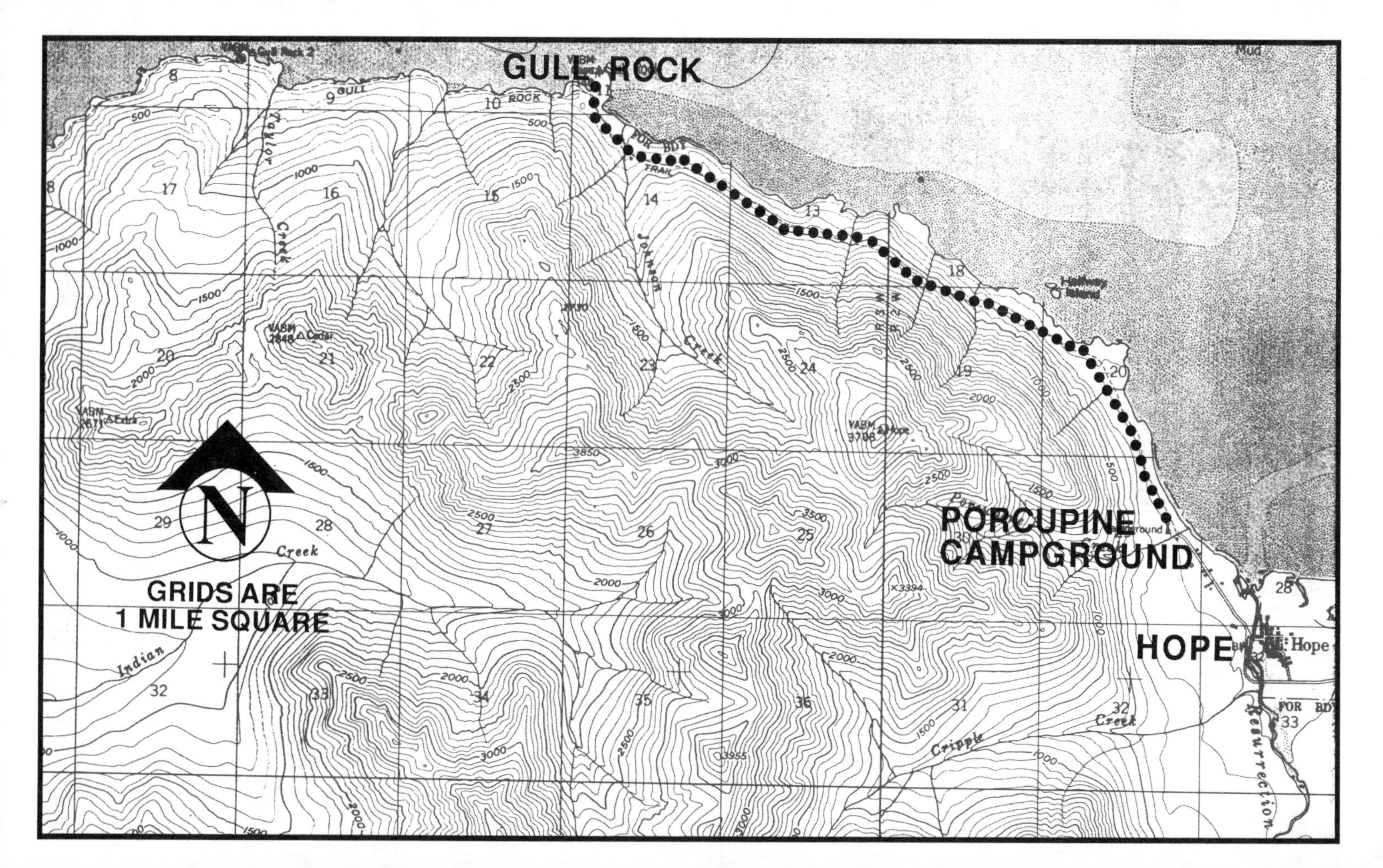
GULL ROCK
PORCUPINE
CAMPGROUND
HOPE
N
GRIDS ARE
1 MILE SQUARE
Taylor
Creek
Johnson
Creek
Indian
Creek
Cripple
Creek
Resurrection
Hope
Mud
FOR BDY
TRAIL
GULL
ROCK

trail 9

GULL ROCK

AT - A - GLANCE

TRAILHEAD:	mile 17.8 Hope Hwy.
FROM ANCHORAGE:	74.5 miles
LENGTH OF TRAIL:	10 miles round trip
RIDING TIME:	2 to 4 hours
DIFFICULTY:	3.5
LOW POINT:	50 ft.
HIGH POINT:	650 ft.
ELEVATION GAIN:	600 ft.
U.S.G.S. MAPS:	Seward D-8, Seward 1 : 250,000

Spectacular views of Turnagain Arm await the skillful rider on this challenging wooded trail where mountains meet water. Turnagain Arm is known for having the second highest tides in the world as well as having spectacular bore tides, where a wall of incoming water meets an outgoing tide. Cycling in and out of the dark, moss-covered hemlock forest provides a beautiful contrast to the vast and sparkling scene you get when the trees part and afford the rider a view of the Arm.

An obvious path takes the rider in and out of sections where tree roots are exposed and interlaced, requiring the skills of an advanced rider who can hop the bike's wheels over and around obstacles. The deft rider will seek the challenge of the rooted tangles while those less skilled should dismount and walk the more troublesome sections. Wet riding conditions can compound the difficulty of this ride.

Gull Rock trailhead is located at the end of the Hope Highway and toward the back of Porcupine Campground (mile 17.8 Hope Hwy.), a U. S. Forest Service-maintained campground offering water, toilets and tables for a small fee. This trail starts out smooth and easy but soon becomes difficult because of tree roots and large rocks. Before long, a smooth trail is under wheel only to succumb to more roots. This scenario of easy and then difficult carries throughout the ride and sets a slow pace for most. About 1 mile from trail's end the rider comes upon a Kenai National Wildlife Refuge (KNWR) sign which marks the refuge boundary. By law, cyclists are not allowed to ride mountain bikes on any of the KNWR trails. Horses yes, bicycles no. Soon you're at Johnson Creek bridge where you can scramble around the ruins of several old cabins and the remains of a sawmill and stables from the 1920s. The trail then breaks out of the trees, revealing Turnagain Arm, which can be seen on two sides of a grassy shoulder. This is a great spot for lunch. A needle-covered trail climbs and winds its way to a tree-covered rocky promontory. Several camp sites are available in this area. Take some time to look around for the one that's just right. For additional riding in this area see Palmer Creek and Resurrection Pass in this chapter.

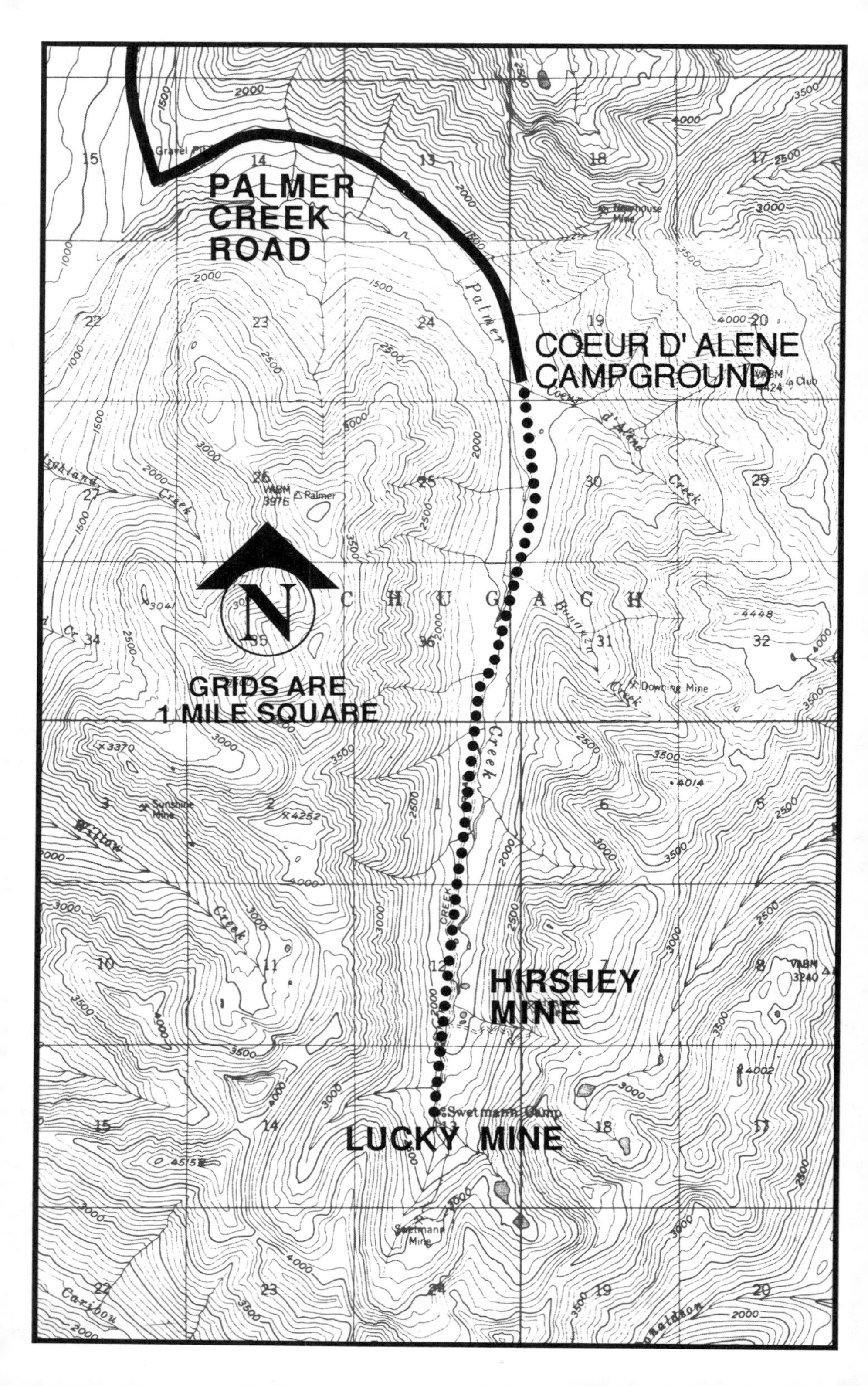
PALMER
CREEK
ROAD
COEUR D' ALENE
CAMPGROUND
GRIDS ARE
1 MILE SQUARE
HIRSHEY
MINE
LUCKY MINE

trail 10

PALMER CREEK

AT - A - GLANCE

TRAILHEAD:	mile 7.2 Palmer Creek Rd.
FROM ANCHORAGE:	80.4 miles
LENGTH OF TRAIL:	9 miles round trip
RIDING TIME:	2 to 4 hours
DIFFICULTY:	3
LOW POINT:	1,400 ft.
HIGH POINT:	2,200 ft.
ELEVATION GAIN:	800 ft.
U.S.G.S. MAPS:	Seward D-7, Seward 1 : 250,000

Enjoy an easy bicycle and hike combination that takes the visitor past beaver ponds and above tree line into glacially carved bowls dotted with alpine lakes (tarns) and wildflowers. Watch the tall trees of the coastal forest slowly give way to alpine tundra as views of Resurrection Creek Valley unfold before you. Cycle into abandoned Lucky Mine, also called Swetmann Mining Camp, a reminder of the gold rush that took place at the turn-of-the-century when thousands of miners worked these northern Kenai Mountains.

An easy-to-follow unmaintained road takes the rider 9 miles (round trip) to the mining camp. Equipment and buildings in the area are private property. Few hazards are encountered and the uphill grade is shallow enough for most skill levels. Cross several ankle-deep creeks as you traverse this lush valley.

Travel south from Anchorage on the Seward Highway to mile 56.3. Take a right onto the Hope Highway and drive 16.2 miles to the Resurrection Creek Road. For those wishing a longer ride, begin cycling here (24.8 miles round trip). Drive .7 of a mile up Resurrection Creek Road to Palmer Creek Road. This scenic gravel road gradually gains altitude as you loosely parallel Palmer Creek. Coeur d'Alene Campground (mile 7.2 Palmer Creek Rd.), near a clear-running stream, offers tent sites, picnic tables, fire pits and an outhouse. Begin cycling here. An unmaintained but still wide and non-technical road slowly ascends to the Lucky Mine. At the ruins, leave your bike behind and climb an obvious hiking trail up a short, steep pitch, passing a waterfall before arriving at the tarns. Spend some time exploring this glacial bowl were thin tundra allows for easy hiking. Surmount a nearby peak and relish the mountain panorama. Additional hiking can be found by climbing the ridge above Hirshey mine and walking up Alder Creek. Two lakes surrounded by 4,000 ft. mountain peaks lie at the head of Alder Creek. In the vicinity of Hope are two other trailheads: Gull Rock and Resurrection Pass Trail (see this chapter for additional information). Porcupine Campground at mile 17.8 of the Hope Highway is maintained by the U. S. Forest Service and offers camp sites, drinking water, tables, fire pits and toilets for a small fee.

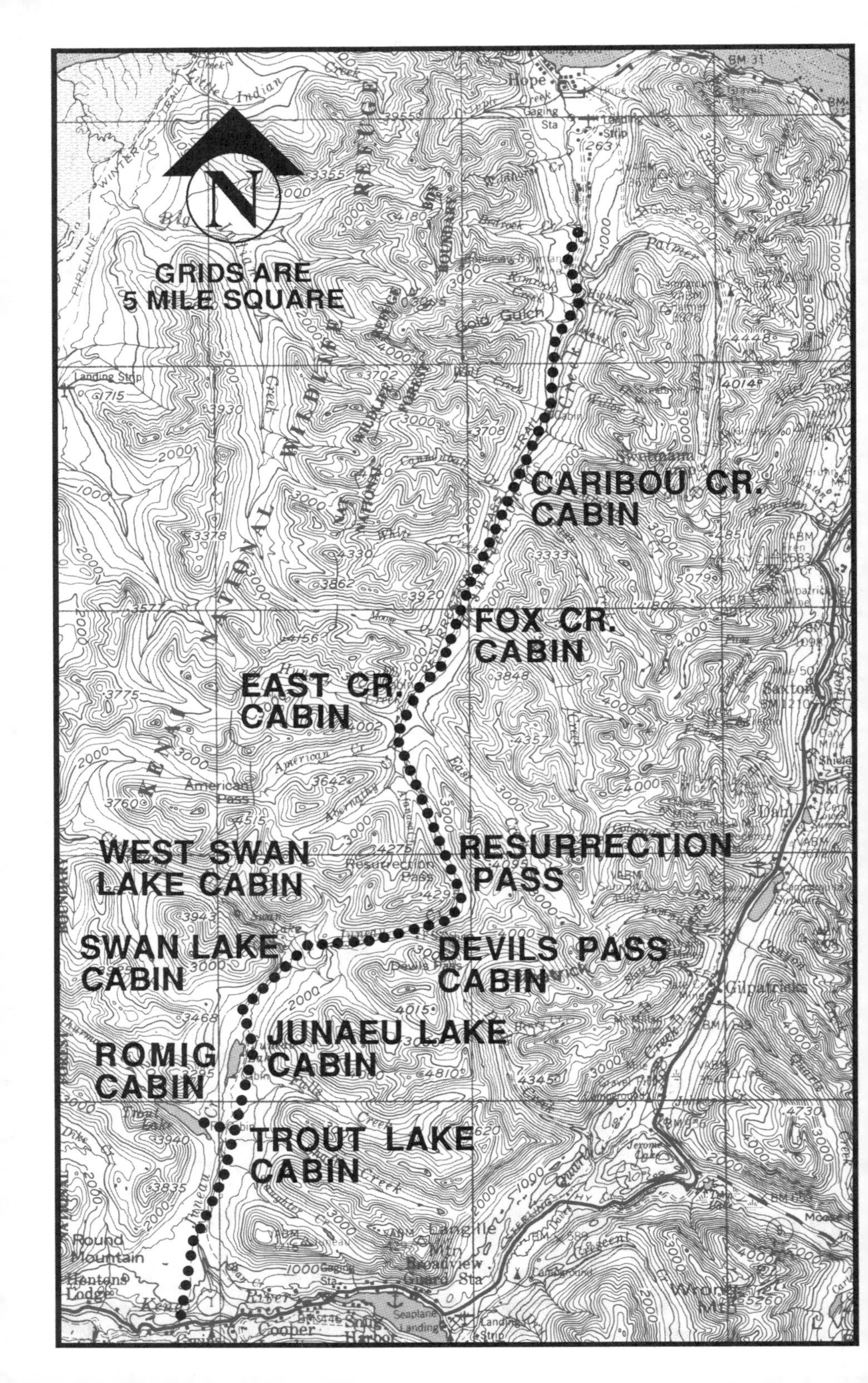
N
GRIDS ARE
5 MILE SQUARE
CARIBOU CR.
CABIN
FOX CR.
CABIN
EAST CR.
CABIN
WEST SWAN
LAKE CABIN
RESURRECTION
PASS
SWAN LAKE
CABIN
DEVILS PASS
CABIN
ROMIG
CABIN
JUNAEU LAKE
CABIN
TROUT LAKE
CABIN
Hope
Resurrection
Pass
American
Pass
Round
Mountain
Cooper
Saxton
Gilpatricks

trail 11

RESURRECTION PASS

Cycle through the impressive Kenai Mountains on a single-track trail as you journey through a land laced with rivers and dotted with alpine lakes. Thick woodlands change slowly to alpine as you advance to the summit of this alluring river valley. Before the turn-of-the-century, miners traveled this route seeking gold-rich claims in Hope. Nine Forest Service cabins offer shelter to the latest wave of travelers on this historic trail, including hikers, bikers and equestrians . For the cyclist who enjoys fishing, all the lakes on this trail have fish. Nearby Russian River is a world-class salmon river and an excellent complement to this alpine adventure. The backcountry traveler should look for moose, bear, sheep, eagles, ptarmigan and other wildlife on this mountainous ride.

AT - A - GLANCE

TRAILHEAD: .....mile 4 Resurrection Rd.

FROM ANCHORAGE: ....76.4 miles

LENGTH OF TRAIL: ...38.6 miles one way

RIDING TIME: ....12 hours to several days

DIFFICULTY: ....3 to 4.5

LOW POINT: ....300 ft.

HIGH POINT: ....2,650 ft.

ELEVATION GAIN: ....2,350 ft.

U.S.G.S. MAPS: ....Seward C-8, D-8, Seward 1 : 250,000

This is a well-maintained soft, earthen trail offering superb traction and a fun ride when dry or damp. In the fall, when wet weather and horses' hooves pound the trail, it quickly becomes a muddy quagmire and should be avoided. Approach erosion control devices with caution. They may cause wheel damage or spill the rider, if crossed improperly.

Three trailheads provide access to this trail system: Hope (mile 4 Resurrection Creek Rd.), Kenai River (mile 53.1 Sterling Hwy.) and Devils Pass (mile 39.5 Seward Hwy.), a 10-mile side trail intersecting near the summit (see Devils Pass). Arrange for transportation at your destination. To start from the Hope trailhead, travel south from Anchorage on the Seward Highway to mile 56.3.Turn right onto the Hope Highway and drive 16.1 miles to Resurrection Creek Road. Turn left and drive 4 miles to the trailhead. Cycle across Resurrection River bridge and begin a slow, steady climb to the summit (2500 ft.) 19.3 miles away. Forest Service cabins, measured from the Hope trailhead, are located at miles 7.1 (Caribou Cr.), 12.5 (Fox Cr.), 14.4 (East Cr.), 21.4 (Devils Pass), 25.8 (Swan and West Swan Lake), 29 & 29.6 (Juneau Lake, Romig) and 30.8 (Trout Lake). Cabins should be reserved in advance with the Forest Service at its Anchorage office (see Agency Information).

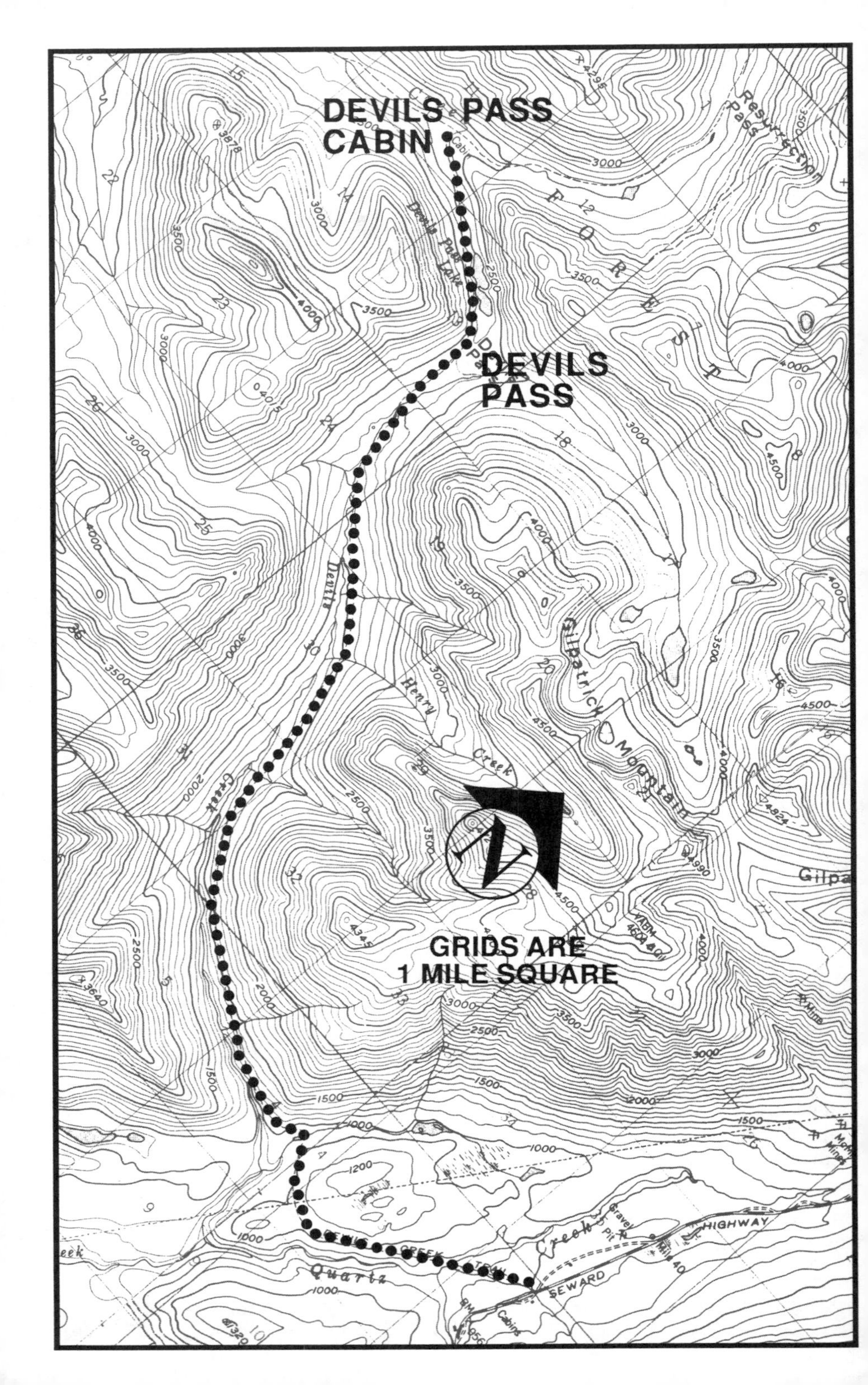
DEVILS PASS CABIN
DEVILS PASS
GRIDS ARE 1 MILE SQUARE
Devils Pass Lake
Resurrection Pass
Devils
Henry Creek
Gilpatrick Mountain
Quartz
HIGHWAY
SEWARD
Gravel Pit
Cabins

trail 12

DEVILS PASS

Craggy peaks and an alpine lake await the cyclist willing to put it in "granny gear" and leave it there as this trail climbs 10 miles into the rugged Kenai Mountains. An "A" frame cabin near the pass invites the mountain biker to invest several days exploring the alpine uplands. This trail connects with the Resurrection Trail System established in the 1890s by waves of gold seekers traveling through the mountains from Seward to Hope. Explore the lake's edge or climb a ridge. Hiking possibilities abound near the pass, where a thin, dry tundra above tree line allows for easy scrambling. Consider biking out via the Resurrection Trail (see Resurrection Trail) to either the Hope trail head (31.6 total miles) or the Kenai River trail head (27.2 total miles). Arrange for transportation or cycle back to the starting point.

AT - A - GLANCE

TRAILHEAD: ......mile 39.5 Seward Hwy.

FROM ANCHORAGE: ....87.5 miles

LENGTH OF TRAIL: ....20 miles round trip

RIDING TIME: ....4 to 6 hours

DIFFICULTY: 4

LOW POINT: ....1,000 ft.

HIGH POINT: ....2,400 ft.

ELEVATION GAIN: ....1,400 ft.

U.S.G.S. MAPS: ....Seward C-7, C-8,
Seward 1 : 250,000

Enjoy a soft, earthen trail with excellent traction (when dry) on this long uphill adventure. Forest Service maintenance keeps this trail, and others in the area, in great shape. Strength, more than skill, is needed to surmount this invigorating mountain ride. All the effort put forth in getting to the top is returned in spades as the downhill ride unfolds. Watch out for traffic, as this is a shared trail with multiple user groups, including other bikers, family hikers, horses and llamas.

Drive south from Anchorage to mile 39.5 of the Seward Highway where a Chugach National Forest sign indicates the trailhead parking lot. An easy-to-follow trail takes the rider across beautiful Quartz Creek on a wide, well-built bridge, then under a power line and over a hill before turning northward into the Kenai Mountains. Parallel Devils Creek from a high bank that winds and climbs as you make your way steadily up the valley. Before long you've reached Devils Pass (2400 ft.) and lofty Devils Pass Lake tucked between narrow mountain walls. Cycle another mile and arrive at Devils Pass Cabin at an intersection with the Resurrection Trail. Cabins, if needed, must be reserved in advance. This popular trail system is well used in the summer. Cabin reservations can be made with the U. S. Forest Service office in Anchorage (see Agency Information).

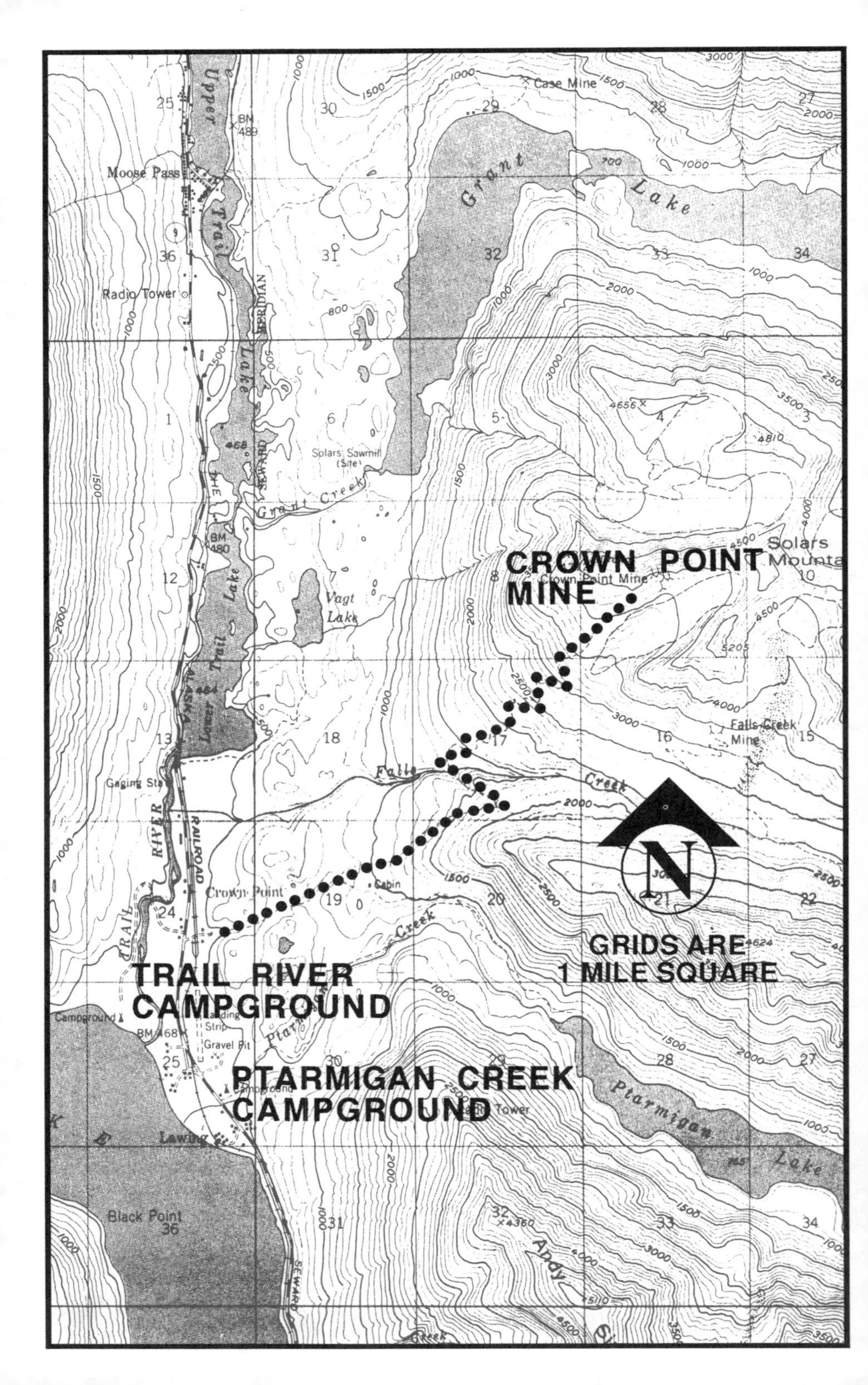
CROWN POINT MINE
TRAIL RIVER CAMPGROUND
PTARMIGAN CREEK CAMPGROUND
GRIDS ARE 1 MILE SQUARE
N
Moose Pass
Upper Trail Lake
Grant Lake
Case Mine
Radio Tower
Solars Sawmill (Site)
Grant Creek
Vagt Lake
Lower Trail Lake
Crown Point Mine
Solars Mountain
Falls Creek Mine
Falls Creek
Crown Point
Cabin
Gaging Sta
Trail River
Alaska Railroad
Campground
Landing Strip
Gravel Pit
Lawing
Black Point
Ptarmigan Lake
Tower

trail 13

CROWN POINT

AT - A - GLANCE

TRAILHEAD:	mile 25.2 Seward Hwy.
FROM ANCHORAGE:	101.4 miles
LENGTH OF TRAIL:	12 miles round trip
RIDING TIME:	3 to 6 hours
DIFFICULTY:	5 (hillclimb)
LOW POINT:	500 ft.
HIGH POINT:	4,200 ft.
ELEVATION GAIN:	3,700 ft.
U.S.G.S. MAPS:	Seward B-7, Seward 1 : 250,000

Stand in a high glacial bowl and absorb the panorama of the snow-capped peaks, rivers, valleys and lakes of the Kenai Mountains. A variety of animals live in these valleys, including moose, bear, Dall sheep, mountain goat, eagles, marmot and ptarmigan. Indulge in this arduous skyward climb to be rewarded with a bird's-eye view of Lower Trail Lake and turquoise Kenai Lake. Present day miners continue to use this road to access gold mines which sit precariously on the cliffs of the upper mountain.

Negotiate dozens of switchbacks on this strenuous ride before reaching trail's end. Possibly the toughest ride on the Kenai Peninsula based solely on climbing, it also rates high for pure scenic beauty. Hike the last leg to the top without your bike for a commanding view of the entire area. This wide road is often rocky and requires considerable stamina to surmount its incline. Several small streams contribute to the erosion of the lower trail, where large rocks force the rider to carefully choose the proper line. Most riders will push their bikes up the steeper grades close to the top. Consider bringing extra clothes for the cooler temperatures near the glacier. Take several breaks on the speedy downhill run to relieve strain on the hands and wrists during hard braking. Make sure all brakes function properly and that a helmet is worn.

Drive south of Anchorage to mile 25.2 of the Seward Highway, just south of Moose Pass. Here, between Trail Creek bridge and Falls Creek bridge turn left and cross the railroad tracks. Park in the vicinity, out of traffic's way. Begin cycling here. Notice a small sign pointing down a country lane indicating Crown Point is 6 miles away. Remain on the main trail as you cycle beyond several private homes before turning left after .5 of a mile and initiating the long uphill climb. Because the upper switchbacks are without water, carry extra. This road ends after 6 miles in a large glacial bowl where active mining continues. Two Forest Service campgrounds, Trail River Campground (mile 24.2 Seward Hwy.) and Ptarmigan Campground (mile 23.1 Seward Hwy.), provide tent sites, drinking water, picnic tables, toilets and fire pits for a small fee .

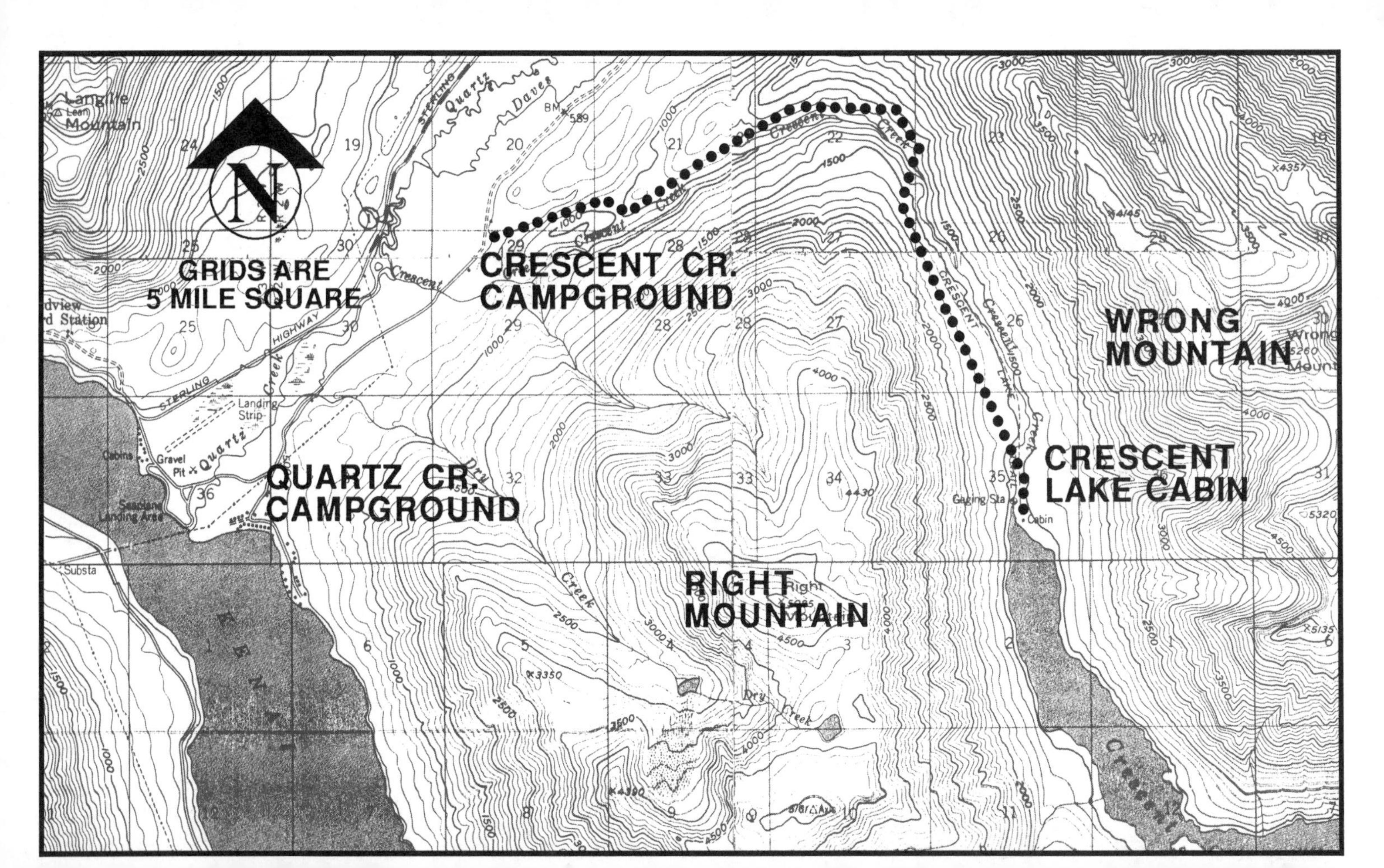
GRIDS ARE
5 MILE SQUARE
CRESCENT CR.
CAMPGROUND
QUARTZ CR.
CAMPGROUND
WRONG
MOUNTAIN
CRESCENT
LAKE CABIN
RIGHT
MOUNTAIN

trail 14 CRESCENT LAKE

This memorable trail takes the rider to a backcountry cabin sitting on a lake's shore with towering mountains reflecting in its waters. As the name implies, this body of water is shaped like a crescent and lies between Right Mountain and Wrong Mountain. Encircled by lofty 5,000-ft. peaks, the rider escapes into a mountain dreamland of flowering meadows and clear-running streams. A U.S. Forest Service cabin, with rowboat, entices the visitor to spend a day or two exploring the area. Paddle around the lake or take a hike into the nearby high country. Fish for trophy sized arctic grayling in the lake .

AT - A - GLANCE

TRAILHEAD: ...mile 3.4 Quartz Creek Rd.

FROM ANCHORAGE: ....101.4 miles

LENGTH OF TRAIL: ..12.8 miles round trip

RIDING TIME: ....3 to 5 hours

DIFFICULTY: ....2.5 to 3

LOW POINT: ....550 ft.

HIGH POINT: ....1,550 ft.

ELEVATION GAIN: ....1,000 ft.

U.S.G.S. MAPS: ....Seward B-7, B-8, C-7, C-8, Seward 1 : 250,000

Expect a leisurely ride on a maintained trail with few hazards to impede the way as you cycle casually up to Crescent Lake. Roll on a hard-pack surface, past birch trees and open fields as this trail meanders gently through a mountain valley. Bridges spanning the largest water crossings along the route help to keep the feet dry. This trail gains less than 1,000 feet in the 6.4 miles you climb to the cabin, and is recommended for most user groups.

At mile 44.9 of the Sterling Highway turn left onto Quartz Creek Road. Two campgrounds on this road, Quartz Creek Campground (mile 0.3 Quartz Creek Rd.) and Crescent Creek Campground (mile 2.7Quartz Creek Rd.), provide tent sites, toilets, water and tables for a small fee. At the end of Quartz Creek Road (mile 3.4) a parking area and signs indicate the trailhead. The U. S. Forest Service requests a travel plan be filed at the trail-use register. This information will be used to better manage this and other trails in the area. Leave the trailhead behind and cycle through the woods and over a hill before crossing the first Crescent Creek bridge (mile 3.4). The trail, at the base of Right and Wrong Mountains, turns in a southerly direction as it loosely follows Crescent Creek up the valley. Cross Crescent Creek a second time, near the lake's mouth, before reaching the cabin (mile 6.4) and the turn around point of your ride. Enjoy a rest as you soak up the magnificent scenery in this mountain getaway.

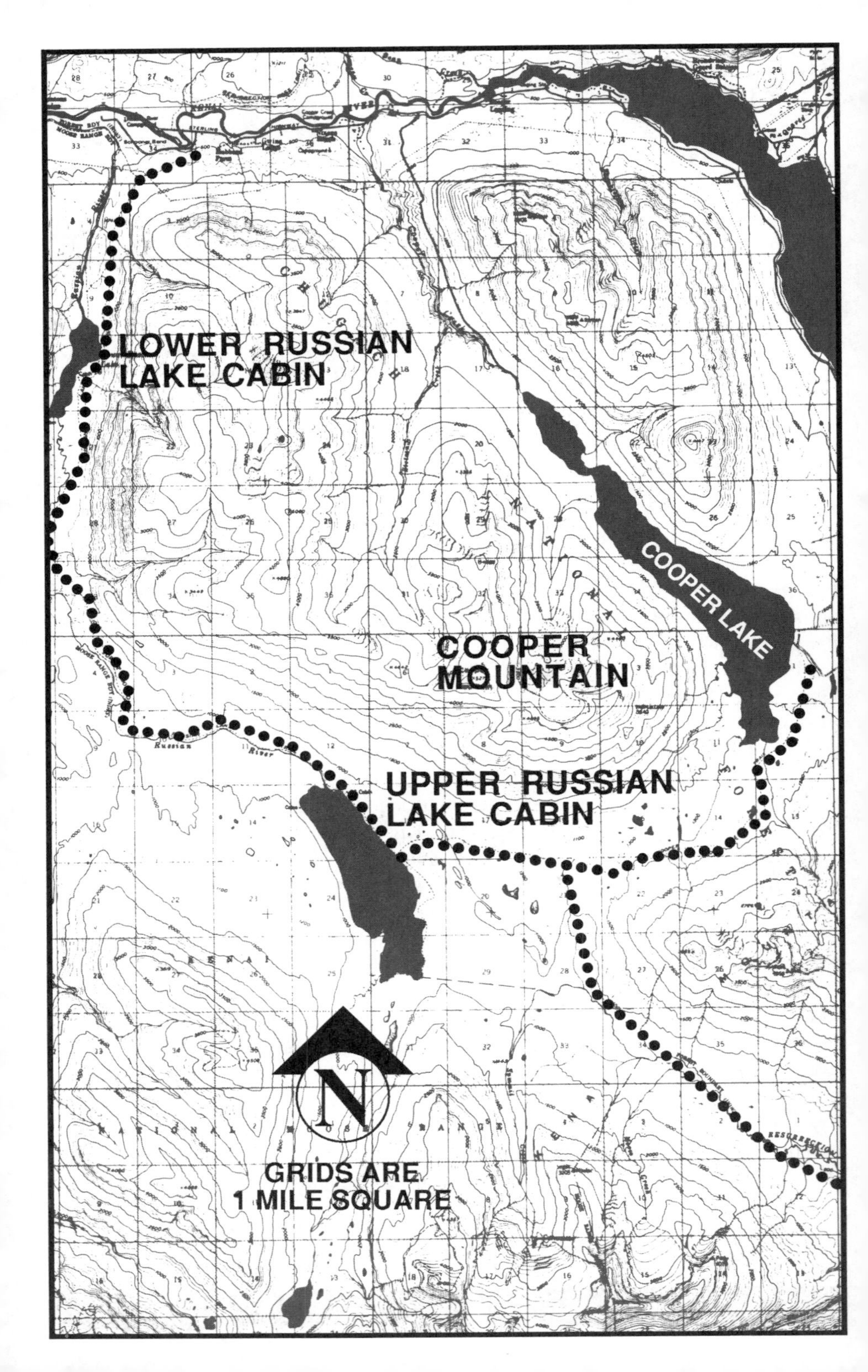

LOWER RUSSIAN
LAKE CABIN
COOPER LAKE
COOPER
MOUNTAIN
UPPER RUSSIAN
LAKE CABIN
N
GRIDS ARE
1 MILE SQUARE

trail 15

RUSSIAN RIVER

AT - A - GLANCE

TRAILHEAD:	mile 52.6 Sterling Hwy.
FROM ANCHORAGE:	105.6 miles
LENGTH OF TRAIL:	21 miles one way
RIDING TIME:	5 to 7 hours
DIFFICULTY:	3 to 4
LOW POINT:	550 ft.
HIGH POINT:	1,475 ft.
ELEVATION GAIN:	925 ft.
U.S.G.S. MAPS:	Seward B-8, Kenai B-1, Seward 1 : 250,000

Enjoy this forested 21-mile ride along the world famous Russian River, where anglers line the banks shoulder-to-shoulder to fish for trophy-sized sockeye (red) and king salmon. Consult with the Dept. of Fish and Game on rules and regulations before fishing in this area (see Agency Information). Brown bear sightings are frequent during salmon season.

Travel through a sub-alpine forest of hemlock, birch and tall grasses on a trail with numerous small hills. A soft, earthen trail allows for easy and enjoyable cycling along this river valley, which passes by the shores of Lower and Upper Russian Lakes. Three U.S. Forest Service cabins are available along this route; Lower Russian Lake (3.6 miles), Aspen Flats (9 miles) and Upper Russian Lake (12 miles). Cabins must be reserved by calling the Forest Service (see Agency Information).

Three trailheads provide access to this popular trail system. The Cooper Lake trailhead can be reached by turning off the Sterling Highway at mile 47.9 and onto Snug Harbor Road. Drive down this maintained dirt road 11 miles, paralleling the beautiful Kenai Lake as you follow U.S. Forest Service signs to a well-marked trailhead. The Russian River trailhead can be accessed at mile 52.6 of the Sterling Highway. Turn into the Russian River Campground to the ranger's shack and pay a small fee for parking before continuing to the well-marked trailhead. If the parking lot is full try parking in the Resurrection Pass parking lot (mile 53.2 of the Sterling Hwy.) and cycling back a short distance to the Russian Lakes trailhead. Stay on the marked main trail as you make your way to lower Russian Lake (mile 2.6), loosely paralleling the wooded Russian River, passing through a recent burn area. Continue on to Upper Russian Lake (mile 12), which sits at the base of Cooper Mountain (5,270 ft.). At mile 16, the Resurrection River trail branches off to the south and continues for 14 miles to the third entrance, Exit Glacier trailhead (see Resurrection River). From this intersection, continue cycling east 5 miles on rolling terrain to the Cooper Lake trail head. Many riders prefer to ride from the Cooper Lake trail head to the Russian Lake trail head. This route has less climbing.

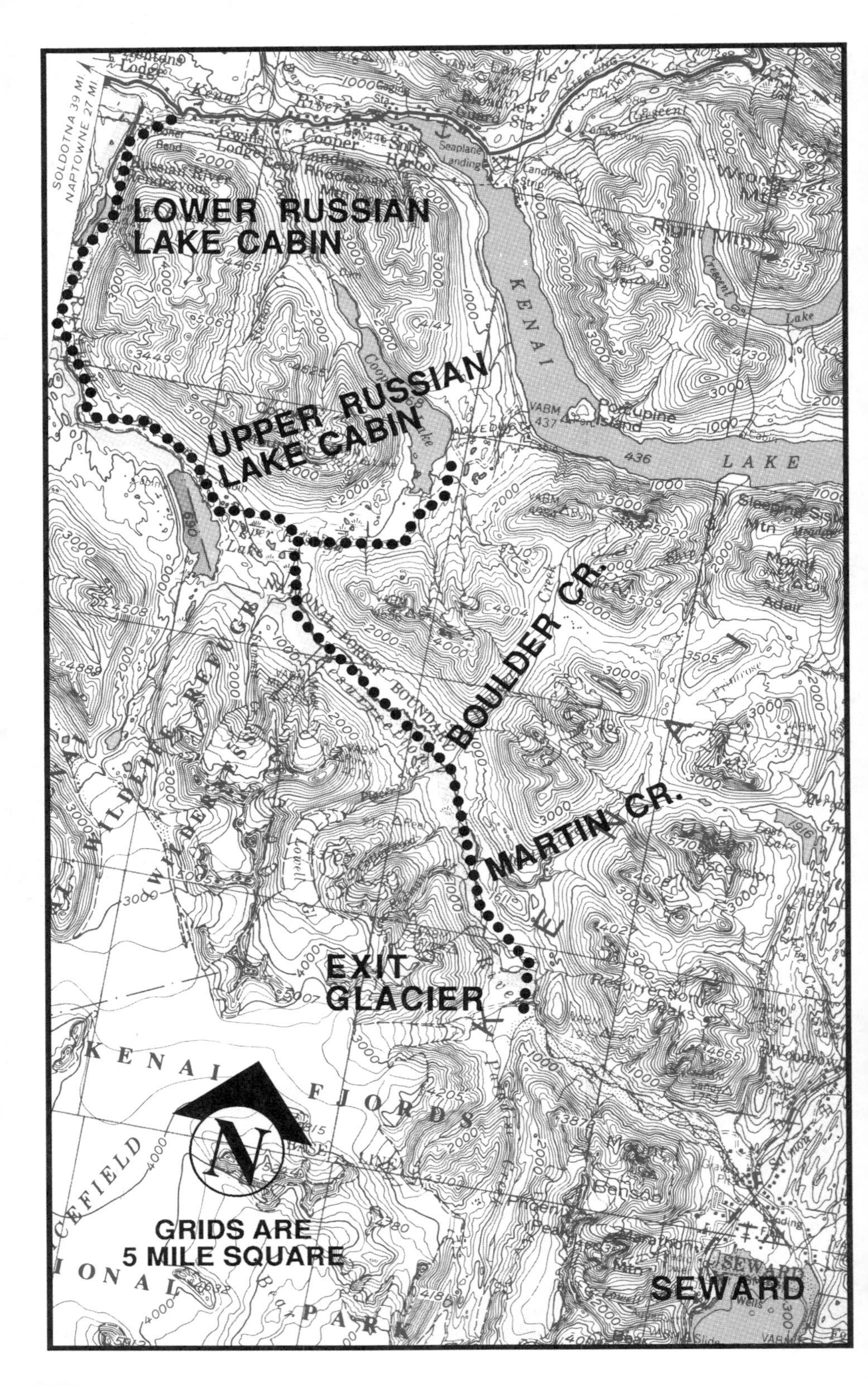
LOWER RUSSIAN LAKE CABIN
UPPER RUSSIAN LAKE CABIN
BOULDER CR.
MARTIN CR.
EXIT GLACIER
SEWARD
GRIDS ARE 5 MILE SQUARE
N
SOLDOTNA 39 MI.
NAPTOWNE 27 MI.

trail 16 RESURRECTION RIVER

Ride a trail lined with tall trees draped in moss as you parallel the Resurrection River and skirt around the gigantic Harding Icefield. The Kenai Mountains rise from the ocean to more than 4,000 feet. This route is the southern leg of the 70-mile Resurrection Trail System, stretching from Seward to Hope. This system, originally established by miners accessing gold claims in the mountains, is now frequented by multiple user groups including hunters, hikers and bikers.

AT - A - GLANCE

TRAILHEAD: ....mile 11 Snug Harbor Rd.

FROM ANCHORAGE: ....111.9 miles

LENGTH OF TRAIL: ....16 miles one way

RIDING TIME: ....8 to 12 hours

DIFFICULTY: 4

LOW POINT: ....400 ft.

HIGH POINT: ....1,475 ft.

ELEVATION GAIN: ....1,075 ft.

U.S.G.S. MAPS: ....Seward A-8, B-8, Seward 1 : 250,000

An earthen trail, loamy on occasion, offers the rider good traction and easy riding during dry conditions but has the potential for being very muddy. One section of boggy ground, approximately 4 miles long, is often wet and slow even during dry times. Erosion control ditches (50 or 60 of them) present the greatest hazard to the cyclist. Approach these with care . They could cause wheel damage or spill the rider if crossed improperly. Stop and enjoy the numerous open glades, which provide an opportunity to view the surrounding mountains. In August and September, black and brown bears gather along the Resurrection River to feed on spawning salmon. Exercise caution, particularly around Boulder and Martin creeks. Please note that the mosquitoes in the area can be very annoying. It is recommended that you bring ample bug dope and head nets .

Three trailheads provide access to this route. Cooper Lake trailhead, the most-favored starting point, can be reached by turning off the Sterling Highway at mile 47.9 onto Snug Harbor Road. Parallel beautiful Kenai Lake as you drive 11 miles down this maintained dirt road to a well-marked U. S. Forest Service trailhead. The Russian River entrance is at mile 52.6 of the Sterling Highway while the Exit Glacier trailhead is approached by turning off the Seward Highway at mile 3.7 onto the Exit Glacier Road. Travel this maintained dirt road 7.5 miles to a marked Forest Service trailhead just before crossing the Resurrection River bridge. All trailheads are well marked and the trail easy to follow. Three U. S. Forest Service campgrounds are located near the trail heads: Cooper Creek (mile 50.7 Sterling Hwy.), Russian River (mile 52.6 Sterling Hwy.) and Primrose Landing (mile 17 Seward Hwy.).

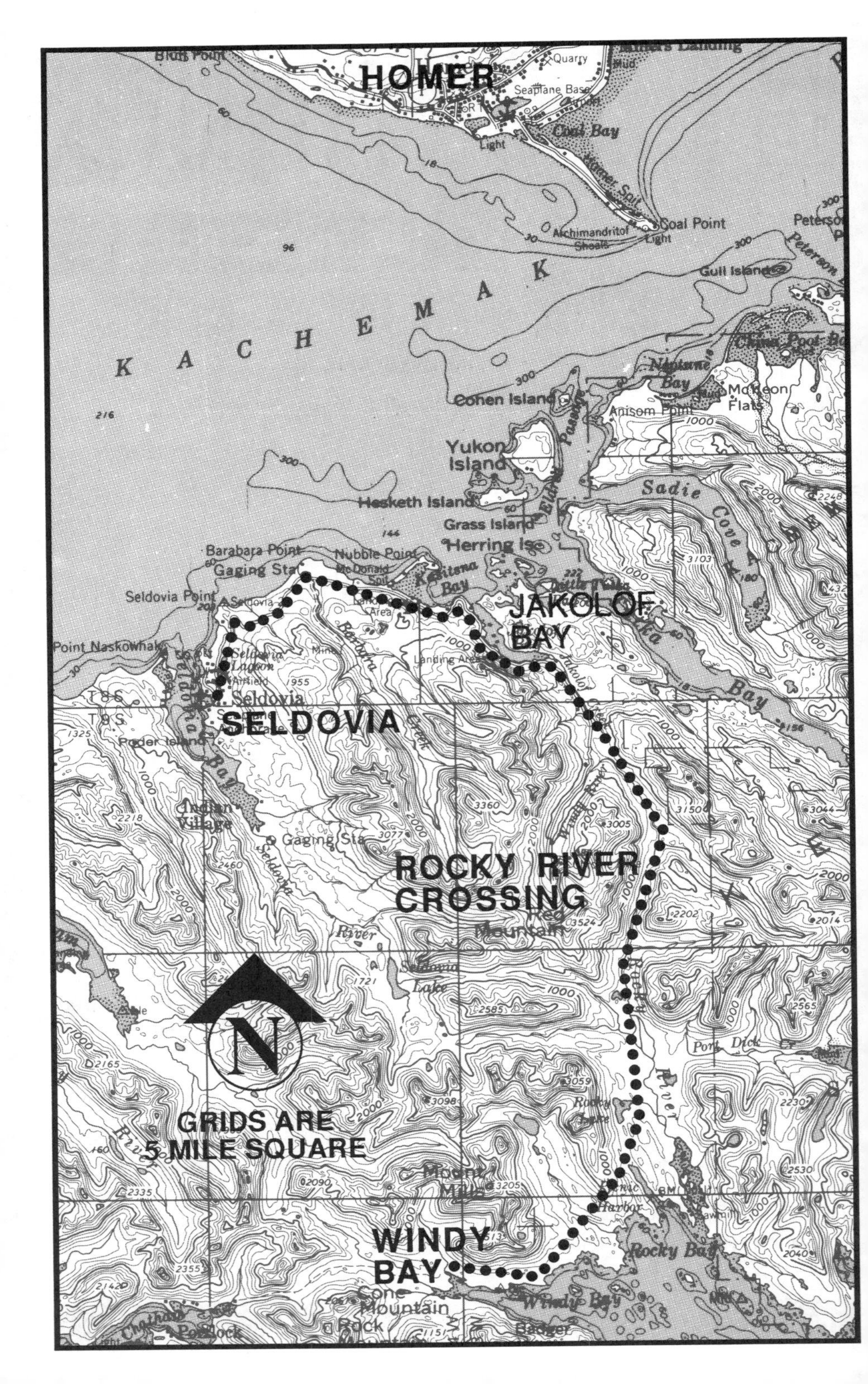
HOMER
Quarry
Seaplane Base
Coal Bay
Light
Coal Point
Archimandritof Shoals
Gull Island
K A C H E M A K
Cohen Island
McKeon Flats
Anisom Point
Yukon Island
Hesketh Island
Grass Island
Herring Is
Sadie Cove
Barabara Point
Gaging Sta
Nubble Point
Seldovia Point
Point Naskowhak
JAKOLOF BAY
Landing Area
SELDOVIA
Indian Village
Gaging Sta
ROCKY RIVER CROSSING
Red Mountain
Seldovia Lake
Port Dick
Rocky Lake
Mount Mills
Rocky Bay
Windy Bay
WINDY BAY
Cone Mountain
Rock
Badger
GRIDS ARE 5 MILE SQUARE
N

trail 17

ROCKY RIVER

AT - A - GLANCE

TRAILHEAD:	Seldovia
FROM ANCHORAGE:	241.8 miles
LENGTH OF TRAIL:	39 miles round trip
RIDING TIME:	10 hours to several days
DIFFICULTY:	4
LOW POINT:	sea level
HIGH POINT:	650 ft.
ELEVATION GAIN:	650 ft.
U.S.G.S. MAPS:	Seldovia B-5, B-4, Seldovia 1 : 250,000

Forested mountains rise from the ocean as waves sparkle below on this scenic coastal ride along Kachemak Bay. Marvel at the enormous glaciers that spill from the Harding Icefield, creating the hundreds of bays and fiords around it. The rich and varied ecosystems of the area — marine, coastal, woodlands and alpine — burst with life during the summer.

A maintained gravel road twists, winds and roller-coasters 12.5 miles to an old wood mill at the back of beautiful Jackalof Bay. From here, an unmaintained remote mountain trail — once a road — crosses rugged terrain with many hazards before traversing the Kenai Mountains to the Gulf of Alaska. For many, the ride to the end of Jakolof Bay is plenty. For others, the backcountry adventure just begins. The powerful forces of erosion have damaged or eliminated several bridges and have washed away large sections of trail. Numerous fallen trees also slow travel. Cyclists must be totally self sufficient on this backcountry trail. There are no services beyond Seldovia. A public easement allows travel (on the roadway only) to Windy Bay. If you intend on camping or hiking off the roadway beyond Jakaolof Bay, call the Port Graham Corporation for a special permit (see Agency Information).

Getting there is half the fun. Leave spectacular Homer Spit aboard the state ferry or a local sea charter and cross Kachemak Bay to the enchanting coastal town of Seldovia. Take in the town before cycling north on the Seldovia Red Mountain Road. Cycle above shoreline on a high bluff overlooking Kachemak Bay. MacDonald Spit (mile 8) offers a distraction for the photographer. From the end of Jakolof Bay (mile 12.5) the road quickly deteriorates and suffers progressively each year from lack of maintenance. Cross numerous creeks that are thigh deep or less. Rocky River (mile 19.5) stops most visitors with its deep, swift water. Great camping and salmon fishing can be found along its banks. Exercise caution crossing this or any moving water. An obvious trail continues for about another 10 miles to Windy Bay on the Gulf of Alaska.

chapter 3

GLENN HIGHWAY

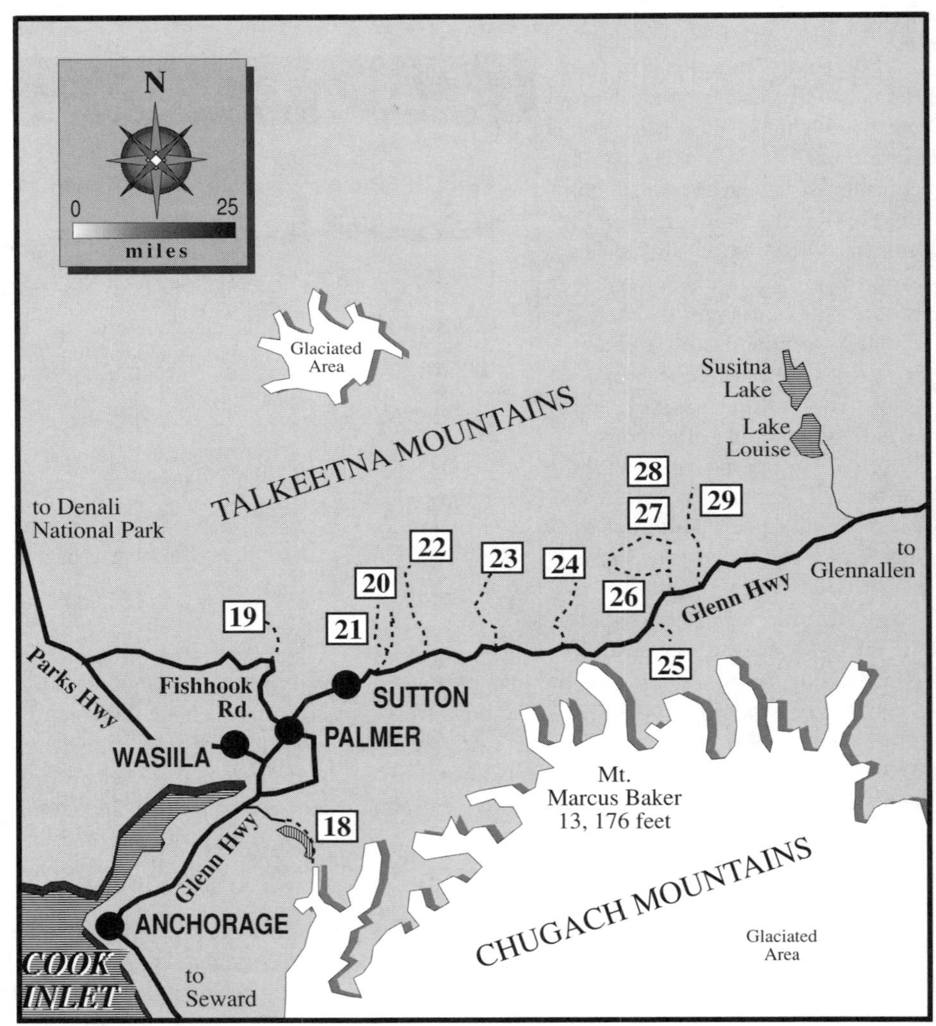

The scenic Glennallen Highway (Glenn Hwy.) travels 189 miles northeast of Anchorage to Glennallen. Along the way you pass countless mountains, rivers and lakes. South of the roadway is the Chugach Mountains and to the north the Talkeetna Mountains. Dozens of mining trails penetrate into the wilderness, allowing the cyclist to explore river bottoms, woodlands, and mountain passes.

Many of the trails in this chapter begin with a steep climb above tree line, affording the visitor with spectacular views of the surrounding area. The easiest rides are trails 18,19, 25 and 26. Trail 18, Eklutna Glacier, is a ride that everyone should do. Trail 28, because of its length, is the hardest, followed by trails 22, 23, and 24.

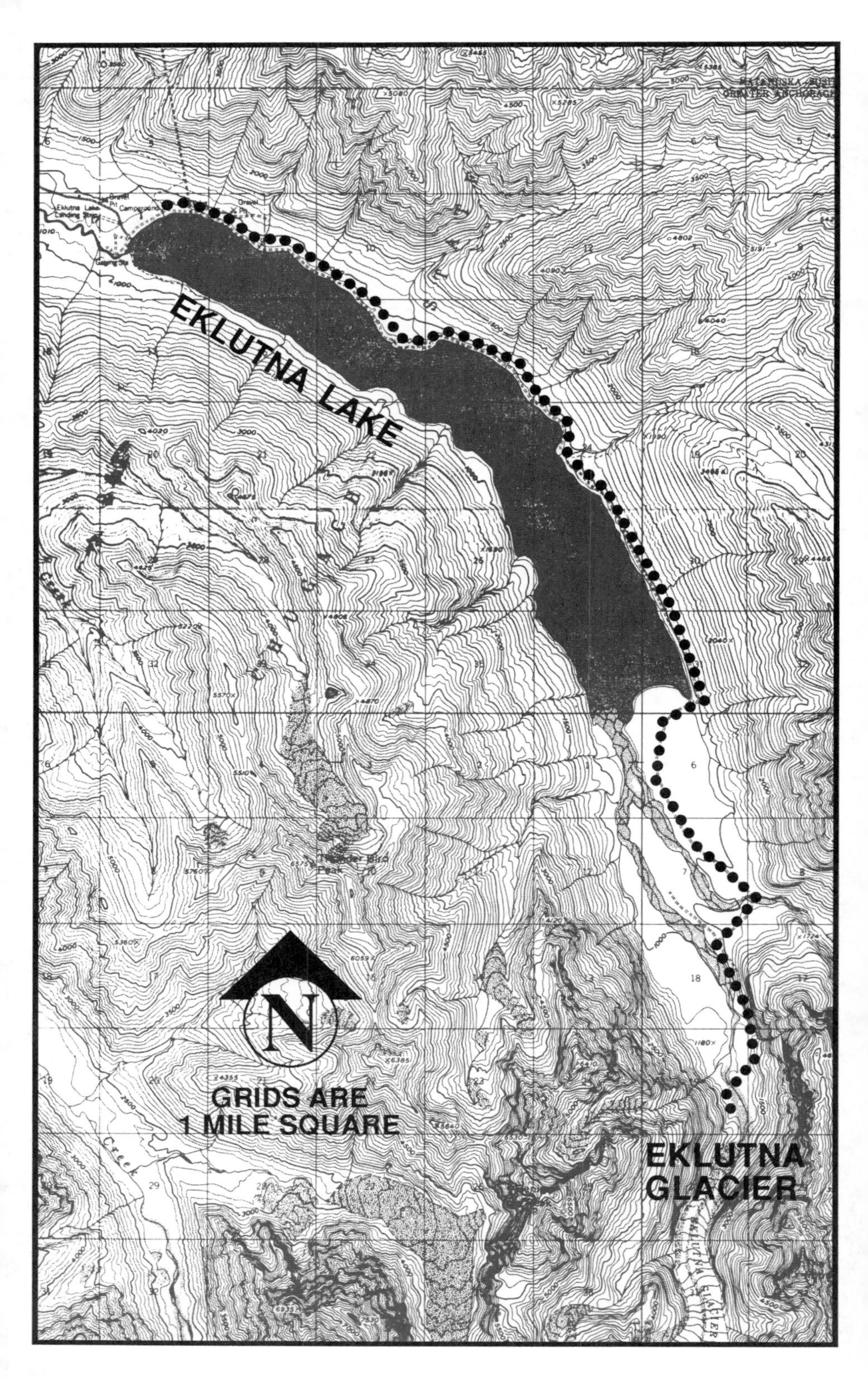
EKLUTNA LAKE
GRIDS ARE
1 MILE SQUARE
EKLUTNA
GLACIER
N
Thunder Bird Peak
MATANUSKA-SUSITNA
CENTER ANCHORAGE

trail 18 EKLUTNA GLACIER

Towering mountains, a turquoise lake and a glacier, combined with a wide, easy road make this ride a must for everyone. This scenic valley is home to Dall sheep, moose, eagles and a few rarely seen bears. The Eklutna Lake Recreation Area has camp sites for 50, a picnic area, boat launch, drinking water, toilets and several hiking trails. Also, several established backcountry camp sites are available, making this trail popular for those who like to load up the bike with camping gear for overnight trips. Many families with children also frequent this trail, either with bike trailers or with children on their own bikes.

AT - A - GLANCE

TRAILHEAD: ....mile 10 Eklutna Lake Rd.
FROM ANCHORAGE: ....36.5 miles
LENGTH OF TRAIL: ....26 miles round trip
RIDING TIME: ....3 to 6 hours
DIFFICULTY: ....2 to 3
LOW POINT: ....850 ft.
HIGH POINT: ....1,100 ft.
ELEVATION GAIN: ....250 ft.
U.S.G.S. MAPS: ....Anchorage B-6,
Anchorage 1 : 250,000

This spacious, unmaintained dirt road allows for a leisurely ride as it follows the shore of beautiful and tranquil Eklutna Lake. Trail hazards, all of which are easily negotiated, include a handful of rocky or sandy sections and several places where erosion has damaged the trail. Most of the road is relatively flat, with only a few small hills to tackle. Park regulations allow for motorized vehicle use on this trail Sunday through Wednesday, leaving Thursday through Saturday for non-motorized uses. If you are seeking a quiet bike ride, and time permits, try going on non-motorized days.

Drive 26 miles east of Anchorage to the Eklutna exit. Go right, taking the frontage road heading back toward Anchorage. Drive .5 of a mile and take a left onto the Eklutna Lake Road. Drive 10 miles on a winding dirt road to the last parking lot. Several large State Park information boards mark the trail head. Cross a small bridge and turn right. You are now on the main road, which is easy to follow, using provided mile markers. A number of side trails branch off, inviting those wishing to explore. At the lake's end (mile 7) the trail continues toward ever-narrowing mountain walls with waterfalls. Eklutna Alex Campsite (mile 8.8), Kanchee Campsite (mile 11) and Cottonwood Campsite (mile 12) are available to the backcountry camper. Kanchee is Athabaskan for porcupine. If you wish to see the glacier, park regulations request (with a big sign at mile 13) that you leave your bike behind and travel on foot a short distance around a glacial moraine. If you have the time, the hike is worthwhile.

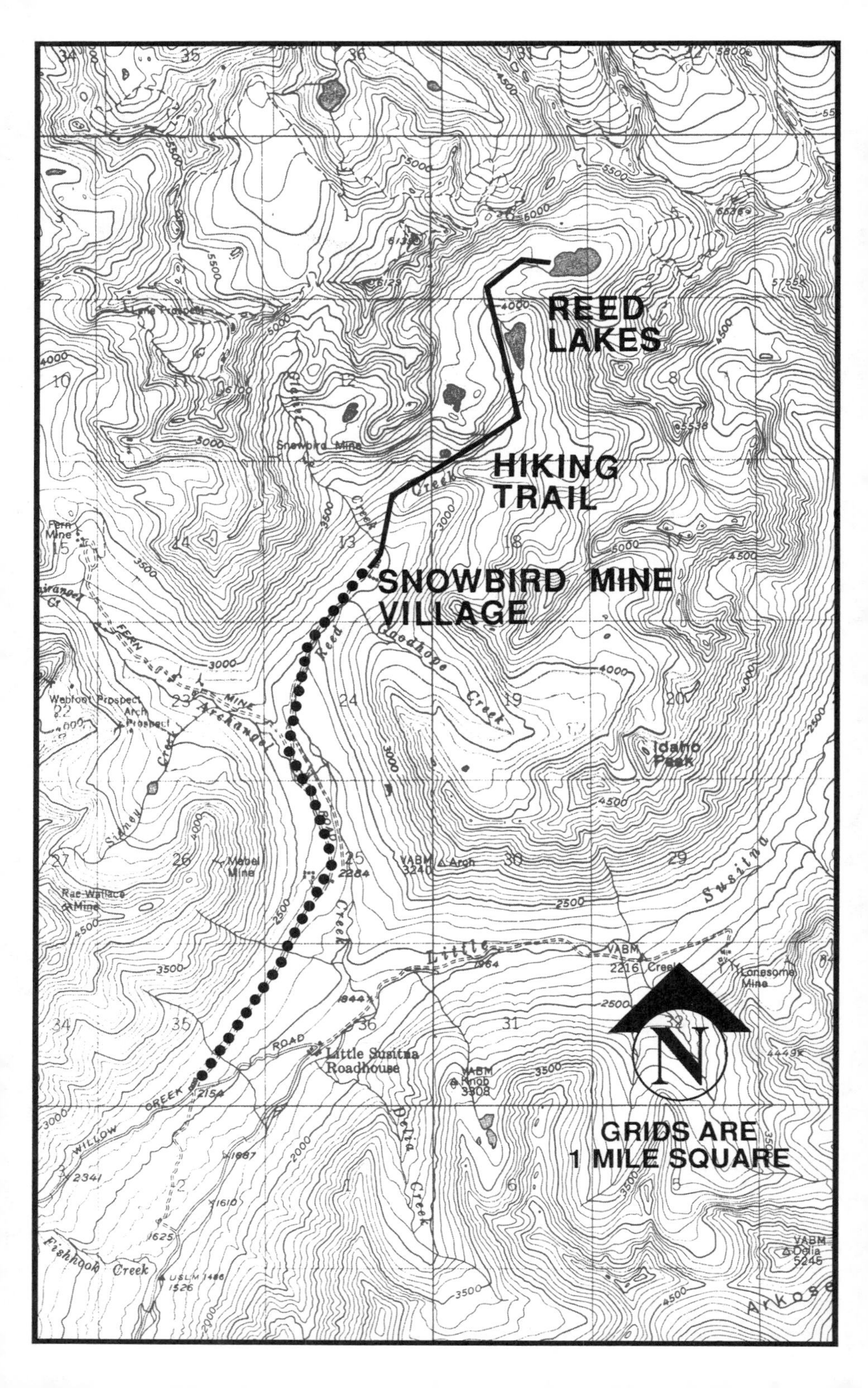
REED LAKES
HIKING TRAIL
SNOWBIRD MINE VILLAGE
GRIDS ARE 1 MILE SQUARE
N
Snowbird Mine
Fern Mine
Webfoot Prospect
Arch Prospect
Mabel Mine
Rae-Wallace Mine
Little Susitna Roadhouse
Lonesome Mine
Idaho Peak
Reed Creek
Goodhope Creek
Archangel Creek
Little Susitna Creek
Delia Creek
Fishhook Creek
Willow Creek Road

trail 19

REED LAKES

AT - A - GLANCE

TRAILHEAD: . . mile 14.6 Hatcher Pass Rd.

FROM ANCHORAGE: . . . . 64.1 miles

LENGTH OF TRAIL: 7 mile bike, 6 mile hike

RIDING TIME: . . . 1.5 hour bike, 5 hour hike

DIFFICULTY: . . . . 3 to 3.5

LOW POINT: . . . . 2,250 ft.

HIGH POINT: . . . . 4,250 ft.

ELEVATION GAIN: . . . . 2,000 ft.

U.S.G.S. MAPS: . . . . Anchorage D-5, Anchorage 1 : 250,000

Visit this magical place tucked into the Talkeetna Mountains, where waterfalls feed alpine lakes and crystal clear pools disappear into boulder fields. This is a wonderful combination trip, consisting of a short bike ride above tree line and a spectacular mountain hike. Miners seeking mineral wealth found gold in these mountains and built these roads to access their claims. Nearby Independence Mine State Park offers informative guided tours through the refurbished remains of the once-flourishing mining industry.

Cycle on hard-pack dirt and through an eroded creek bed before hiking on a well established foot trail. The foot path is in good condition with a few damaged areas. In one section the hiker must hop from boulder to boulder. In the fall, blueberries line the steep mountainsides. Rock climbers are often seen on the exposed rock faces along this trail.

Drive east of Anchorage to mile 49.5 of the Glenn Highway. Turn left onto the Fishhook-Willow Road (also called Hatcher Pass Rd.) which turns to gravel after 7 miles. Pass a lodge and make a hairpin turn going up mountain. The next right, at mile 14.6, is the trailhead. Park here, out of traffic's way. Cycle along this road, crossing a bridge over Archangel Creek. Turn right into a small parking area (mile 2) and cycle down an unmaintained trail damaged by erosion. Hide and lock your bikes in the tall brush surrounding the abandoned Snowbird Mine Village (mile 3.5). Just past the abandoned buildings, cross Reed Creek on boulders and follow a foot path up a steep hill. Scramble through a boulder field toward ever narrowing mountain walls. Between these walls lie a string of beautiful pools with sandy bottoms that tempt the visitor on hot days to take a dip. Dry off in the thick green grass and wild flowers that line these pools. Beyond are the beautiful Reed Lakes, each a little higher in the valley, and a cascading waterfall. It is about a 6 mile round trip hike to Upper Reed Lake from Snowbird Mine Village. There are no maintained campgrounds in this area. Off-the-trail camping however, abounds. Several lodges and Bed and Breakfasts in the area provide most services.

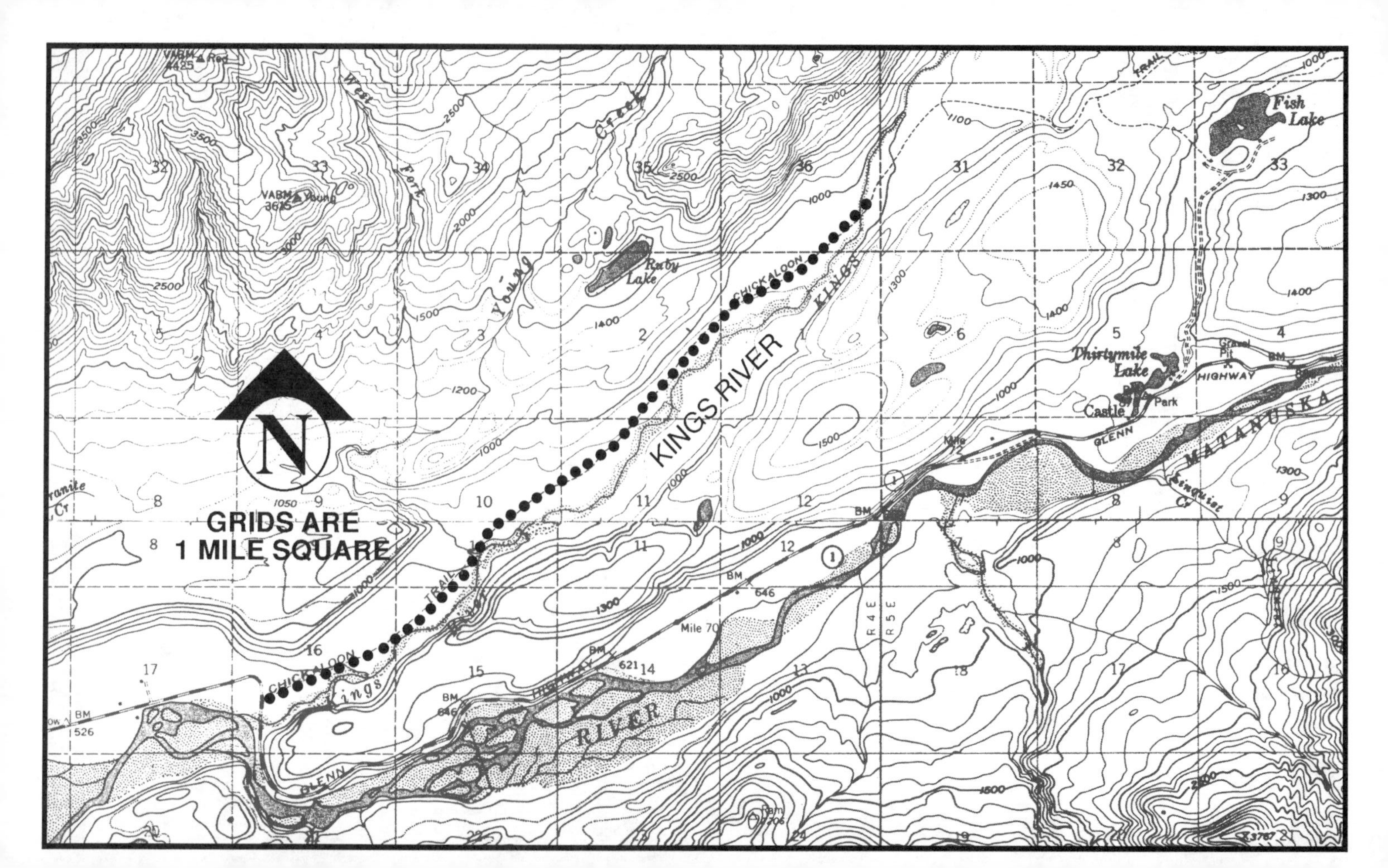

N
GRIDS ARE
1 MILE SQUARE
KINGS RIVER
CHICKALOON
KINGS
TRAIL
Kings
Ruby Lake
Young Creek
West Fork
Fish Lake
Thirtymile Lake
Castle
Park
Gravel Pit
HIGHWAY
GLENN
MATANUSKA
RIVER
Kinquist Cr
Mile 70
R 4 E
R 5 E
VABM Red 4425
VABM Young 3615

trail 20

KINGS RIVER

AT - A - GLANCE

TRAILHEAD: ....mile 66.7 Glenn Hwy.

FROM ANCHORAGE: ....66.7 miles

LENGTH OF TRAIL: ....10 miles round trip

RIDING TIME: ....2 to 4 hours

DIFFICULTY: 3

LOW POINT: ....550 ft.

HIGH POINT: ....900 ft.

ELEVATION GAIN: ....350 ft.

U.S.G.S. MAPS: .....Anchorage C-5, D-5, Anchorage 1 : 250,000

In the fall, brilliant light pours through openings in this dense woodland and dances on the blanket of fallen leaves and shrubs under wheel. This lush forest in the Talkeetna Mountains supports a variety of flowering plants, berries and mushrooms. Mining activity in the Nelchina area prompted the building of this trail in 1914. Today it is shared by mountain bikers, hikers, equestrians, ORVs and hunters. This trail lies within the Matanuska Valley Moose Range and is recognized as important moose winter habitat.

For the most part, this level trail is soft and earthy, providing good traction as it loosely parallels the Kings River. Several hazards exist in this forested ride. They include numerous fallen trees, tree roots and rocky sections. Riding is slow but not strenuous and all hazards are easily negotiated.

At mile 66.7 of the Glenn Highway, just before the highway crosses the Kings River, pull into a large parking area on the left and secure a place out of the way. Begin cycling here. The trail crosses under a telephone line and parallels the Kings River. Numerous campsites exist along this early section of trail. Do not enter land that is posted as private property. Soon the trail becomes rocky as you near Young Creek, which is swift and knee deep. Try crossing the creek on a large fallen cottonwood 100 feet down river. Enter a tall cottonwood grove, which often is wet. At about mile 2.5 the trail makes an obvious split. The left trail goes immediately up a steep hill. This is the Young Creek trail (see Young Creek). Keep right, continuing to parallel the Kings River. This trail rambles over bumpy roots and around numerous downed trees. Soon you'll be riding a beautiful trail high on a river bank with a wonderful view of Pinnacle Mountain and Kings Mountain in the nearby Chugach Mountains. The trail ends on the banks of Kings River (mile 5). The water here is swift and often deep. Enjoy lunch under tall cottonwoods on the banks of the river as you take in the view. A small foot path leads up river. State-maintained King Mountain Campground (mile 76 Glenn Hwy.) provides tent sites, drinking water and toilets for a small fee.

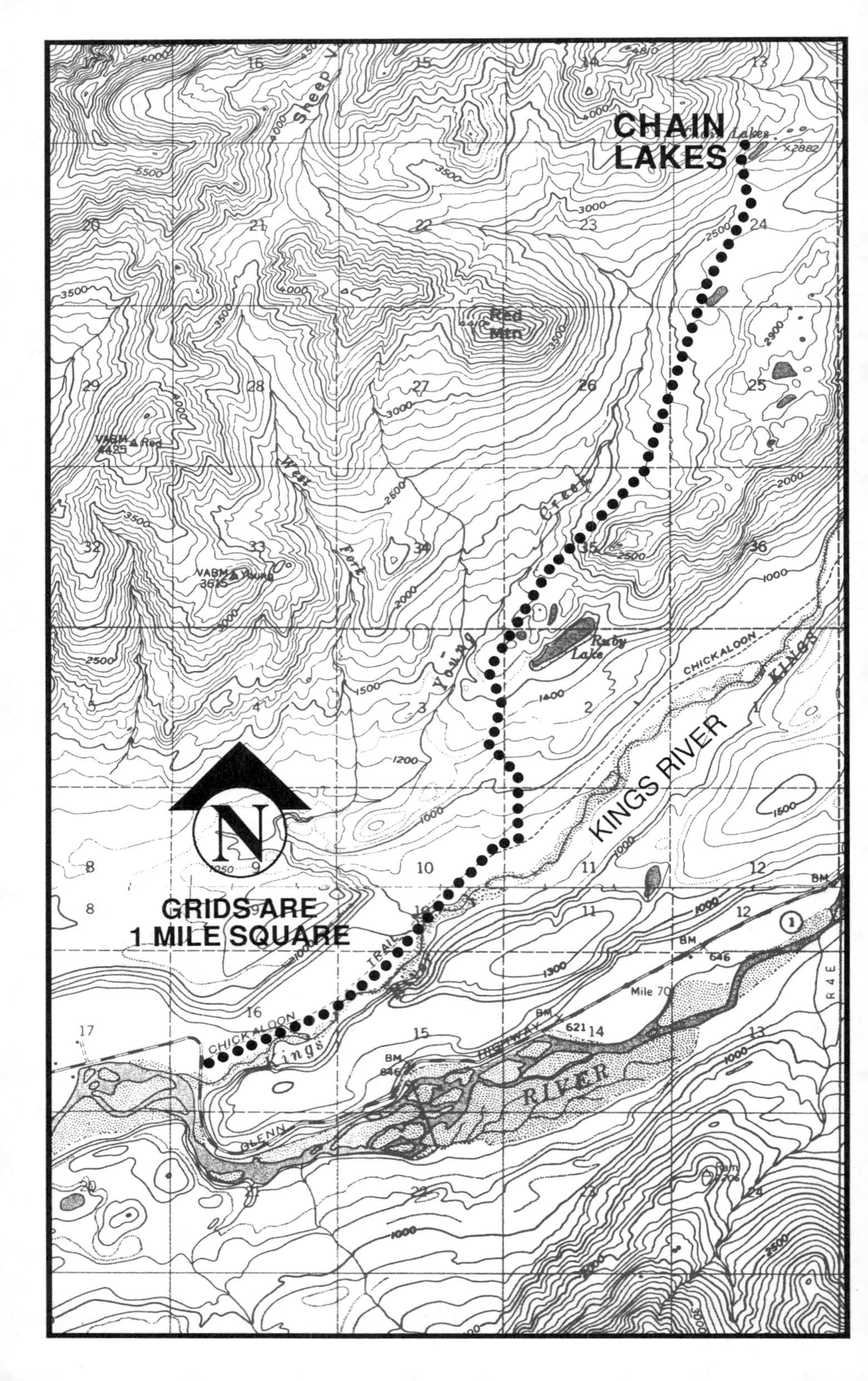

CHAIN LAKES
Red Mtn
Sheep
West Fork
Young Creek
Ruby Lake
CHICKALOON
KINGS RIVER
Kings
RIVER
TRAIL
HIGHWAY
GLENN
Mile 70
GRIDS ARE 1 MILE SQUARE
N
VABM 4425 Red
VABM 3615 Young
R 4 E

trail 21

YOUNG CREEK

Climb this roller-coaster trail into the Talkeetna Mountains to a high perch above the Kings River, affording the cyclist a fantastic view of the valley below and of mighty Castle Mountain. Looking southwest, the rider can gaze across the Palmer Flats, viewing – Knik Arm, the Chugach Mountains and the Anchorage Bowl. This trail starts out on the historic Chickaloon-Knik-Nelchina Trail System, constructed in 1914, before the Glenn Highway was built.

AT - A - GLANCE

TRAILHEAD: ....mile 66.7 Glenn Hwy.

FROM ANCHORAGE: ....66.7 miles

LENGTH OF TRAIL: ....13 miles round trip

RIDING TIME: ....3 to 5 hours

DIFFICULTY: ....3.5 to 4.5

LOW POINT: ....550 ft.

HIGH POINT: ....2,550 ft.

ELEVATION GAIN: ....1689 ft.

U.S.G.S. MAPS: .....Anchorage C-5, D-5, Anchorage 1 : 250,000

The trail is mostly hard-pack dirt with occasional rocky areas, where erosion has damaged the route. Several perennial mud holes are easily negotiated. The rider should expect ample climbing as this trail surmounts small hills, which level out only to climb again. Weak legs may have to walk one or two of these inclines, but the panorama at the top and the downhill descent are the payoffs for the arduous investment.

East of Anchorage, just before the Glenn Highway crosses the Kings River (mile 66.7), pull into an large parking area. Begin cycling here. The trail crosses under a telephone line and parallels the Kings River going upstream. Several fine camp sites are found along this early section of trail. Do not enter land that is posted as private property. Soon the trail becomes rocky as you near swift, knee-deep Young Creek. Cross the creek (look 100 feet downstream for a log crossing) and enter a tall cottonwood grove, which often is wet. At about mile 2.5 the trail splits, with the lower trail going right, paralleling the Kings River (see Kings River). Take the left trail and climb a steep hill with good traction. Stay on this trail as you pass by several side trails, and a large mud hole with an old green truck in it. Climb through a forest of tall trees to a level area where the trail forks (mile 4.3). A left takes you to a crossing of Young Creek, where a trail leads the rider up and around Red Mountain. Take the right trail, which is not obvious, and climb through a wet area and past several beautiful lakes with first-rate camp sites. Continue on to a high ridge above tree line and past an alpine lake for a superb vista of massive Castle Mountain (mile 6.5).

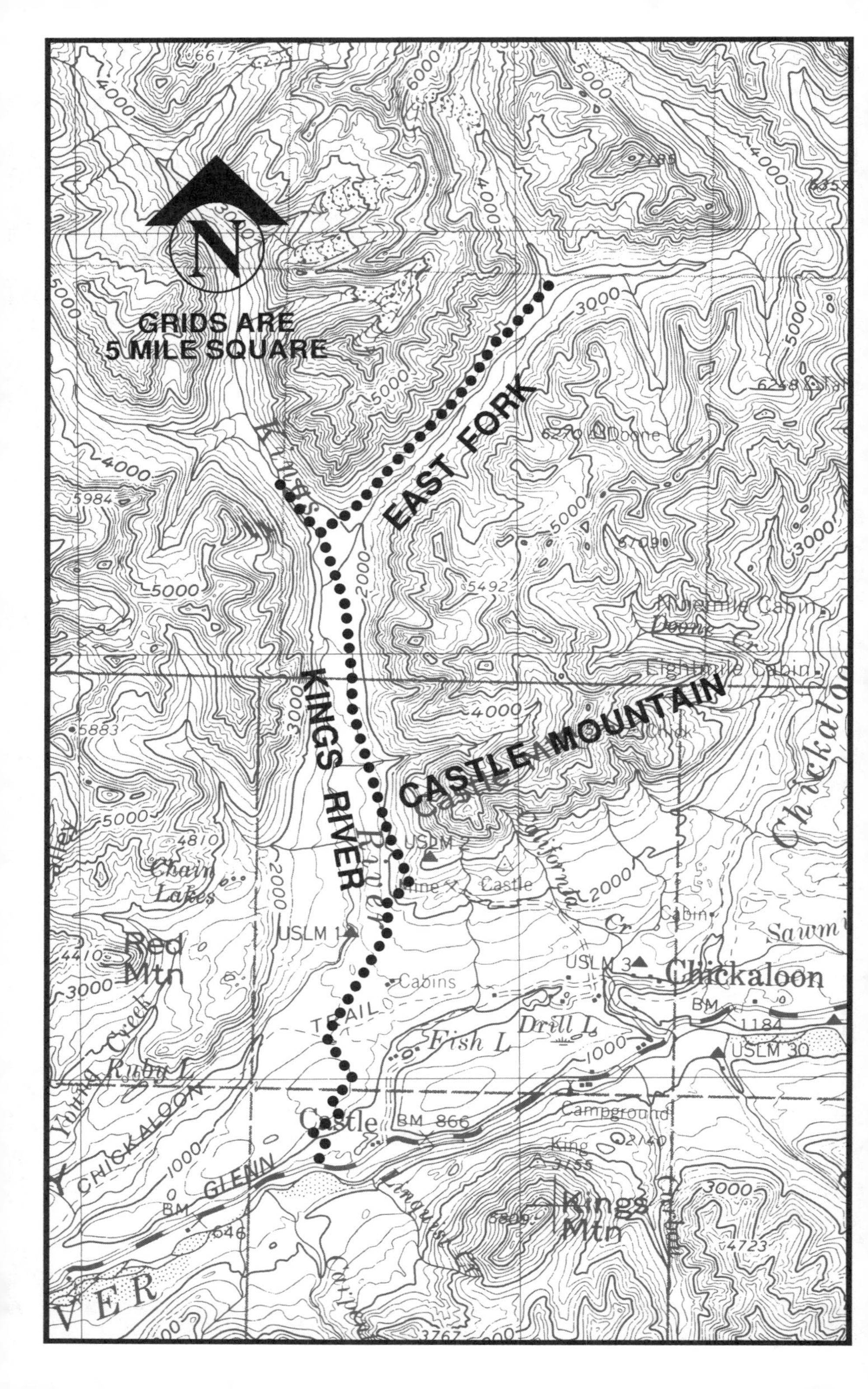

N
GRIDS ARE
5 MILE SQUARE
EAST FORK
KINGS RIVER
CASTLE MOUNTAIN
Red Mtn
Chain Lakes
Chickaloon
Kings Mtn
Castle
Cabins
TRAIL
Fish L
Drill L
Ruby L
Young Creek
CHICKALOON
GLENN
Campground
Eightmile Cabin
Doone Cr
USLM 1
USLM 3
USLM 30
BM 866
Mine
Cabin

trail 22

PERMANENTE RD.

Impressive Castle Mountain towers above as the cyclist scrambles about on its lower flank. Kings River flows below, fed by numerous creeks and a multitude of glaciers sweeping off 6,000 ft. peaks. A dense forest crowds itself from river bank to mountainside like a thick, green carpet. Watch for moose, Dall sheep and bear. This road was built in the 1960s to access various limestone claims in the valley. It offers a long ride, complete with impressive views of steep, glaciated mountains, timbered countryside and wild rivers. Permanenti Road is also known as Permanente, Permenenti and Castle Mountain Trail.

AT - A - GLANCE

TRAILHEAD: ....mile 71.5 Glenn Hwy.

FROM ANCHORAGE: ....71.5 miles

LENGTH OF TRAIL: ....37 miles round trip

RIDING TIME: ....8 to 12 hours

DIFFICULTY: 4

LOW POINT: ....700 ft.

HIGH POINT: ....2,600 ft.

ELEVATION GAIN: ....1,900 ft.

U.S.G.S. MAPS: ....Anchorage D-5,
Anchorage 1 : 250,000

Wide and unmaintained, this miner's road rolls through thick woodlands and a rocky river bottom. On occasion, growing alders and water erosion choke the route. This is particularly evident on the hills, which should be ridden with caution. This will be a challenging ride for some, because of its length and the number of hills. Trail conditions vary from muddy to hard-pack to rocky riverbed. Several water crossings, knee deep or less, are easily negotiated.

From Anchorage, travel east on the Glenn Highway to mile 71.5. Turn left (north) onto a small, easy-to-miss side road. Park out of the way in an obvious parking area. Cycle north and climb a maintained gravel road. Veer right at the first intersection (mile .75), leaving the maintained road. A homemade street sign nailed to a tree just beyond a private drive indicates this trail as "Permanenti Rd." Continue going north (straight) at an intersection with the Chickaloon-Knik-Nelchina Trail System (mile 2.75). At the top of a steep, rough hill (mile 5.6) take a left, passing a less-used side trail. Continue on the main trail, climbing small hills and crossing several creeks. Exceptional camp sites can be found near mile 7.5 and mile 10.5. Cross the east fork of Kings River and enter a grove of tall trees. Take a right at the next intersection (mile 12) and loosely parallel the northeast fork of the river until the trail ends in a boulder field with excellent views of the valley (mile 18.5).

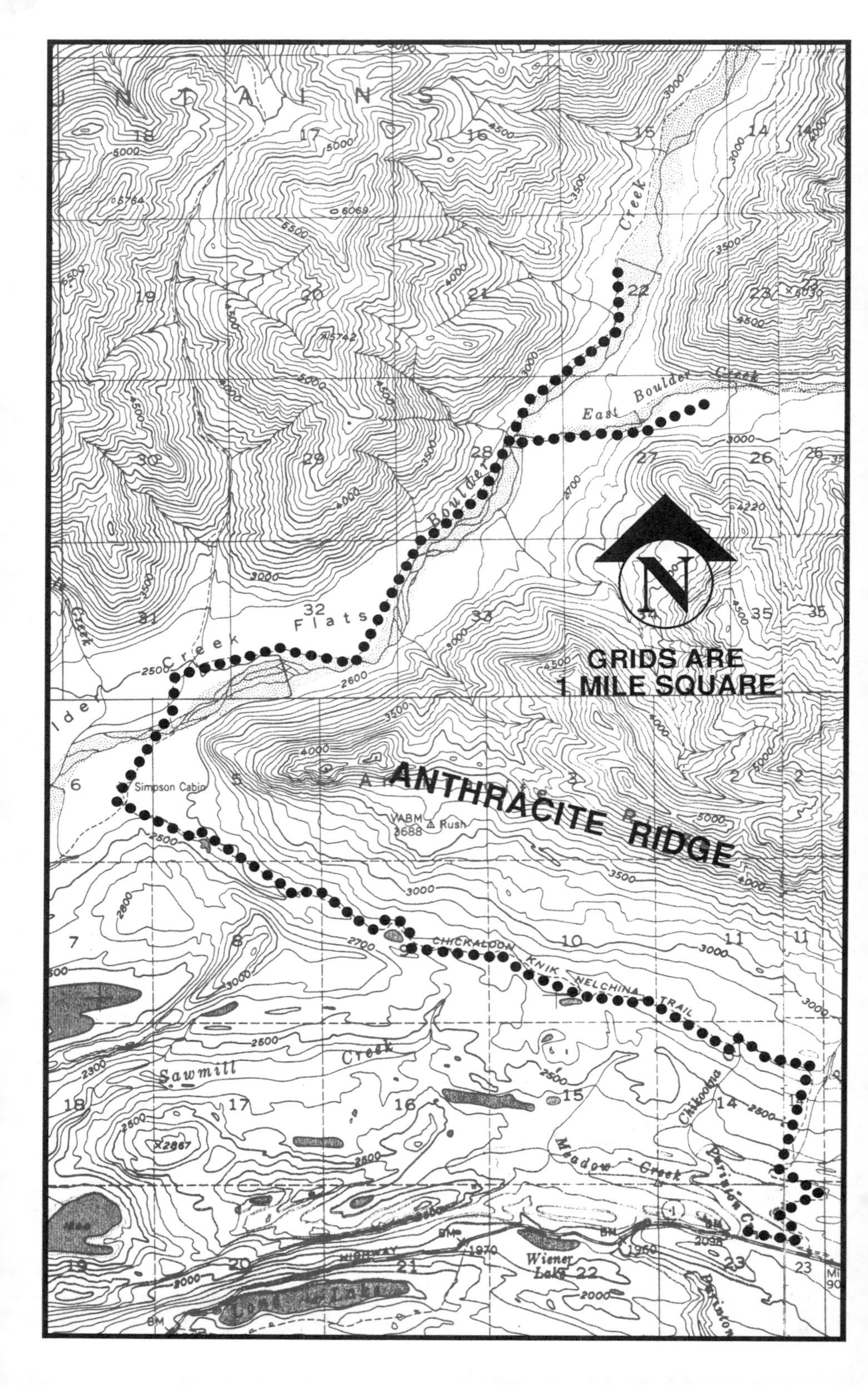
GRIDS ARE
1 MILE SQUARE
ANTHRACITE RIDGE
Simpson Cabin
Boulder
Creek
Flats
East Boulder Creek
CHICKALOON KNIK NELCHINA TRAIL
Sawmill
Creek
Meadow Creek
Chikoona
Wiener Lake
HIGHWAY
VABM 3688 Rush

trail 23

PURINTON CREEK

AT - A - GLANCE	
TRAILHEAD:	89 Glenn Hwy
FROM ANCHORAGE:	89 miles
LENGTH OF TRAIL:	22 miles round trip
RIDING TIME:	8 to 12 hours
DIFFICULTY:	4
LOW POINT:	2,100 ft.
HIGH POINT:	2,800 ft.
ELEVATION GAIN:	700 ft.
U.S.G.S. MAPS:	Anchorage D-4, D-5, Anchorage 1 : 250,000

Cycle above tree line and witness an incredible panorama of two mountain ranges towering face-to-face. The Chugach Mountains (south) and the Talkeetna Mountains (north) rise out of the silty Matanuska River Valley. A multitude of rivers and streams flow from these mountaintops, feeding the rich and varied ecosystem below. Moose, bear, caribou and Dall sheep are a few of the inhabitants in this drainage. Flowering plants and berries abound.

A wide, easy-to-follow, unmaintained trail, more of a road at times, immediately climbs a ridge and parallels striking Anthracite Ridge. Climb numerous short, steep hills and easily negotiate the perennial mud holes. Pass through several miles of blueberry fields and by a series of beautiful sub-alpine lakes offering ideal spots for lunch. The trail surface starts out as hard-pack dirt (mud when wet) and gradually gets rocky as you round Anthracite Ridge and drop into Boulder Valley. Here you ride on rocky river bottom and gravel bars as you cross the braided, knee-deep Boulder River numerous times.

East of Anchorage, at mile 89 of the Glenn Highway, park in a pullout at the Purinton Creek bridge (a state highway sign spells it Puritan). Do not block a natural embankment used to load ORVs. Cycle east a short distance, crossing Purinton Creek bridge and take the first left onto a dirt road. The rider now crosses private property for a short distance. Do not park or camp on this land. Turn left (.3 of a mile) and climb a ridge. At mile 1, turn left. Ride along this ridge a short distance before turning right (mile 1.2) and descend, only to climb again. At mile 2.1 turn left and follow Anthracite Ridge. Several established camp sites can be found along this section. Just after mile 4 the trail splits again, providing alternate routes to the same location. Start dropping into Boulder Creek valley as you round Anthracite Ridge (mile 6.6). Once at the river (mile 7.6), travel upstream on a rocky riverbed, picking the best route that day. At mile 11, the east fork of the Boulder meets the main river at a wide flood plain. The adventurous can find additional exploring up either creek. Nearby Long Lake state campground (mile 85.3 Glenn Hwy.) offers camp sites, drinking water, toilets and fishing.

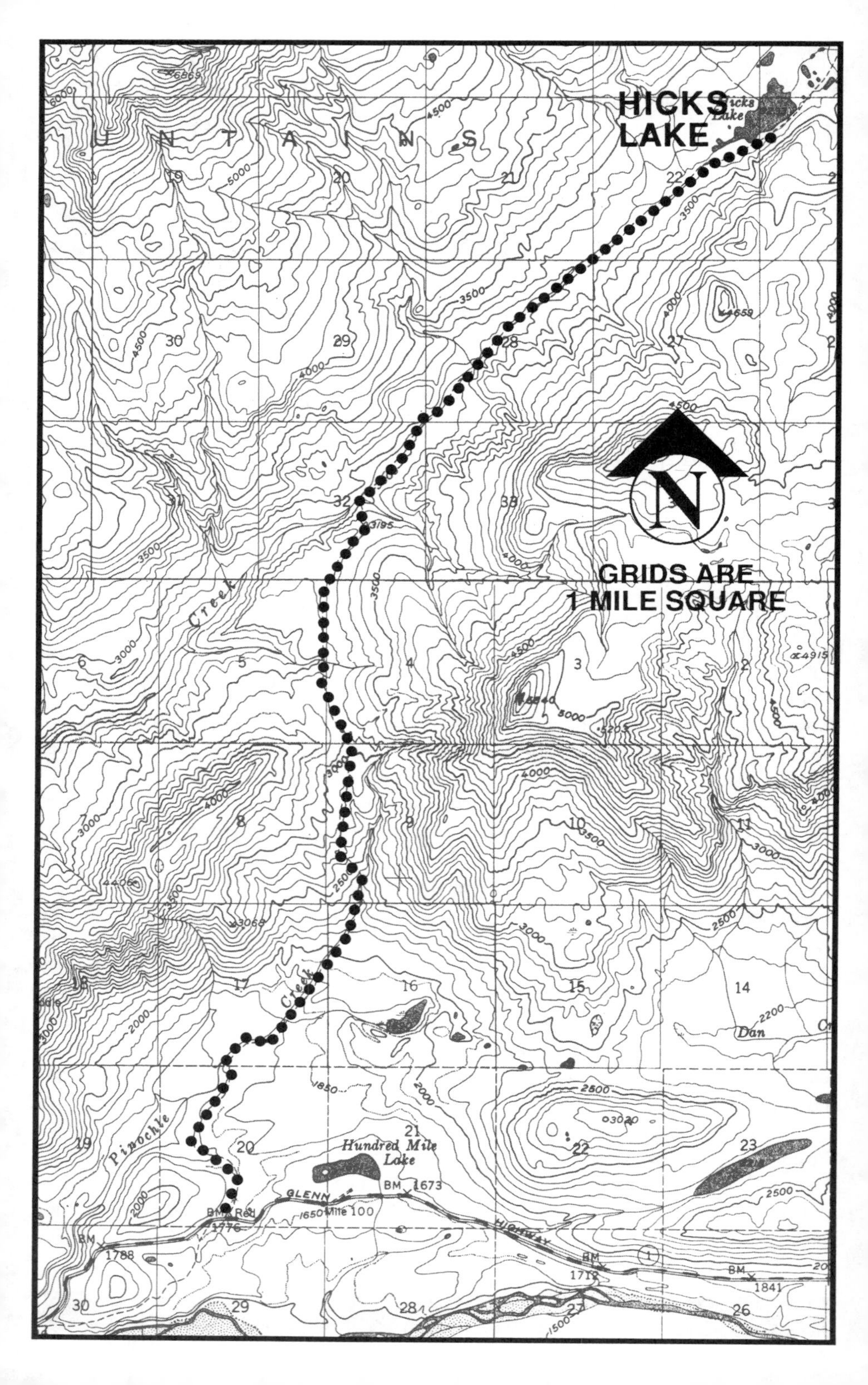
HICKS LAKE
GRIDS ARE 1 MILE SQUARE
N
Creek
Creek
Pinochle
Hundred Mile Lake
GLENN HIGHWAY
Mile 100
Dan

trail 24

PINOCHLE CREEK

AT - A - GLANCE

TRAILHEAD: ....mile 99.2 Glenn Hwy.

FROM ANCHORAGE: ....99.2 miles

LENGTH OF TRAIL: ..18.4 miles round trip

RIDING TIME: ....6 to 8 hours

DIFFICULTY: 4

LOW POINT: ....1,750 ft.

HIGH POINT: ....3,200 ft.

ELEVATION GAIN: ....1,400 ft.

U.S.G.S. MAPS: .....Anchorage C-3, D-2, Anchorage 1 : 250,000

Flowing off 13,176-foot Mt. Marcus Baker in the Chugach Mountains, the Matanuska Glacier, 3.5 miles wide at its terminus, is the dominant feature at this trail head. Thousands of years ago this river of blue ice stretched down the valley nearly reaching the city of Palmer 60 miles away. The Pinochle trail was built by turn-of-the-century miners who hauled needed equipment to mining claims along the creeks and rivers in the Talkeetna Mountains. Hunting and recreation now provide most of the traffic into this mountainous playground.

This historic trail, which is wide and easy to follow, takes the biker past several alpine lakes and into the Caribou Creek drainage. Climb a steep mountain pass on a dirt trail. Cyclists should expect wet feet as this trail crosses several shallow creeks and two swampy areas. Because of the earthen surface a muddy trail can quickly develop during wet conditions.

Turn south into a large gravel pullout at mile 99.2 of the Glenn Highway. Park here, out of traffic's way. Cycle directly across the highway to the north side, up a dirt road. Ride through a swampy area, where numerous ORV trails skirt muddy sections. Stay on the main trail heading north. Smaller, less used trails branch off to private land. Climb out of the wet lowlands through a small wooded section to a particularly steep, long hill. Some of it is ridable, but for many this will be a walk. Soon you've crested the pass and are in wide open country (mile 4). Follow the trail down and then around a hillside, where half a dozen paralleling ORV trails have scarred this traverse. Pick the best route that day. A long, steep hill drops the rider into Hicks Creek, where remnants of mining still linger. A wide gravel road climbs slowly to Hicks Lake (mile 9.2) and the smaller lakes beyond. For many, this will be a good place to turn around. Water erosion from Divide Creek has damaged the trail to Caribou Creek. Hiking trails, however, continue going up and down Caribou Creek. Nearby Matanuska Glacier State Recreation Site (mile 101 Glenn Hwy.) offers camp sites, water, tables and toilets for a small fee. Hiking trails near the campground provide wonderful opportunities for photographing the glacier.

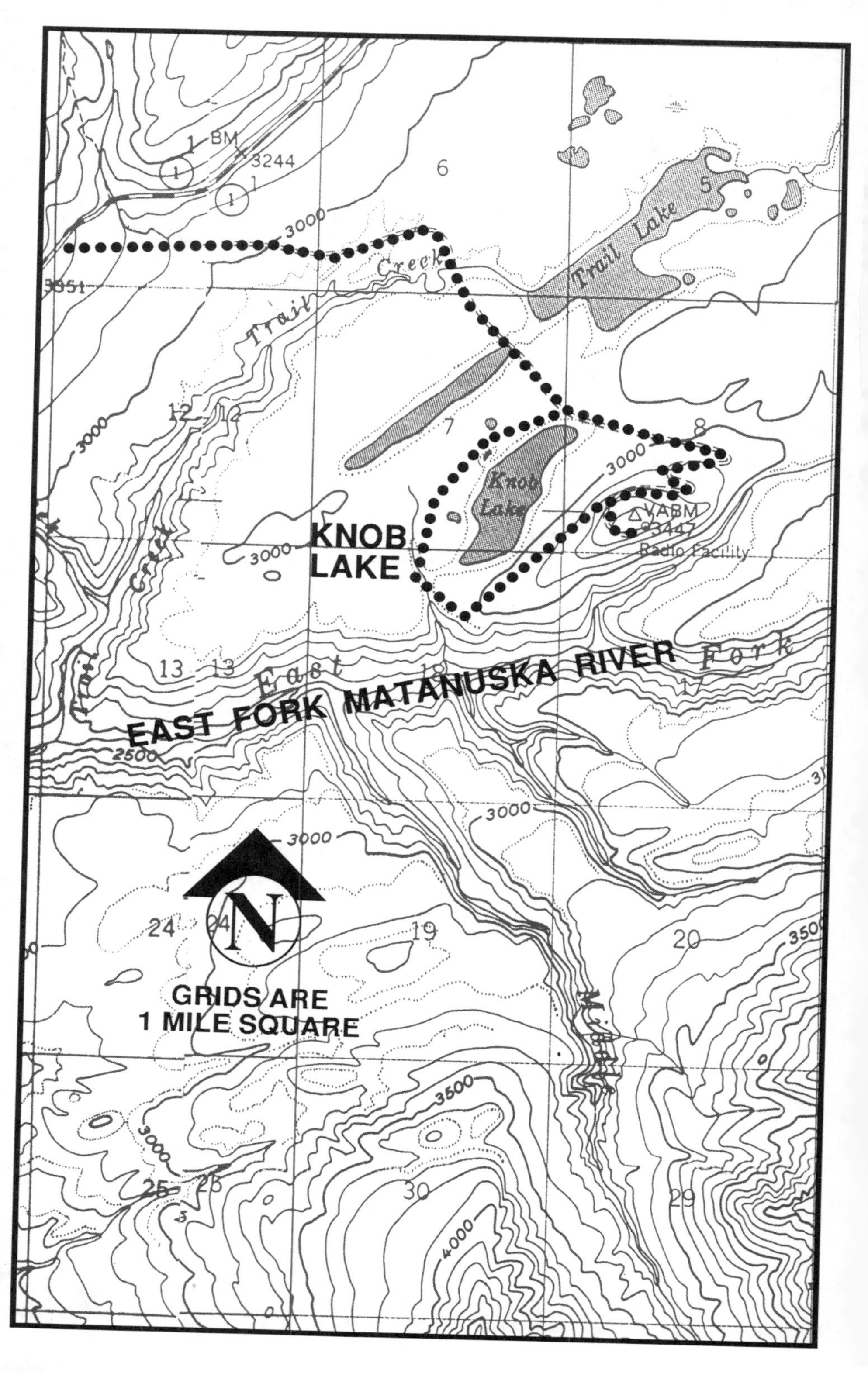
KNOB
LAKE
EAST FORK MATANUSKA RIVER
Trail Lake
Trail Creek
Knob Lake
VABM
3447
Radio Facility
BM
3244
East Fork
GRIDS ARE
1 MILE SQUARE
N
3000
2500
3500
4000

trail 25 KNOB LAKE

This fall, fill your empty containers with fat, juicy blueberries while surrounded by lakes that lie at the feet of the mighty Chugach and Talkeetna mountains. Climb Knob Hill for a bird's-eye view of broad, lake-studded Tahneta Pass. To the west is Gunsight Mountain, Sheep Mountain and Lion Head, all popular landmarks. Cycle along the high banks of the East Fork of the Matanuska River which carved this 300-foot-deep ravine. Scramble down this steep bank to the glacial-fed waters and explore this seldom-visited area.

AT - A - GLANCE

TRAILHEAD: ......mile 118.5 Glenn Hwy.

FROM ANCHORAGE: ....118.5 miles

LENGTH OF TRAIL: ...8.5 miles round trip

RIDING TIME: ....2 to 3 hours

DIFFICULTY: 2

LOW POINT: ....2,950 ft.

HIGH POINT: ....3,350 ft.

ELEVATION GAIN: ....400 ft.

U.S.G.S. MAPS: ....Anchorage D-1, Anchorage 1 : 250,000

This fun and relatively easy ride takes the visitor first across a maintained gravel road and then through brushy country on a soft, earthen path that circles Knob Lake. In late fall, ride through a rainbow of colors as the bushes and tundra make their seasonal change. Blueberries abound in the short brush of this sub-alpine ecosystem. You will fill your containers in no time as the berries are easy to pick and quite plentiful.

Park in a gravel pullout at mile 118.5 of the Glenn Highway out of traffic's way. Those wishing to can drive several miles more, parking along the road near Knob Hill. This reduces an 8.5-mile ride by almost half. Either way, travel down this maintained, fireweed-lined dirt road towards an obvious "knob" hill with an FAA tower sitting on top of it. Scale this short hill for a sweeping panorama of the area. To ride around Knob Lake, climb the first switchback of Knob Hill and take a right onto a less used dirt trail. Follow this trail through shoulder-high brush along the banks of the East Fork River. The trail then circles Knob Lake, leading the cyclist back to the gravel road. Several smaller trails invite the backcountry rider to explore the surrounding area. In particular, an ORV trail can be seen from the top of Knob Hill heading east past Hunter Lake to the vicinity of Goober Lake. Nearby Matanuska Glacier Campground (mile 101 Glenn Hwy.) is state maintained and offers 12 camp sites, drinking water and toilets for a small fee. Here, a foot path leads the visitor to a great view of the glacier. Numerous lodges in the area offer food, drink, lodging and gas.

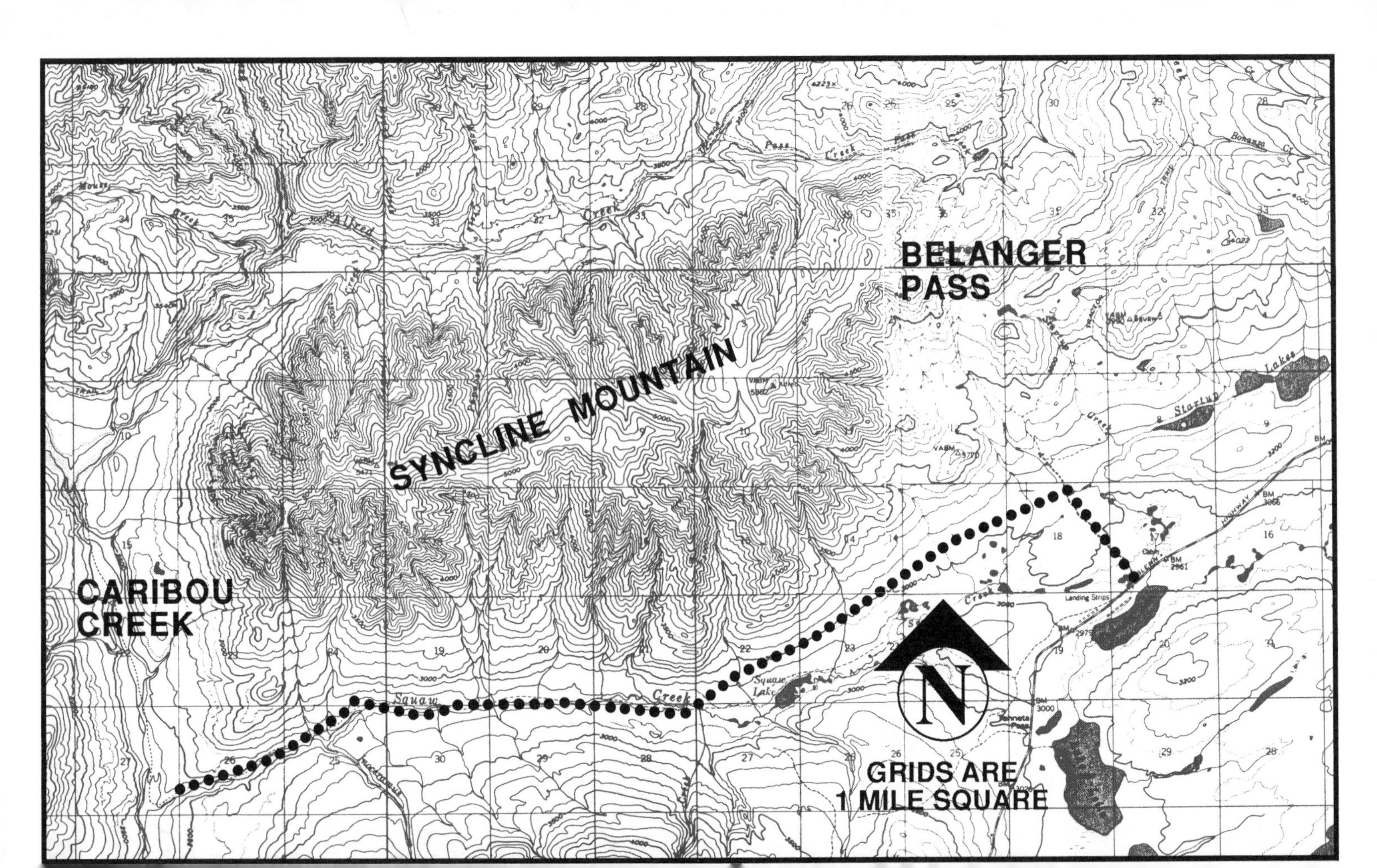
BELANGER
PASS
SYNCLINE MOUNTAIN
CARIBOU
CREEK
N
GRIDS ARE
1 MILE SQUARE

trail 26

SQUAW CREEK

Ride into the wild and untamed Talkeetna Mountains, rich in wildlife and mineral wealth. Mining activity along Squaw Creek, Albert Creek and Alfred Creek brought hordes of gold miners into the area at the turn-of-the-century seeking fame and fortune. Although there are several active mining claims in the area, it is now outdoors enthusiasts who visit these valleys in great numbers, seeking the beauty and tranquility of the mountains. Look for sheep, moose, caribou and bear in this forested valley.

AT - A - GLANCE

TRAILHEAD: ....123.3 Glenn Hwy.

FROM ANCHORAGE: ....123.3 miles

LENGTH OF TRAIL: ....23 miles round trip

RIDING TIME: ....4 to 6 hours

DIFFICULTY: 3

LOW POINT: ....2,300 ft.

HIGH POINT: ....2,950 ft.

ELEVATION GAIN: ....650 ft.

U.S.G.S. MAPS: .....Anchorage D-1, D-5, Anchorage 1 : 250,000

A relatively level trail travels the length of wooded Squaw Creek 11.5 miles before merging with Caribou Creek. Cross clear-running knee-deep Squaw Creek several times on a wide mining road that changes from dirt to gravel and then back again. Numerous muddy sections are easily skirted on fat-tired mountain bikes.

Drive east of Anchorage to mile 123.3 of the Glenn Highway. A large wood sign indicates this side road as part of the Chickaloon-Knik-Nelchina Trail System. Park in the general vicinity of the sign, out of traffic's way. Cycle 1.4 miles up this dirt road and take a left onto well-used Squaw Creek trail (which looks more like a road at this point). Travel through dense woodlands past Squaw Lake and cross Squaw Creek (mile 9.5) numerous times. Soon you're riding between 5,471 ft. Syncline Mountain and 6,441 ft. Gunsight Mountain (with its noticeable notch), both popular with hikers. The trail then drops into the Caribou Creek drainage (mile 11.5), affording the cyclist a view around Syncline Mountain and up Caribou Creek. For further adventures, a well used trail continues, following Caribou Creek upstream for several miles to a narrow canyon and airstrip. Cabins and mining equipment in the area are private property. A less used trail circles Syncline Mountain via Alfred Creek and Pass Creek before climbing to Belanger Pass (see Syncline Mt. Loop and Belanger Pass). The state-maintained Matanuska Glacier Campground (mile 101 Glenn Hwy.) offers tent sites, drinking water and toilets for a small fee. The Long Rifle Lodge (mile 102.2), Sheep Mountain Lodge (mile 113.5) and Eureka Lodge (mile 128) offer full services.

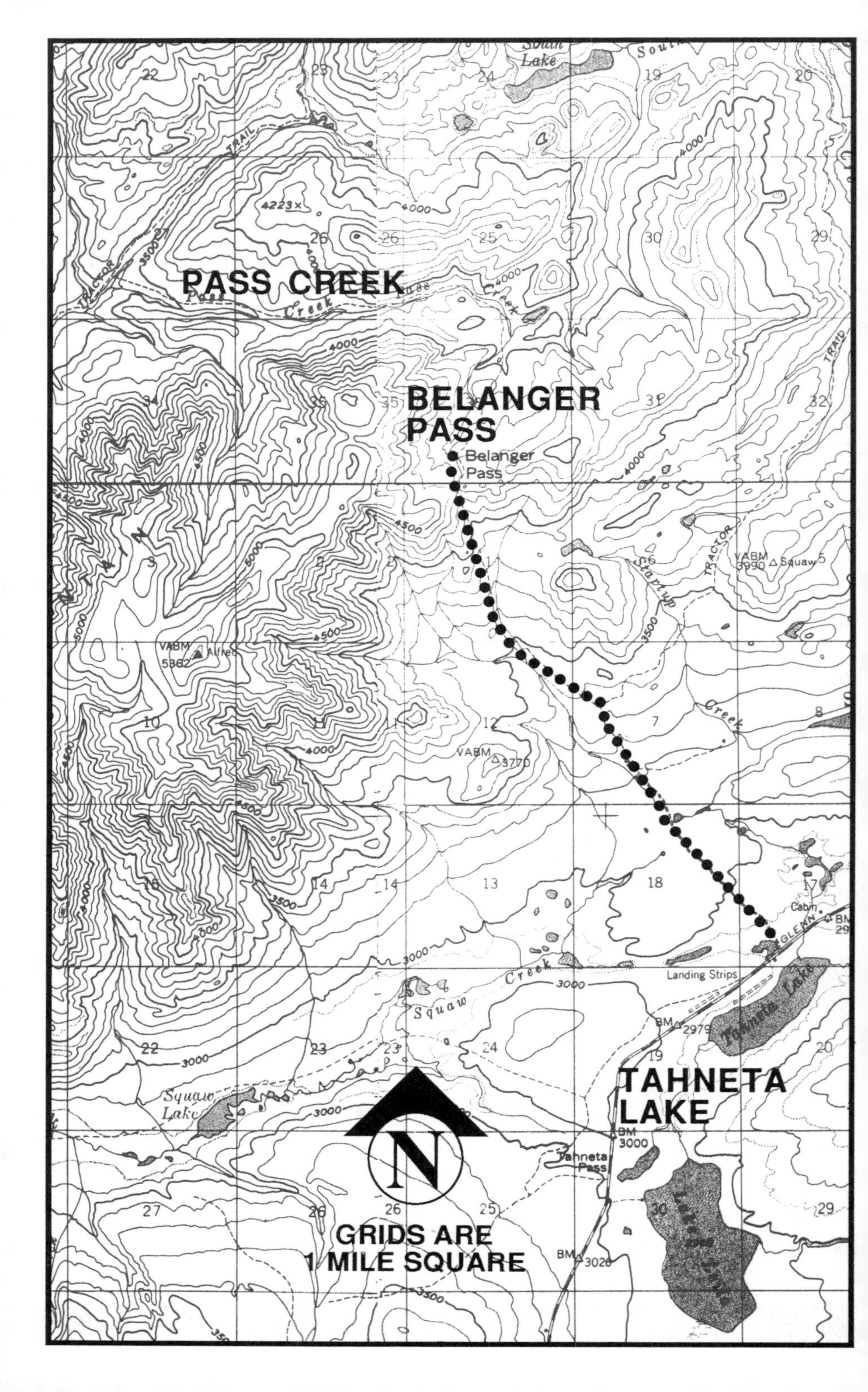
PASS CREEK
BELANGER PASS
Belanger Pass
TAHNETA LAKE
Tahneta Lake
Tahneta Pass
Squaw Lake
Squaw Creek
Landing Strips
Cabin
TRACTOR TRAIL
VABM 5862 Alfred
VABM 3770
VABM 3990 Squaw
BM 2979
BM 3000
BM 3020
N
GRIDS ARE
1 MILE SQUARE

trail 27 BELANGER PASS

This historic mining trail takes the cyclist above tree line into the Talkeetna Mountains and provides expansive views of lake-studded Tahneta Pass. The Nelchina caribou herd migrate through here in great numbers during the fall. This is land rich in both fauna and flora. Mining activity after the turn-of-the-century developed this trail, allowing present day hunters and outdoors enthusiasts access to the numerous trails beyond.

The mining roads in this area crisscross these mountains for miles, mainly traveling up and down different creek drainages. For the most part, these wide and easy-to-follow trails are composed of hard-pack earth and loose gravel. Steep hills with erosion are occasionally encountered. Creek crossings are generally knee-deep or less, except Caribou Creek, which can be thigh deep or more. However, water levels can change quickly due to snow-melt and precipitation in the higher country. Exercise caution when crossing any moving water.

AT - A - GLANCE

TRAILHEAD: ......mile 123.3 Glenn Hwy.

FROM ANCHORAGE: .... 123.3 miles

LENGTH OF TRAIL: ....10 miles round trip

RIDING TIME: ....3 to 4 hours

DIFFICULTY: ....4 (hillclimb)

LOW POINT: ....2,950 ft.

HIGH POINT: ....4,350 ft.

ELEVATION GAIN: ....1,400 ft.

U.S.G.S. MAPS: ....Anchorage D-1, Anchorage 1 : 250,000

The "Chikaloon-Knik-Nelchina Trail System" sign at mile 123.3 of the Glenn Highway marks the trailhead. Park in the general vicinity, out of traffic's way. The trail is clearly visible, climbing the mountainside to an obvious pass. Cycle up a rutted dirt road past Squaw Creek trail, which goes left at mile 1.4 (see Squaw Creek). Skirt right, around private property, and continue going up into Belanger Pass, climbing a long grade where the view keeps getting better. Delight in the perspective from the top of the pass (mile 5). The thin tundra here allows for easy hiking in almost any direction. For those wishing a longer ride, drop down into Pass Creek, where steep canyon walls slowly give way to high rolling hills. At mile 8.5, Pass Creek merges with Alfred Creek. Here the Alfred Creek trail continues in two directions. Upstream (northeast) takes you to Albert Creek and then the Crooked Creek trail. Downstream (west) will take you to the Caribou Creek drainage (see Syncline Mt. Loop). Nearby state-run Little Nelchina Campground (mile 137.4 Glenn Hwy.) has 11 sites with toilets. Drinking water is not available here. All services are available at the Eureka Lodge (mile 128 Glenn Hwy.).

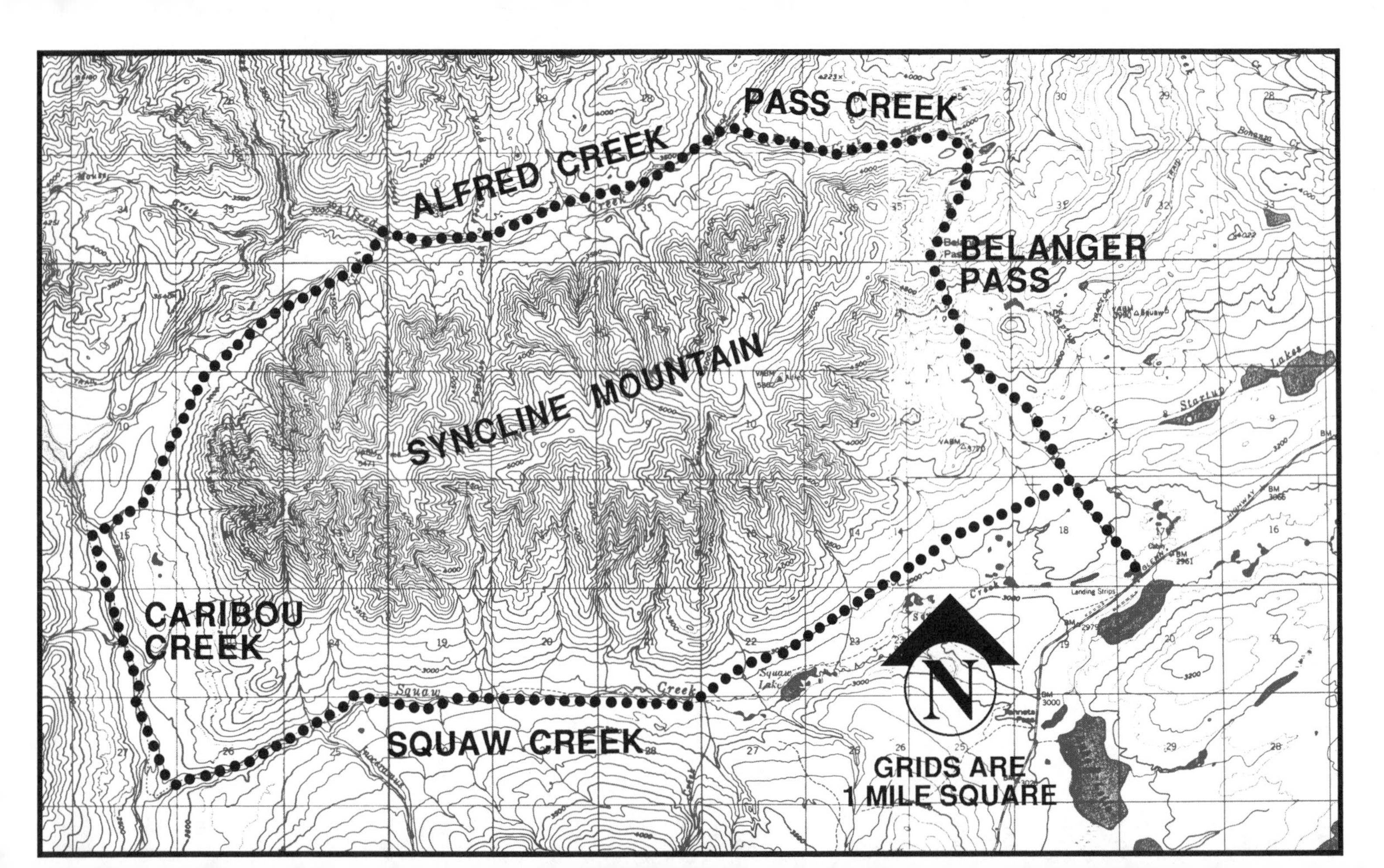

PASS CREEK
ALFRED CREEK
BELANGER PASS
SYNCLINE MOUNTAIN
CARIBOU CREEK
N
SQUAW CREEK
GRIDS ARE 1 MILE SQUARE

trail 28

SYNCLINE MT. LOOP

AT - A - GLANCE	
TRAILHEAD:	mile 123.3 Glenn Hwy.
FROM ANCHORAGE:	123.3 miles
LENGTH OF TRAIL:	31 miles one way
RIDING TIME:	8 to 12 hours
DIFFICULTY:	4 to 5
LOW POINT:	2,300 ft.
HIGH POINT:	4,350 ft.
ELEVATION GAIN:	2,050 ft.
U.S.G.S. MAPS:	Anchorage D-1, D-2, Anchorage 1 : 250,000

The hardy adventurer will accept the challenge of this multi-trail ride which encircles Syncline Mountain for an all-day adventure. Cycle through the rugged Talkeetna Mountains on mining trails that traverse the drainages of Squaw Creek, Caribou Creek, Alfred Creek and finally Pass Creek before climbing up Belanger Pass. A wide variety of animals live in these mountains including bear, sheep, moose, porcupine and caribou. Birds and wildflowers abound. The view of Tahetna Pass and the Chugach Mountains from the top of Belanger Pass is both expansive and spectacular.

Start early and pack an extra large lunch for this 31-mile backcountry adventure. Mountainous country provides the biker with a generous serving of hill climbing and enough water crossings to keep the feet wet all day. Caribou Creek, the deepest crossing, often is only thigh deep but water levels change constantly. Exercise caution and use good judgment when crossing any moving water.

Just east of Gunsight Mountain Lodge, a wood sign at mile 123.3 of the Glenn Highway indicates this as part of the Chickaloon-Knik-Nelchina Trail System. Because of limited parking you should ask permission at the lodge to park there. Cycle up this dirt road 1.4 miles to a well used intersection. Here the cyclist has an option to either go up Belanger Pass or go down Squaw Creek (see Belanger Pass and Squaw Creek). Caribou Creek must be crossed in order to complete the loop. If it is impassable you must backtrack. Take a left at the intersection and cycle down wooded Squaw Creek to Caribou Creek (mile 11.5). Follow a well used trail to the right, traveling up Caribou Creek and crossing it several times. At the end of an old gravel airstrip (mile 13.6), go right, scrambling up a small, rocky creek bed. This less used trail climbs up and traverses the lower flank of Syncline Mountain before dropping into Albert Creek (mile 16.5). Cabins and mining equipment in the area are private property. Bike up Albert Creek to the confluence of Pass Creek (mile 23). Take a right and cycle up this drainage to the top of Belanger Pass (mile 26) before dropping to the trail head.

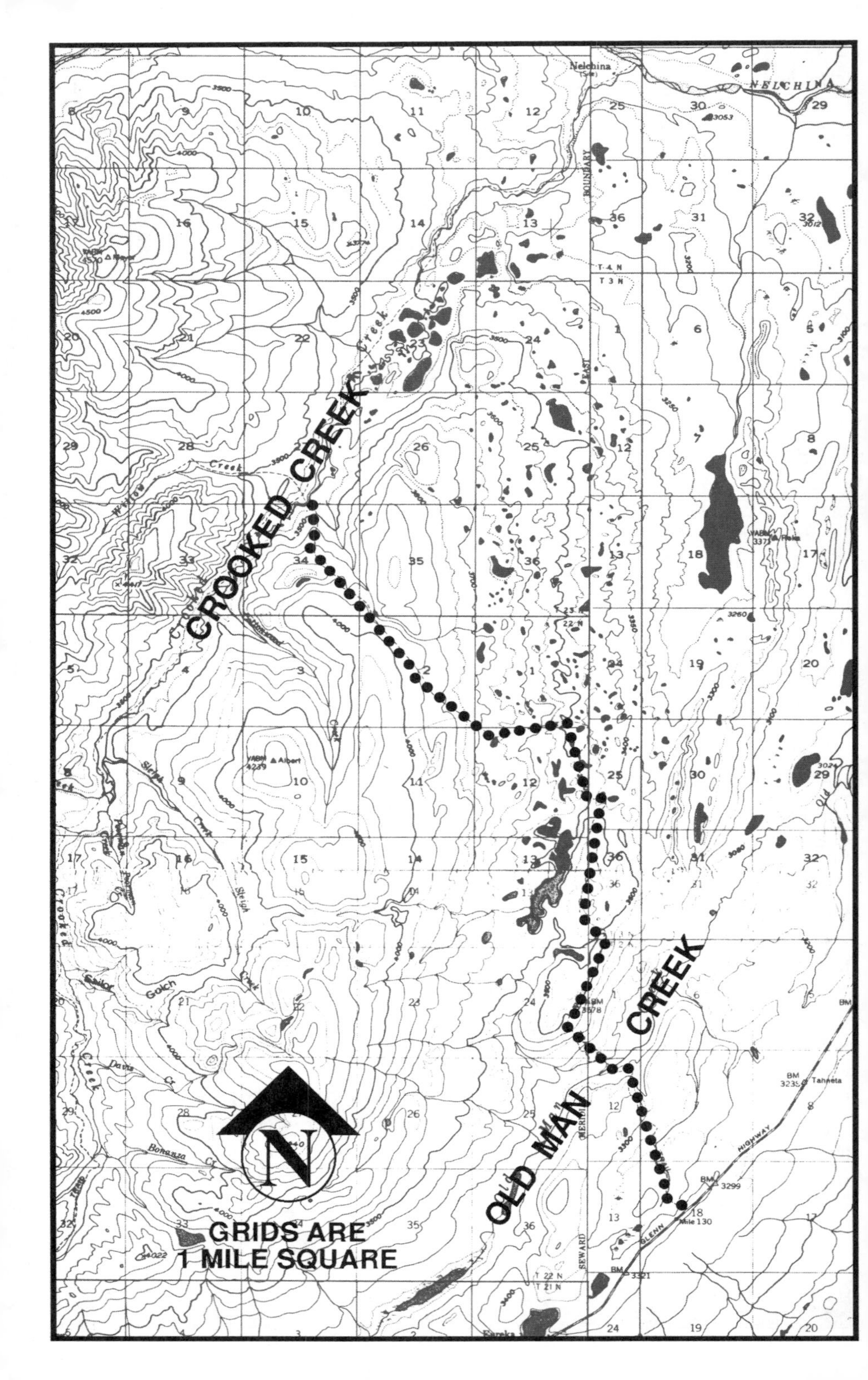
CROOKED CREEK
OLD MAN CREEK
N
GRIDS ARE
1 MILE SQUARE
Nelchina
NELCHINA
HIGHWAY
GLENN
Mile 130

trail 29

OLD MAN CREEK

AT - A - GLANCE

TRAILHEAD: ......mile 130.3 Glenn Hwy.

FROM ANCHORAGE: ....130.3 miles

LENGTH OF TRAIL: ....18 miles round trip

RIDING TIME: ....5 to 7 hours

DIFFICULTY: 3.5

LOW POINT: ....3,250 ft.

HIGH POINT: ....4,500 ft.

ELEVATION GAIN: ....1,250 ft.

U.S.G.S. MAPS: ....Anchorage D-1, Talkeetna Mt. A-1, Anchorage 1 : 250,000

On a clear day, the visiting cyclist is rewarded with a sweeping panorama that includes four mountain ranges rising and encircling the rider. Standing on the lower flanks of the Talkeetna Mountains look northward and view the Alaska Range. To the east the Wrangell Mountains. To the south the Chugach Mountains. These rolling hills of the lower Talkeetna Mountains support the Nelchina caribou herd as well as moose and bear. In the fall a rainbow of colors surround the cyclist exploring this treeless land with many trails.

Cycle across high country on a wide gravel ORV road that slowly gains elevation. Occasionally, the trail will drop into a creek drainage forcing the cyclist to climb steep grades up the other side. Mud holes are encountered in low, wet areas but for the most part this trail is usually high, dry and dusty. Numerous ORV roads crisscross these foothills, providing plenty of exploring options for day rides or over-nighters. Water is plentiful but firewood is sparse or nonexistent in this sub-alpine and alpine environment.

At mile 130.3 of the Glenn Highway, pull into a large gravel parking lot. A large wood sign indicates this as an entrance to the Chickaloon-Knik-Nelchina Trail System. Looking north, you can be see the trail heading north climbing hills and traversing the countryside. Approach this trail from the northwest corner of the gravel parking lot. The trail splits many times to avoid muddy sections. Drop into and cross Old Man Creek before climbing back out up a long, steep hill. Continue going straight at mile 4.2, where an optional side trail to the right leads the rider to the largest lake in the area and then on to the confluence of Crooked Creek and Little Nelchina River. Near mile 7 the trail splits again. Go straight at this intersection and in 2 miles drop into beautiful Crooked Creek (mile 9), a wonderful lunch spot. An additional trail continues across the creek and up a long, steep hill. This is Monument Trail, it climbs and then drops into the valley surrounding the Little Nelchina River. Additional riding and exploring abound in a treeless land with sweeping vistas.

chapter 4

PARKS HIGHWAY

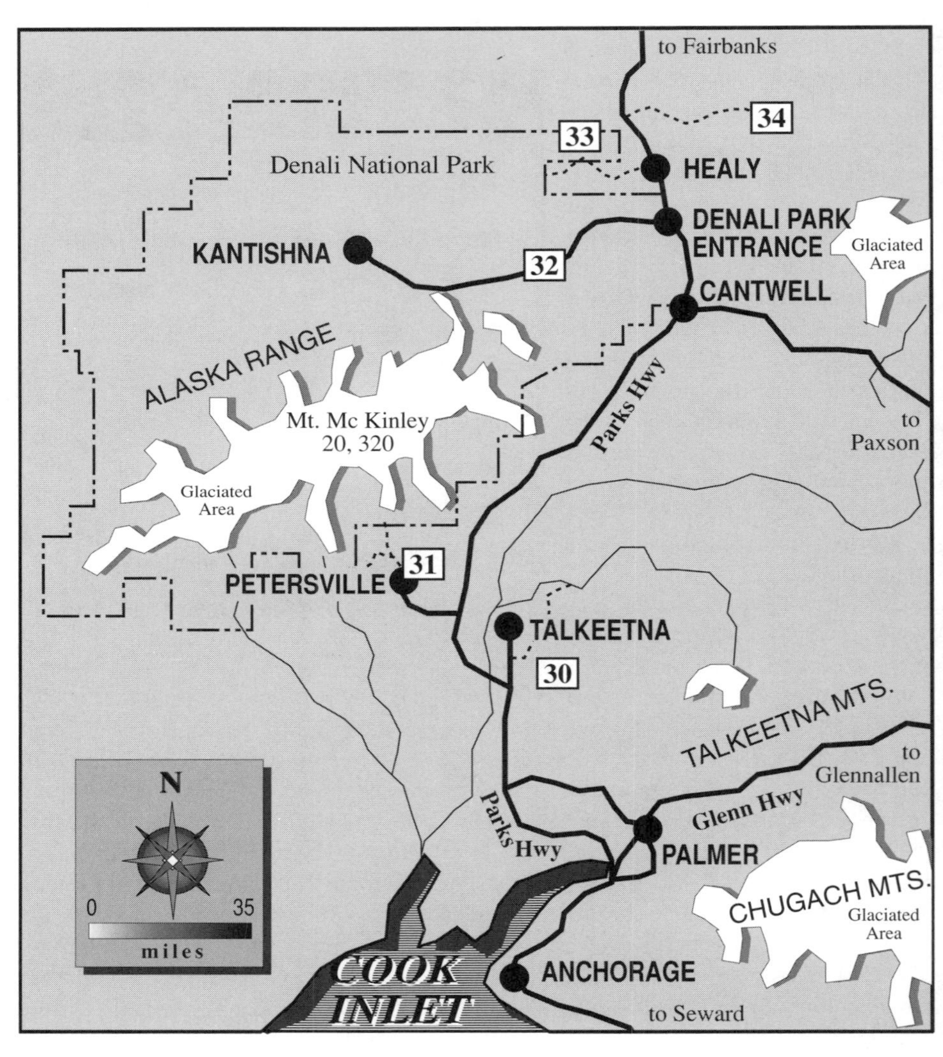

The Parks Highway (also called the George Parks Highway) travels 323 miles north from Anchorage to Fairbanks. This roadway passes over several major rivers as it skirts around the Talkeetna Mountains before crossing the Alaska Range, home to Mt. McKinley (20,230 ft.). Denali National Park and Preserve draws thousands of visitors each year to view the wild animals and inspiring landscape.

Three of the trails in this chapter, 31, 32 and 34, offers views of this mighty mountain. Trails 32 and 33 allows the rider to cycle into Denali National Park. The easiest ride is trail 31, while trails 32 and 34 are the hardest because of their length.

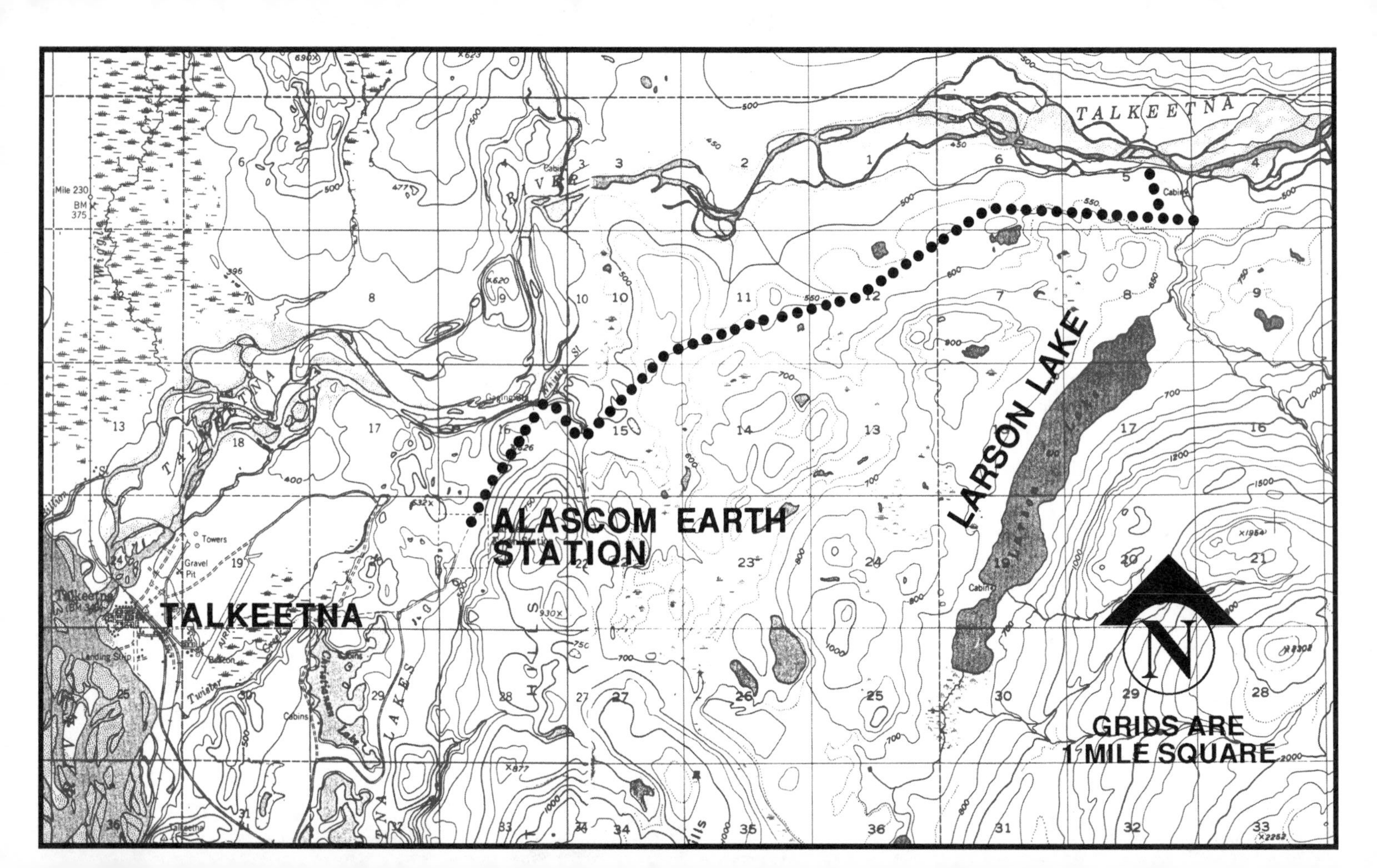

LARSON LAKE
ALASCOM EARTH STATION
TALKEETNA
GRIDS ARE 1 MILE SQUARE
N

trail 30 TALKEETNA RIVER

AT - A - GLANCE	
TRAILHEAD:	end of Comsat Rd.
FROM ANCHORAGE:	114 miles
LENGTH OF TRAIL:	20 miles round trip
RIDING TIME:	4 to 6 hours
DIFFICULTY:	3
LOW POINT:	450 ft.
HIGH POINT:	700 ft.
ELEVATION GAIN:	250 ft.
U.S.G.S. MAPS:	Talkeetna B-1, Talkeetna Mt. B-6, Talkeetna Mt. 1 : 250,000

The people of Talkeetna call their town the "Gateway to Mt. McKinley." Local Indians, the Tanaina, say Talkeetna means "river of plenty." Both names fit. More than 1,000 high-altitude thrill seekers from around the world descend upon this sleepy little town each summer to attempt the summit of 20,320-foot Mt. McKinley. Scenic glacier flights leave hourly for the imposing massif of Mt. McKinley and the enormous rivers of ice that flow from its upper slopes. Three rivers join together near this town, the Talkeetna, the Chulitna and the mighty Susitna, which has the second largest run of migrating salmon in the world. Nearly a dozen river guides cater to the angler seeking trophy sized salmon (5 species), trout and grayling in these rivers. Rafting, scenic boating and big game hunting also are very popular.

This wide and easy-to-follow earthen path leads the cyclist through tall birch and cottonwood to fantastic fishing along Larson Creek and the Talkeetna River.

Drive north of Anchorage to mile 98.7 of the Parks Highway. Turn right onto the Talkeetna Spur Road. At mile 12, take a right onto paved Comsat Road (unmarked), driving to its end, near a large Alascom Earth Station satellite dish. Park out of the way. Enter the ski trails and cycle .36 of a mile. Turn right and climb a hill rutted by erosion. Continue on this dirt (muddy, when wet) ORV trail that climbs, drops and rolls through the woods. Under a power line (mile 5), a less used trail crosses this one. Continue on the main trail, crossing under the power line and passing by several smaller trails. At mile 7.6, you come to a "Y" in the trail. Stay right and soon you'll arrive at Larson Creek. A small wood bridge allows for easy crossing. The trail, after a mile or so, slowly turns into a bushwhack. If you take a left at the "Y," a well-used trail will drop you down to the Talkeetna River. Fun exploring and great fishing can be had up and down this river. Riverside camping, hotels, gas stations and restaurants provide the visitor with accommodations while in Talkeetna (mile 14 Talkeetna Spur Road).

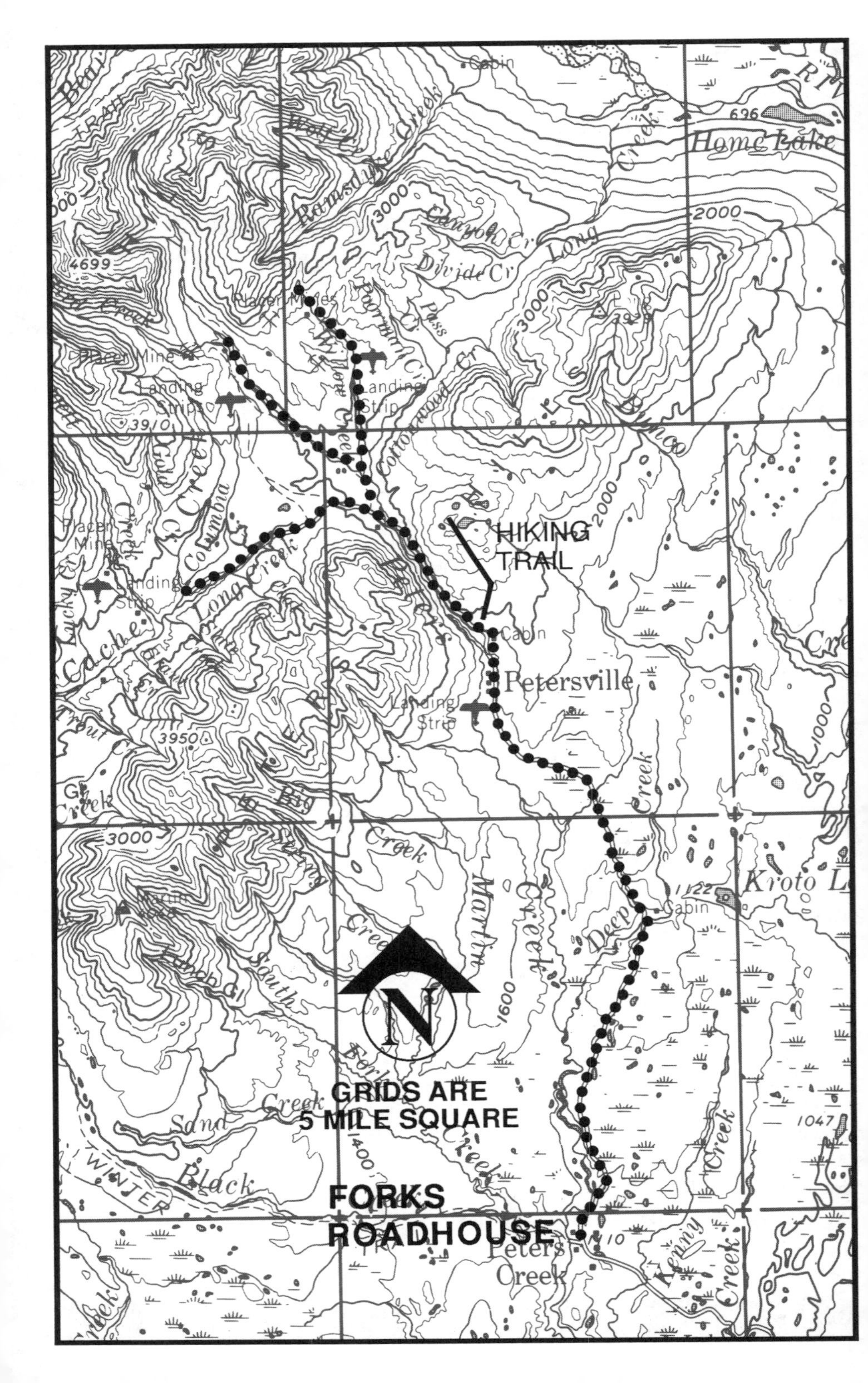

HIKING TRAIL
Petersville
GRIDS ARE 5 MILE SQUARE
FORKS ROADHOUSE
N

PETERSVILLE RD.

View Mt. McKinley as you ride into the Peters Hills, southern foothills of the Alaska Range, and deep into gold country. Miners built this road in the 1920s and several active claims are being worked today. Famed Alaskan artist Sydney Laurence painted several of his Mt. McKinley canvases in these hills. With a little effort, a fantastic panorama of the Alaska Range, with Mt. McKinley, can be experienced when riders leave their bikes below and hike to the top of nearby peaks.

This wide and easy dirt road slowly gains elevation as it makes its way beyond Petersville, a quiet mining community, and into the Dutch Hills. Several large mud holes generally stop most 4-wheel drives early in the season but pose no problem for the cyclist.

AT - A - GLANCE

TRAILHEAD: ......mile 19 Petersville Rd.

FROM ANCHORAGE: ....113.8 miles

LENGTH OF TRAIL: ....34 miles round trip

RIDING TIME: .....6 hours to several days

DIFFICULTY: ....3 to 4

LOW POINT: ....1,100 ft.

HIGH POINT: ....2,500 ft.

ELEVATION GAIN: ....1,400 ft.

U.S.G.S. MAPS: ....Talkeetna B-2, C-2, Talkeetna 1 : 250,000

North of Anchorage, at mile 114.8 of the Parks Highway, take the Petersville Road 19 miles to the Forks Roadhouse, a full-service lodge. Ask if road conditions will allow further car travel. For many, this is a good point to begin riding. Take a right at the Forks Roadhouse and cycle 11 miles north to Petersville. Watch the skyline for views of Mt. McKinley. Less than a mile past Petersville, a tracked vehicle trail heads right and up a steep hill. For a wonderful view of the surrounding area and Mt. McKinley, hide your bikes, stay left and hike 2 miles up the northwest ridge to the top. The main road descends into a river canyon, which, at the bottom, offers fine camping on the banks of Peters Creek. After crossing the creek bridge you come to a "Y." Continue on the main road to the left, cycling up a hill. You are now between the Peters and Dutch hills and have a great view of the entire valley. This road, after several easy miles, drops down into aspens and willows paralleling Long Creek and then into Cache Creek, where private land stops further riding. Additional riding can be found by taking a right at the "Y." Cross several braids of a knee-deep creek before coming to another "Y" in the trail. Both of the trails before you offer fun biking and access to Denali State Park. Hikes with views of Mt. McKinley abound.

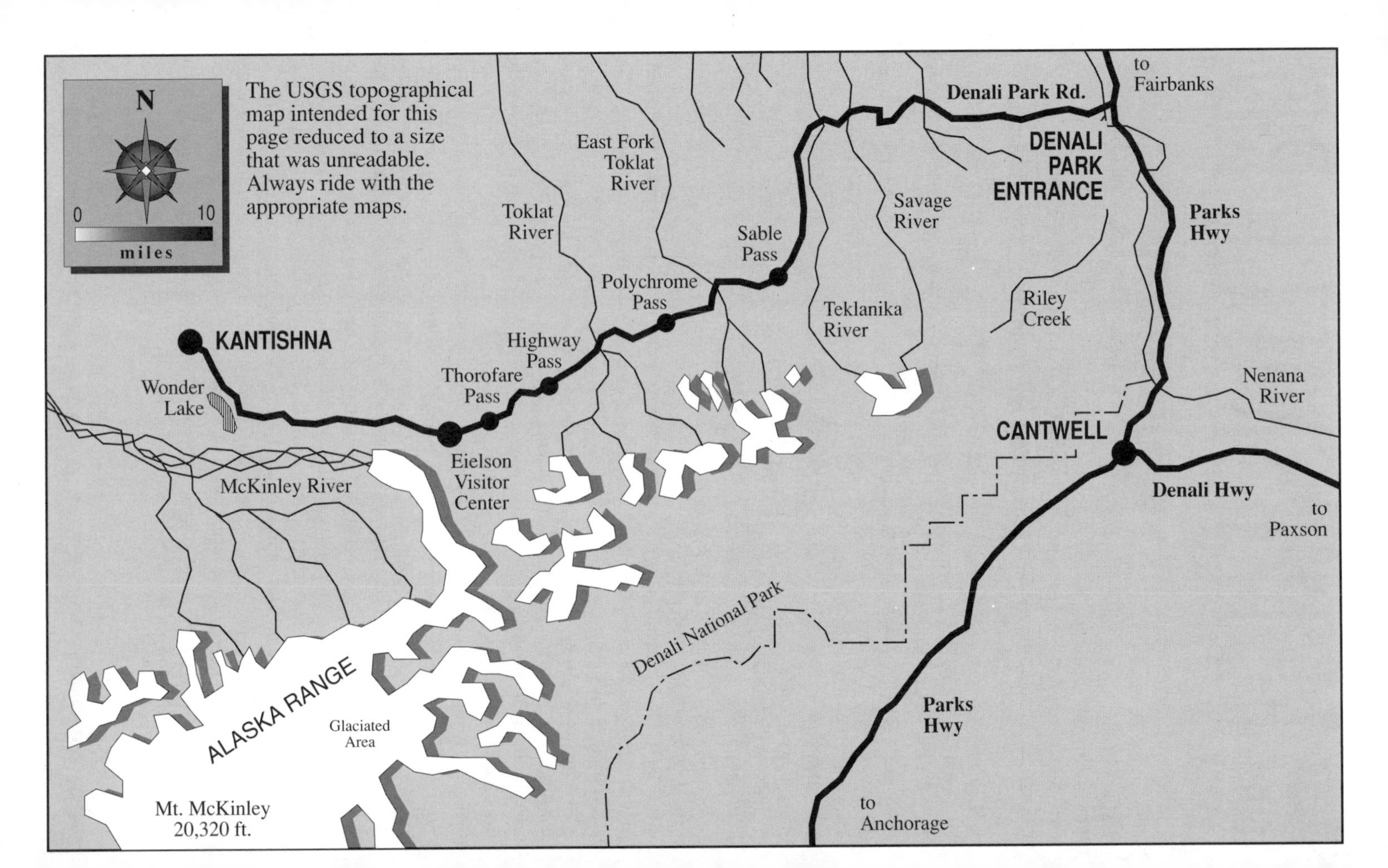
N
0
10
miles
The USGS topographical map intended for this page reduced to a size that was unreadable. Always ride with the appropriate maps.
KANTISHNA
Wonder Lake
McKinley River
Eielson Visitor Center
Thorofare Pass
Highway Pass
Polychrome Pass
Sable Pass
Toklat River
East Fork Toklat River
Teklanika River
Savage River
Denali Park Rd.
DENALI PARK ENTRANCE
to Fairbanks
Parks Hwy
Riley Creek
Nenana River
CANTWELL
Denali Hwy
to Paxson
Parks Hwy
to Anchorage
Denali National Park
ALASKA RANGE
Glaciated Area
Mt. McKinley 20,320 ft.

trail 32

DENALI PARK ROAD

Ride your bike into a cornucopia of wildlife, plant life and geological wonders where every turn of the road offers the rider something new to observe and relish. Few places equal the unfolding of miles of spectacular scenery like Denali National Park. Established in 1917, the park's 6 million acres make it larger than the state of Massachusetts and almost as wild and unspoiled as the early explorers first saw it. With more than 430 types of flowering plants, 37 species of mammals and 157 different varieties of birds, it's easy to fall in love with this unique country. And mighty Mt. McKinley, at 23,320 feet, the largest mountain in the world measured from base to summit, is the crowning jewel of this 90-plus mile ride.

AT - A - GLANCE

TRAILHEAD: ....mile 237 Parks Hwy.

FROM ANCHORAGE: ....237 miles

LENGTH OF TRAIL: ....90 miles one way

RIDING TIME: ....12 hours to several days

DIFFICULTY: ....5 (4 mt. passes)

LOW POINT: ....1,850 ft.

HIGH POINT: ....3,980 ft.

ELEVATION GAIN: ....2,130 ft.

U.S.G.S. MAPS: ....Mt. McKinley and Healy 1 : 250,000, Denali Park map

Except for the first 12 miles, which are paved, this maintained gravel road, with four mountain passes and limited automobile traffic, offers the rider miles of wilderness through the heart of Alaska. Do not forget your camera and plenty of film. There are full service lodges at the park entrance and in the mining district of Kantishna, but no services along this road except for toilets and water. Several of the park buses can accommodate bicycles, allowing the visitor to be shuttled in or out. Talk to lodge owners and park rangers for assistance in planning your ride. Take advantage of the midnight sun and begin cycling in late afternoon to miss much of the bus traffic on this dusty road.

Travel east from the park entrance (mile 237 Parks Hwy.) on a paved road to the visitor's center, where a small fee is paid and knowledgeable park employees will assist you with your questions about park rules. Pick up a copy of the park map. Begin cycling here. Savage Creek is the next stop. Here park rangers turn away those who have not paid or are without permits. The gravel starts here. Climb Primrose Ridge, Sable Pass, beautiful Polychrome Pass (mile 45.3), Highway Pass, Stony Hill and Thorofare Pass before dropping into Eielson Visitor Center (mile 65.2). Enjoy the downhill ride and rolling terrain to Wonder Lake (mile 85) or Kantishna with Mt. McKinley by you're side as you finish this long, scenic ride.

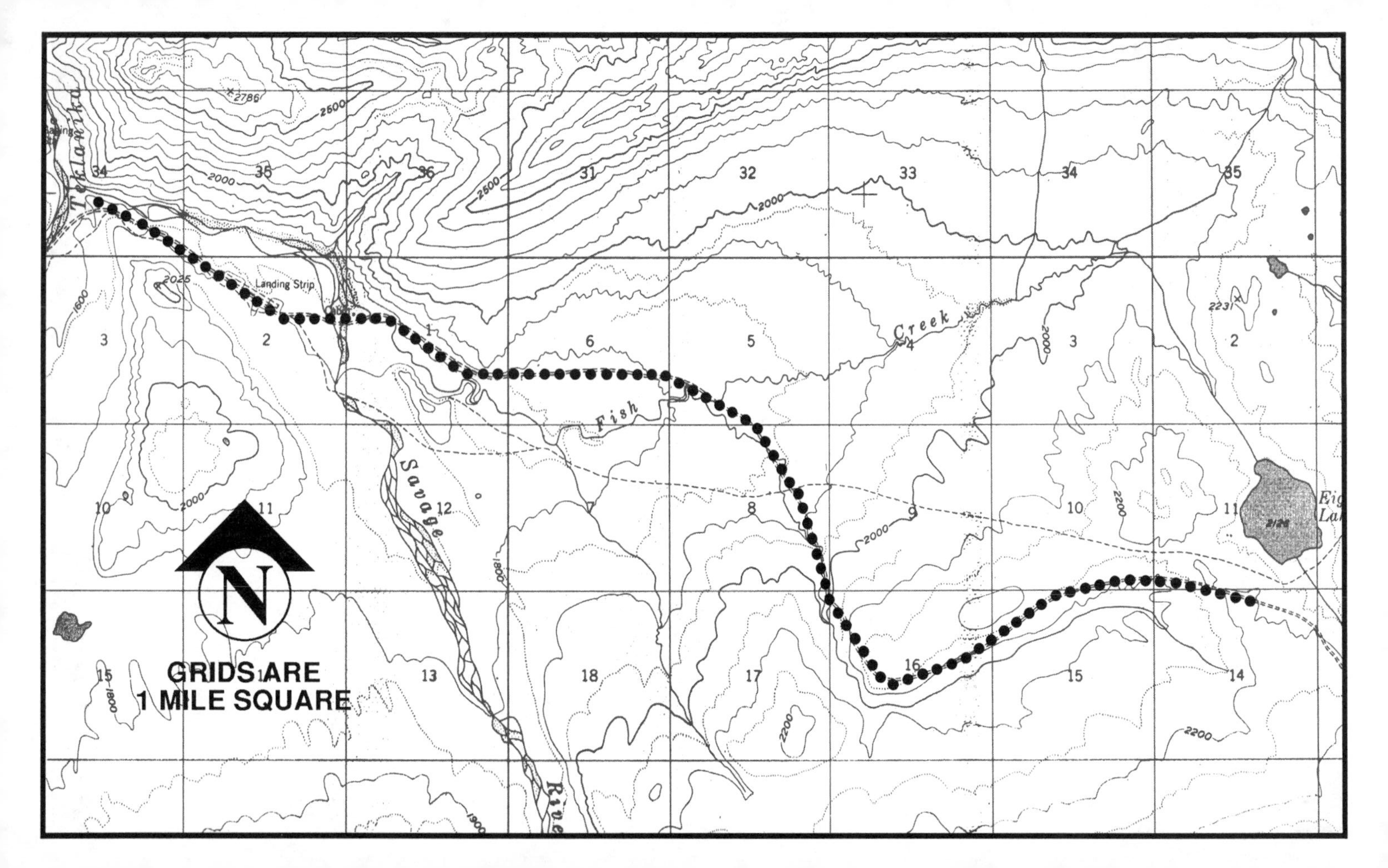

Teklanika
Landing Strip
Fish
Creek
Savage
Rive
N
GRIDS ARE
1 MILE SQUARE

trail 33

STAMPEDE TRAIL

Traverse the northern foothills of the Alaska Range on the original trail miners used in the early 1900s to access claims in the mineral-rich Kantishna Hills. This is vast open country with rolling hills, taiga and an abundance of rivers and streams. Congress in 1980 expanded Denali National Park to include the Kantishna Hills and lands just north of the existing park. However, a large tract of land was omitted, allowing multiple user groups — including motorized vehicles — access to 30-plus miles of the Stampede Trail.

AT - A - GLANCE

TRAILHEAD: ......mile 251.4 Parks Hwy.
FROM ANCHORAGE: ....251.4 miles
LENGTH OF TRAIL: ....20 miles round trip
RIDING TIME: ....5 to 7 hours
DIFFICULTY: ....3 to 3.5
LOW POINT: ....1,550 ft.
HIGH POINT: ....2,200 ft.
ELEVATION GAIN: ....650 ft.
U.S.G.S. MAPS: ....Healy D-5, Healy 1 : 250,000

The main trail is well worn and easy to follow, though a bit muddy in some places. Several water crossings and a dry creek bed must be negotiated along the way. ORVs have made numerous side trails, most of which go off into swampy terrain that is unridable.

Less than 15 miles north of the Denali National Park entrance, at mile 251.4 of the Parks Highway, turn left (west) onto Stampede Road. Follow this maintained gravel road for about 8 miles. An obvious parking area off 8 Mile Lake is the trailhead. Park here, out of the way. A well-defined ORV trail continues west, crossing a handful of mud holes, which are easily skirted. A tributary of Fish Creek must be crossed many times. The soft gravel bottom of this shallow creek forces most cyclists to walk this section. Climb out of a wet area onto a high bank above a beaver pond and observe the beautiful valley that lies ahead. Cross the Savage River, which normally is only knee deep, and cycle by a park boundary marker (mile 7.5) You are now riding legally within Denali National Park. Descend a long hill and go right on a less used trail. Discover a wonderful campsite at the confluence of the Savage and Teklanika rivers (mile 10). This, for most, will be the end of the ride. The Stampede Trail continues however, on the other side of the deep and swift Teklanika. Depending on water levels, a raft may required to cross this river. Use extreme caution in crossing this or any moving water. Park rules forbid cyclists from crossing park boundaries near the Sushana River and cycling further into the park. The nearest maintained campground is Riley Creek (mile 1 Denali Park Rd.). Lodges and hotels at Healy and Lynx Creek (just outside the park entrance) provide full services.

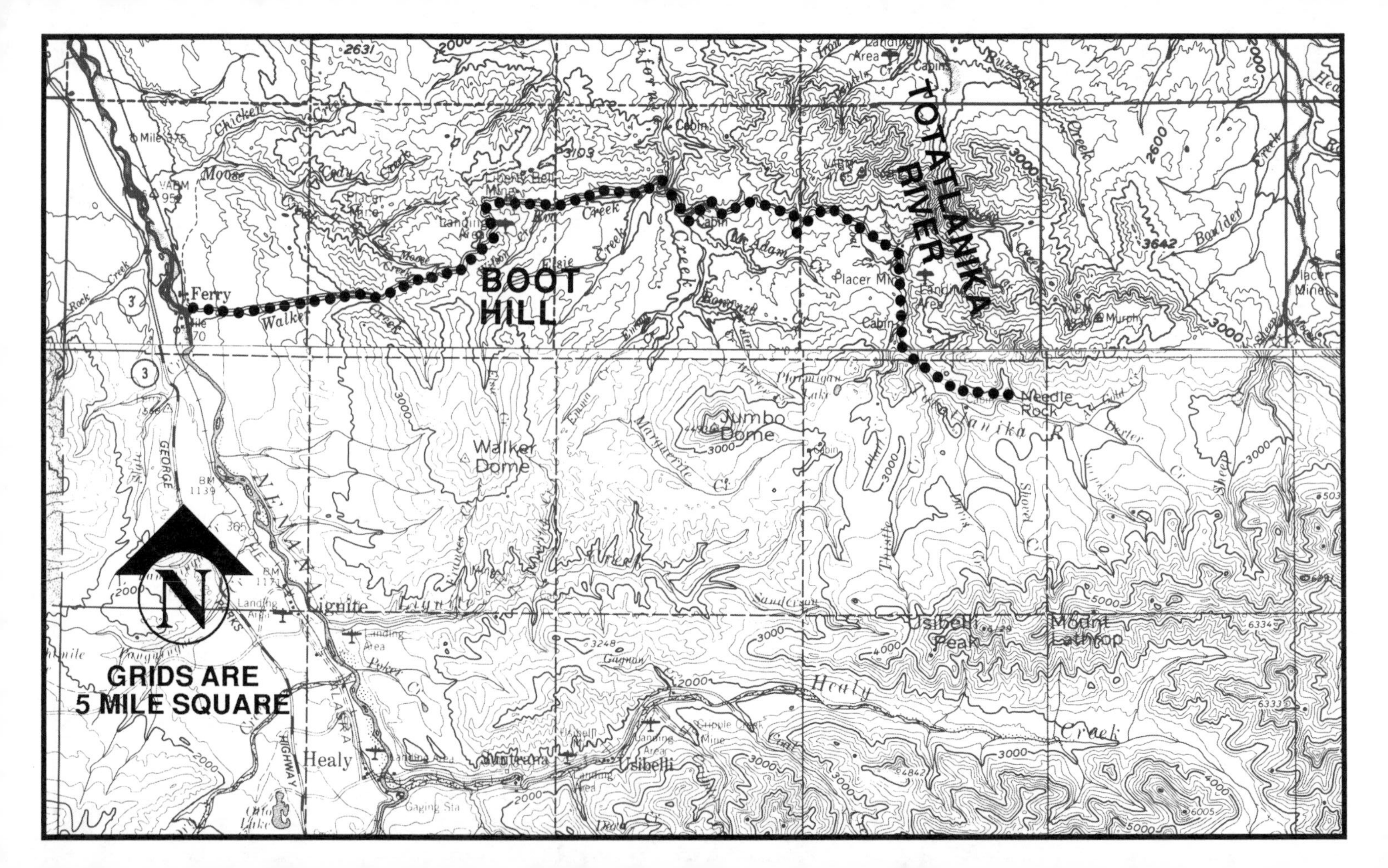
BOOT
HILL
TOTATLANIKA
RIVER
GRIDS ARE
5 MILE SQUARE
N
Ferry
Walker Dome
Jumbo Dome
Needle Rock
Usibelli Peak
Mount Lathrop
Healy
Lignite
Usibelli
Placer Mine
Cabin
Landing Area
Healy Creek
Gaging Sta
HIGHWAY
GEORGE

trail 34

FERRY TRAIL

Escape into the Alaska wilds as you ride within the northern foothills of the Alaska Range and through the Liberty Bell mining district on this historic mining road. Cyclists will enjoy a varied and changing terrain that includes ridge running with panoramic views: aspen-lined river canyons and towering white sandstone spires juxtaposed with snow-covered Mt. McKinley. Visit "Boot Hill," where generations of local miners and their families have placed a multitude of worn-out boots in a cemetery-like setting. All this and more awaits the enthusiast willing to explore this imposing country 22 miles northeast of Denali National Park.

AT - A - GLANCE

TRAILHEAD: ......mile 259.4 Parks Hwy.

FROM ANCHORAGE: ....259.4 miles

LENGTH OF TRAIL: ....50 miles round trip

RIDING TIME: ....12 hours to several days

DIFFICULTY: .... 3 to 4

LOW POINT: ....1,000 ft.

HIGH POINT:...................2,950 ft.

ELEVATION GAIN: ....1,950 ft.

U.S.G.S. MAPS: ....Fairbanks A-5, A-4, Fairbanks 1 : 250,000

A well-defined, gravel road winds and twists for more than 25 miles (one-way) on this remote backcountry tour. Expect trail conditions to change under wheel each time the cyclist climbs out of one creek drainage and drops into the next. In general, this trail is in good shape with few hazards to impede the two-wheeled visitor. The length of this trail is more of a factor than the obstacles encountered, which include isolated erosion, loose gravel or sandy sections, hill climbs and several water crossings.

North of Healy, at milepost 259.4 of the Parks Highway, take a right onto a gravel road and travel to its end at the Nenana River. Park out of traffic's way. Climb up and onto the railroad grade and cross the river on a boardwalk built onto the railroad bridge. Drop down and cycle a short distance. Cross the tracks and go right. Continue on this the main trail, passing a well used side trail at mile 4. Climb above Moose Creek before surmounting Boot Hill (mile 9), where the cyclist is treated to a view of Mt. McKinley. Stay right at the next "Y" and drop into beautiful Eva Creek. Old mining buildings still stand here in the Liberty Bell mining area. Cross calf-deep Eva Creek and then thigh-deep California Creek (mile 15.4) before climbing a long hill where Mt. McKinley is again visible. At mile 21.7, a small path leads the visitor a short distance down to the curious sandstone spires. The trail soon drops to the swift, thigh-deep Totatlanika River (mile 25). Although the trail continues, high water will stop most riders here. Additional riding and exploring abound.

chapter 5

RICHARDSON HWY.

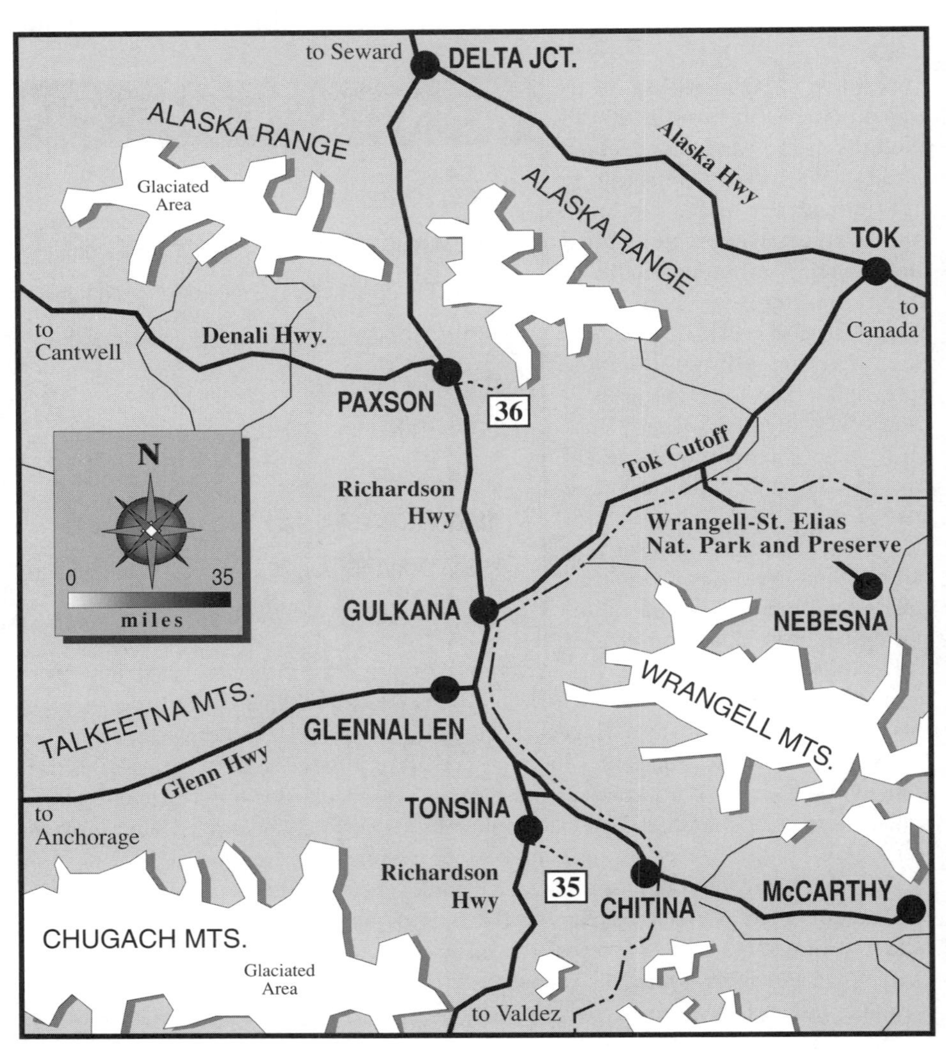

trail		page
35	BERNARD CREEK	82
36	ONE MILE CREEK	84

The Richardson Highway travels 368 miles north from Valdez to Fairbanks, an expansive country punctuated by 4 mountains ranges and hundreds of river. The Trans Alaska Pipeline loosely follows this roadway. Use the Richardson Highway to access trails on the Denali Highway and the Edgerton Highway.

Two trails are featured along this highway. The southern most, trail 35, takes the rider into the Chugach Mountains and to a BLM recreation cabin. Trail 36 drops you onto the valley floor of the Gakona River, which is fed by glaciers in the Alaska Range. Bears and other wild animals are abundant on both rides.

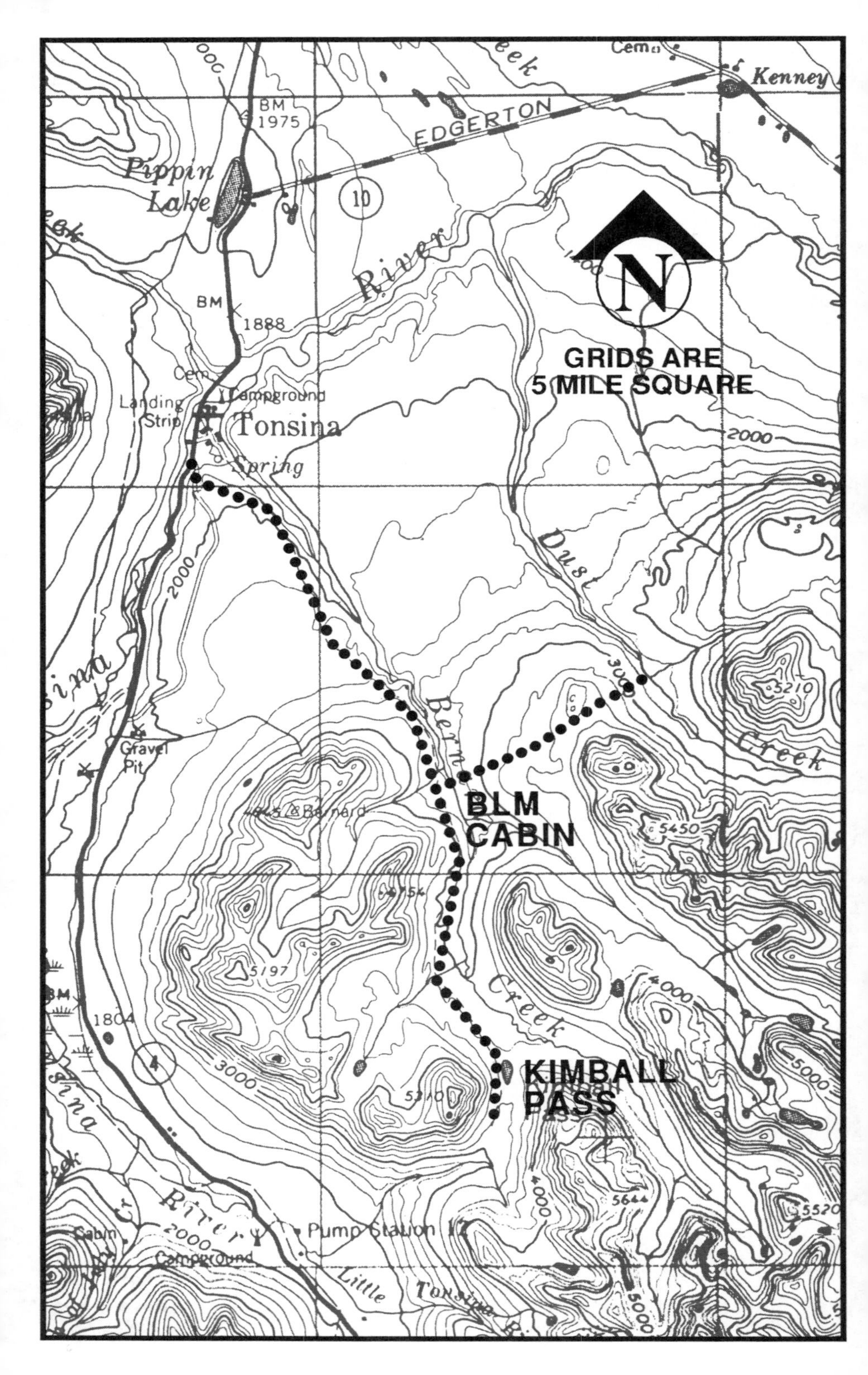

GRIDS ARE
5 MILE SQUARE
BLM
CABIN
KIMBALL
PASS
Tonsina
Pippin
Lake
EDGERTON
River
Dust
Creek
Campground
Landing
Strip
Spring
Gravel
Pit
Pump Station 12
Little
Kenney

trail 35

BERNARD CREEK

This wooded BLM trail takes the rider into the Chugach Mountains and slowly above tree line, deep into moose country. Rise out of the tree-covered Tonsina River Valley as you parallel Bernard Creek on your way to high country. A fully equipped BLM cabin sits next to swift, clear-running Bernard Creek and is available for public use on a first-come, first-use basis. Look for fox, wolves, wolverine, ermine, bear and moose. Bears may be present in large numbers, exercise caution.

AT - A - GLANCE

TRAILHEAD: ....78.6 Richardson Hwy.

FROM ANCHORAGE: ....225.4 miles

LENGTH OF TRAIL: ....24 miles

RIDING TIME: ....6 to 10 hours

DIFFICULTY: 3.5

LOW POINT: ....1,550 ft.

HIGH POINT: ....3,550 ft.

ELEVATION GAIN: ....1,800 ft.

U.S.G.S. MAPS: ....Valdez C-3, C-4, Valdez 1 : 250,000

A well-defined earthen ORV trail changes from gravel to hardpack several times during the ride. The occasional mud hole is easily skirted. Look for animal tracks around the wetter sections. Traction, in general, is quite good. Several short, steep, rocky slopes must be negotiated.

An Alaska Dept. of Fish and Game sign, at milepost 78.6 of the Richardson Hwy., identifies this trail and reads "TONSINA CONTROLLED USE AREA." Find a place to park that is off the road and out of traffic's way. Stay on the main trail, passing another hunting sign and around two badly eroded hillsides. Climb a long gravel road and take the first left (mile 1.3) and then a right (mile 1.5). A BLM sign with map and sign-in sheet mark the trailhead. Bike along a woodsy lane that slowly gains elevation, dropping occasionally to cross small, clear-running streams. A great overlook at mile 4 gives the rider a view of Bernard Creek canyon and the surrounding area. Stay on the main trail and in several miles you will drop upon a BLM public cabin (mile 7) nestled against a hill and within earshot of Bernard Creek. The rider has two trails to chose from, the Kimball Pass trail or the Dusty Creek access trail. The Kimball Pass trail heads out from behind the cabin, goes up a short, steep pitch and continues going in a southerly direction. The Dusty Creek access trail crosses Bernard Creek at the cabin and goes in an easterly direction. Both trails are well-defined and easy-to-follow as they cross brushy, rolling terrain for 4 or 5 miles before fading out. State-maintained Squirrel Creek Campground (mile 79.5 Richardson Hwy.) and the Little Tonsina River State Rec Site (mile 65.1) provides tent sites, drinking water, toilets and fishing for a small fee.

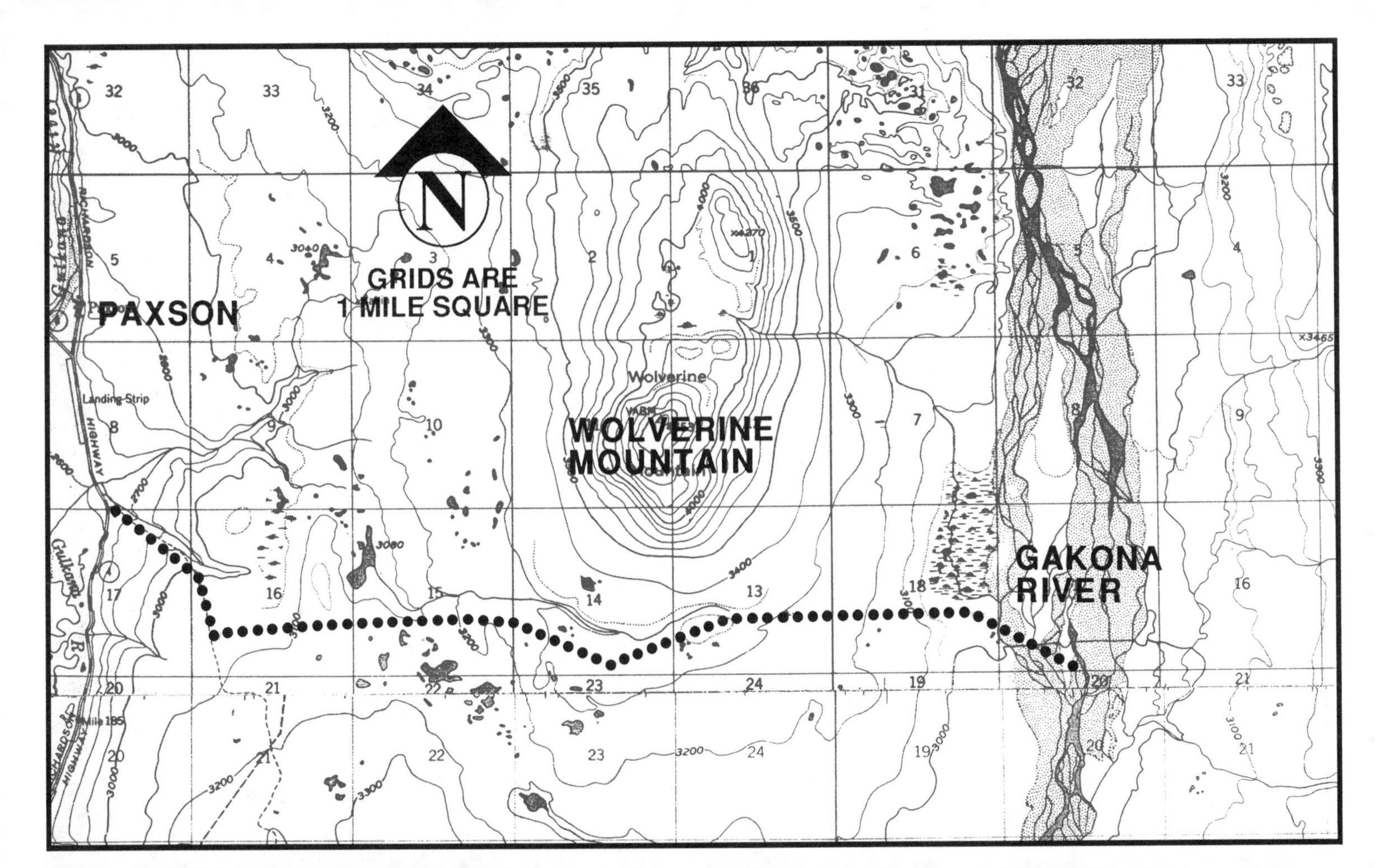

N
GRIDS ARE
1 MILE SQUARE
PAXSON
WOLVERINE
MOUNTAIN
Wolverine
GAKONA
RIVER
Landing Strip
RICHARDSON
HIGHWAY
Gulkana
R
Mile 185

trail 36 ONE MILE TRAIL

AT - A - GLANCE	
TRAILHEAD:	mile 184..5
FROM ANCHORAGE:	258.5 miles
LENGTH OF TRAIL:	14 miles round trip
RIDING TIME:	6 to 8 hours
DIFFICULTY:	3.5
LOW POINT:	2,600 ft.
HIGH POINT:	3,350 ft.
ELEVATION GAIN:	750 ft.
U.S.G.S. MAPS:	Mt. Hayes A-3, Mt. Hayes 1 : 250,000

Ride your bike under the Trans Alaska Pipeline and past Wolverine Mountain before descending into the Gakona River drainage. This remote ORV trail provides hunting access to river systems flowing south from nearby glaciers in the eastern Alaska Range. The area's lush rolling hills, numerous lakes and broad river valleys are home to a great number of wild animals. Examine the edges of drying mud holes for animal tracks. It's possible to observe bear, wolf, moose and other animals along this trail.

Climb out of the Gulkana River Valley on a well-defined trail that makes its way up and onto the southern shoulder of Wolverine Mountain. Dropping down in a series of steps the rider is soon on the gravel river bottom of the Gakona River. Though this trail is mostly hard-pack dirt, several sections of boggy tundra must be negotiated. For this reason, the cyclist should expect wet feet.

About 1 mile south of Paxson Lodge is One Mile Creek (mile 184.5 Richardson Hwy.) and just south of that is an ORV trail that heads east. Find a place to park that's off the road and out of traffic's way. The first mile is all uphill and quite steep. Be prepared to push your bike up this, the hardest section of the ride. Less than two miles into the journey you will encounter the world famous Trans Alaska Pipeline. The trail continues after crossing under the pipeline and soon drops into a bog where the trails split. Take the left trail, which goes through the bog and past a small lake with resident water birds. You'll soon crest the highest point and begin the downhill ride into the Gakona River Valley. Cycle on the river bed, where small rocks and glacial silt allow for easy biking in almost any direction. Lots of exploring and great camping possibilities abound along the bank. For most, this is the end of the ride (mile 7). An ORV trail continues, crossing the many braids of water in this flood plain to the other side. Although most of the braids are only knee deep the Gakona River is swift-running, glacier-fed and always changing. Exercise caution when crossing this or any moving water. From here, the trail can be seen climbing to the top of a far hill. It then drops down the other side into the Chistochina River drainage.

chapter 6

DENALI HIGHWAY

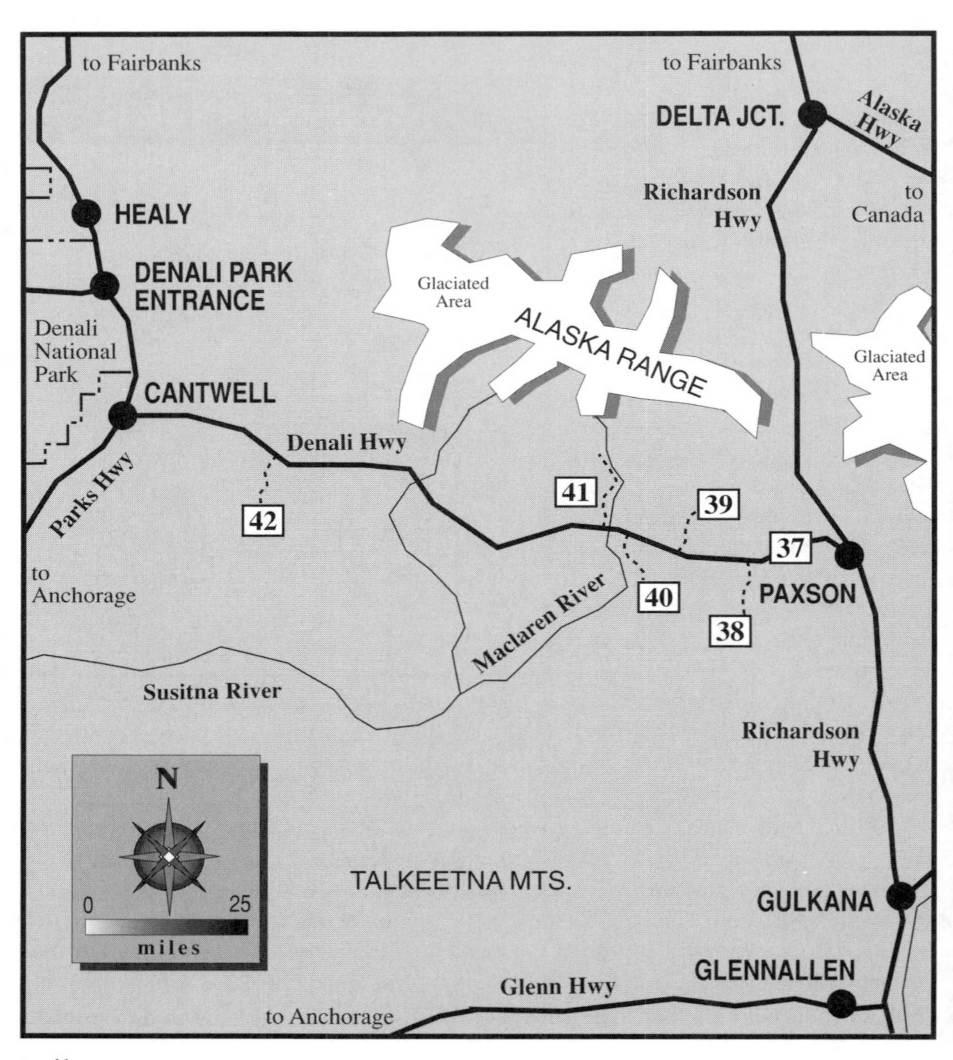

The Denali Highway travels 137.5 miles, east to west, from Paxson to Cantwell. A gravel road, except for the first 22 miles, it traverses the southern flank of the Alaska Range, crossing several major river drainages.

Although many of the trails in this chapter are short, they take the cyclists into interesting and beautiful country. Trails 38 and 42 are noted for great fishing. The easiest rides are trails 38, 39, and 41. The hardest trails are 37 and 40.

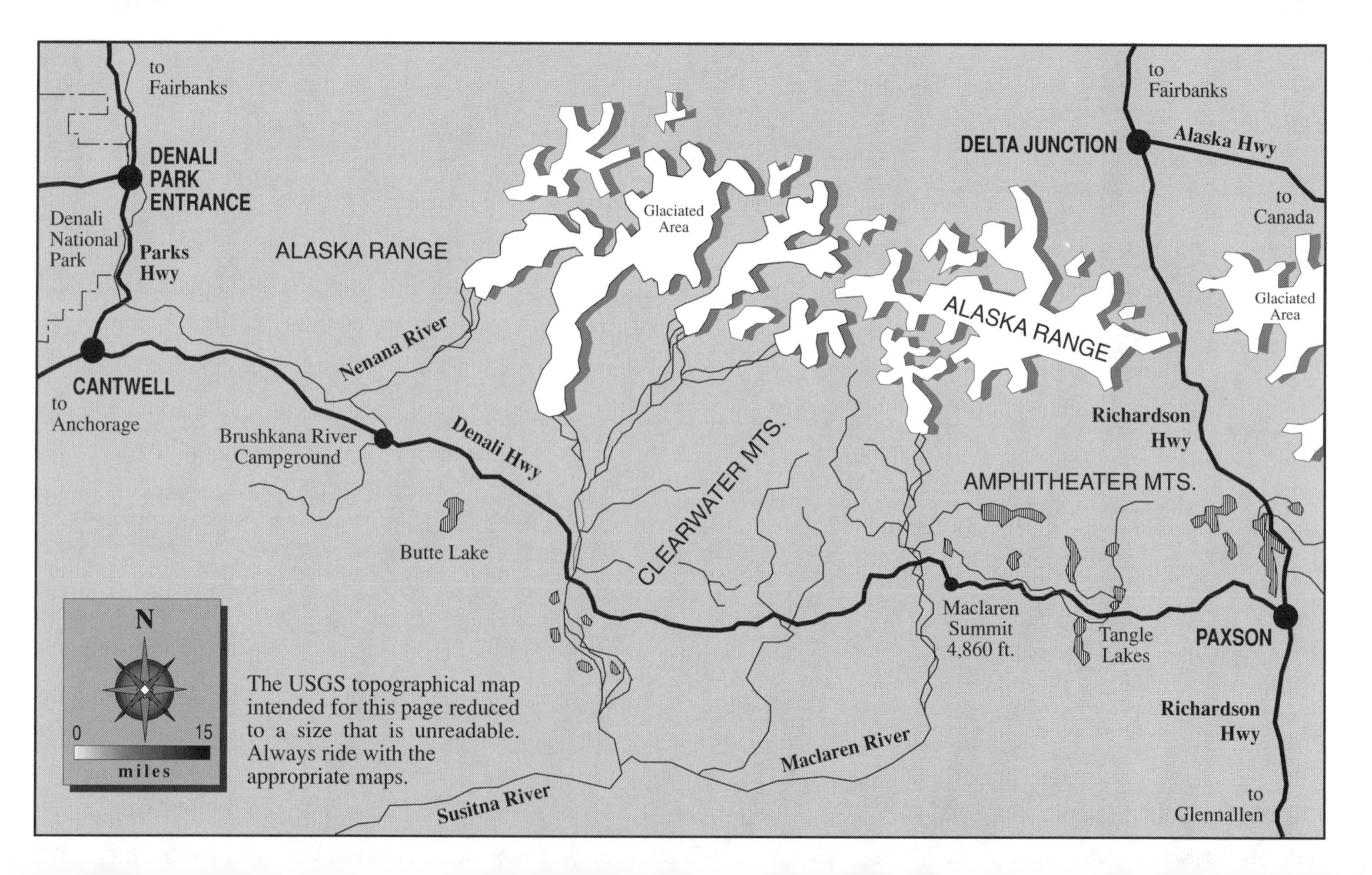

The USGS topographical map intended for this page reduced to a size that is unreadable. Always ride with the appropriate maps.

trail 37

DENALI HIGHWAY

AT - A - GLANCE	
TRAILHEAD	..:mile 185.5 Richardson Hwy.
FROM ANCHORAGE:	........259.5 miles
LENGTH OF TRAIL:	.135.5 miles one way
RIDING TIME:	...............1 to 3 days
DIFFICULTY:	..................2.5 to 3
LOW POINT:	..................2,450 ft.
HIGH POINT:	..................4,086 ft.
ELEVATION GAIN:	.............1,636 ft.
U.S.G.S. MAPS:	..........Mt. Hayes and Healy 1 : 250,000, BLM points of interest map

The grandeur of Alaska is slowly unwrapped like a prized Christmas present as you ride across the 137.5 mile Denali Highway. The road, completed in 1957, was built so motorized vehicles could access Mt. McKinley National Park (now called Denali National Park). It traverses the southern slopes of the ice-capped Alaska Range and crosses three major river drainages as it travels from Paxson to Cantwell. The cycling angler will delight in the fishing along this roadway.

A maintained gravel surface changes texture and composition often. The occasional washboard, sandy section, pothole and long uphill climb are all easily negotiated. Much of the road surface travels on or next to the ancient remains of retreating glaciers, giving us names such eskers, kettle lake, kames and pingos. Close to a dozen rideable trails leave the roadway and travel to a remote lake or river. (see this chapter for additional trails and information.)

Although this ride can be done from either direction, mileposts run east to west, as does this description. Starting in Paxson (mile 185.5 of the Richardson Hwy. and mile 0 of the Denali Hwy.), cycle west on the Denali Highway, the first 21 miles of which are paved. The Tangle River Inn, Sleeping Lady Lodge and two BLM campgrounds provide services at the impressive Tangle Lakes (mile 21.5). Cycle past Landmark Gap Lake and Glacier Lake as you traverse the Amphitheater Mountains. Climb to Maclaren Summit (mile 36), which at 4,086 feet, is the second highest highway pass in Alaska. Maclaren Lodge (mile 42) offers full services and sits on the banks of the Maclaren River. Climb up and through "Crazy Notch" (mile 46) before rounding the Clearwater Mountains and crossing the Susitna River (mile 79.5). Gracious House is a full service lodge at mile 82. Hike a small hill (mile 85) for a fantastic view of Mt. Deborah (12,339 feet) and Mt. Hess (11, 940 feet) . Watch below for caribou, which migrate through this habitat. BLM-maintained Brushkana River Campground (mile 104) has numerous camp sites with fire pits, toilets, tables and drinking water. Soon you're cycling above the silty Nenana River. At mile 130, look for a wonderful view of Mt. McKinley, a fitting finish to the 135.5 mile Denali Highway tour.

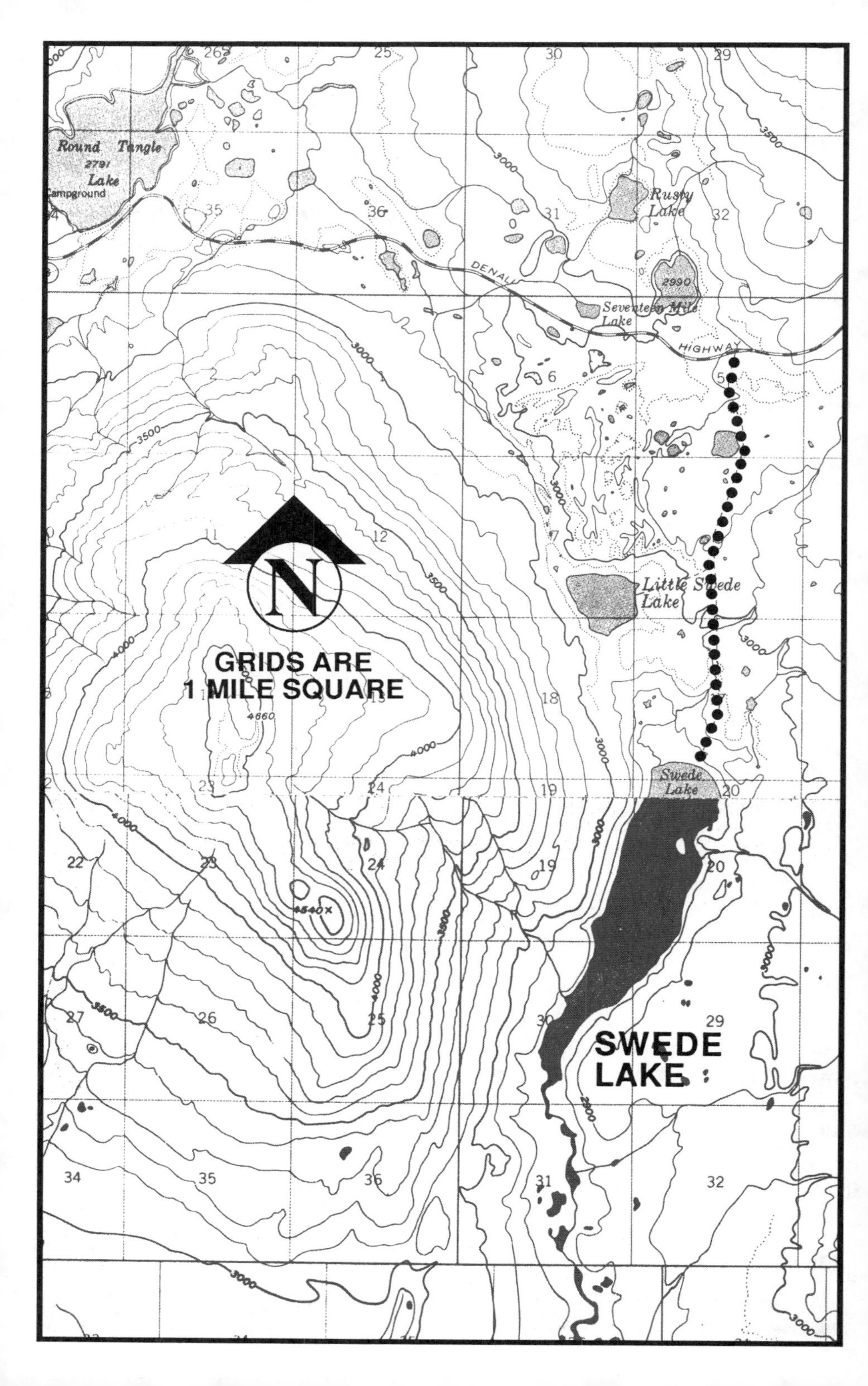
Round Tangle Lake
2791
Campground
Rusty Lake
2990
Seventeen Mile Lake
DENALI HIGHWAY
Little Swede Lake
Swede Lake
GRIDS ARE 1 MILE SQUARE
N
4660
4540
SWEDE LAKE

trail 38

SWEDE LAKE

Welcome to high country, with rolling hills, hundreds of lakes and snow-capped mountains. To the southwest are the Wrangell Mountains and to the north, the Alaska Range. You are just inside the eastern boundary of the Tangle Lakes Archaeological District, which was established to protect prehistoric human sites in the area. The nearby Tangle Lakes offers a variety of outdoor options that include fishing, scenic photography, canoeing and a float on the Delta National Wild, Scenic and Recreational River. This river flows through the Amphitheater Mountains to the Tanana River and then to the mighty Yukon River.

AT - A - GLANCE

TRAILHEAD: . . . . . . .mile 16.8 Denali Hwy.

FROM ANCHORAGE: . . . . .276.3 miles

LENGTH OF TRAIL: . . .5.2 miles round trip

RIDING TIME: . . . . .2 to 4 hours

DIFFICULTY: . . . . .2.5 to 3

LOW POINT: . . . . .2,750 ft.

HIGH POINT: . . . . .3,100 ft.

ELEVATION GAIN: . . . . .350 ft.

U.S.G.S. MAPS: . . . . .Mt. Hayes A-4, Gulkana D-4, Mt. Hayes 1 : 250,000

A smooth earthen trail takes the rider south across country that is open and treeless to Big Swede Lake. This lake is a fisherman's dream for lake trout, burbot and grayling. Inquire locally for information on fishing in this area. Look for caribou, bear and moose in this area. A hunting trail continues beyond Big Swede Lake to the Middle Fork of the Gulkana River, where other hunting trails provide access to Dickey Lake and the Alphabet Hills. In wet conditions, many parts of this trail will be extremely muddy.

The trailhead, at milepost 16.8, is on the south side of the Denali Highway and marked with a BLM sign, map and visitor's log. Find a parking spot out of the way. Looking south, you can see the trail cross high, brushy country. In the distance, Big Swede Lake is nestled against the toe of a mountain. Occasionally, the trail will fork around a muddy section as motorized vehicles, seeking firmer ground, tear up new vegetation. Select the driest route that day. Approximately 1.9 miles into the ride the trail splits. The right trail, after .7 of a mile, offers a wonderful lunch site with a fantastic view of the lake from a high bank. There is easy access to the lake for fishing or exploring. The left trail takes you around the lake on a ridge, past private property and then down into the Middle Fork drainage. Two BLM campgrounds, Tangle Lakes (mile 21.5 Denali Hwy.) and Tangle River (mile 21.7 Denali Hwy.), have camp sites, toilets, tables, drinking water and boat ramps. Tangle River Inn (mile 20 Denali Hwy) and Sleeping Lady Lodge (mile 22 Denali Hwy.) provide full services.

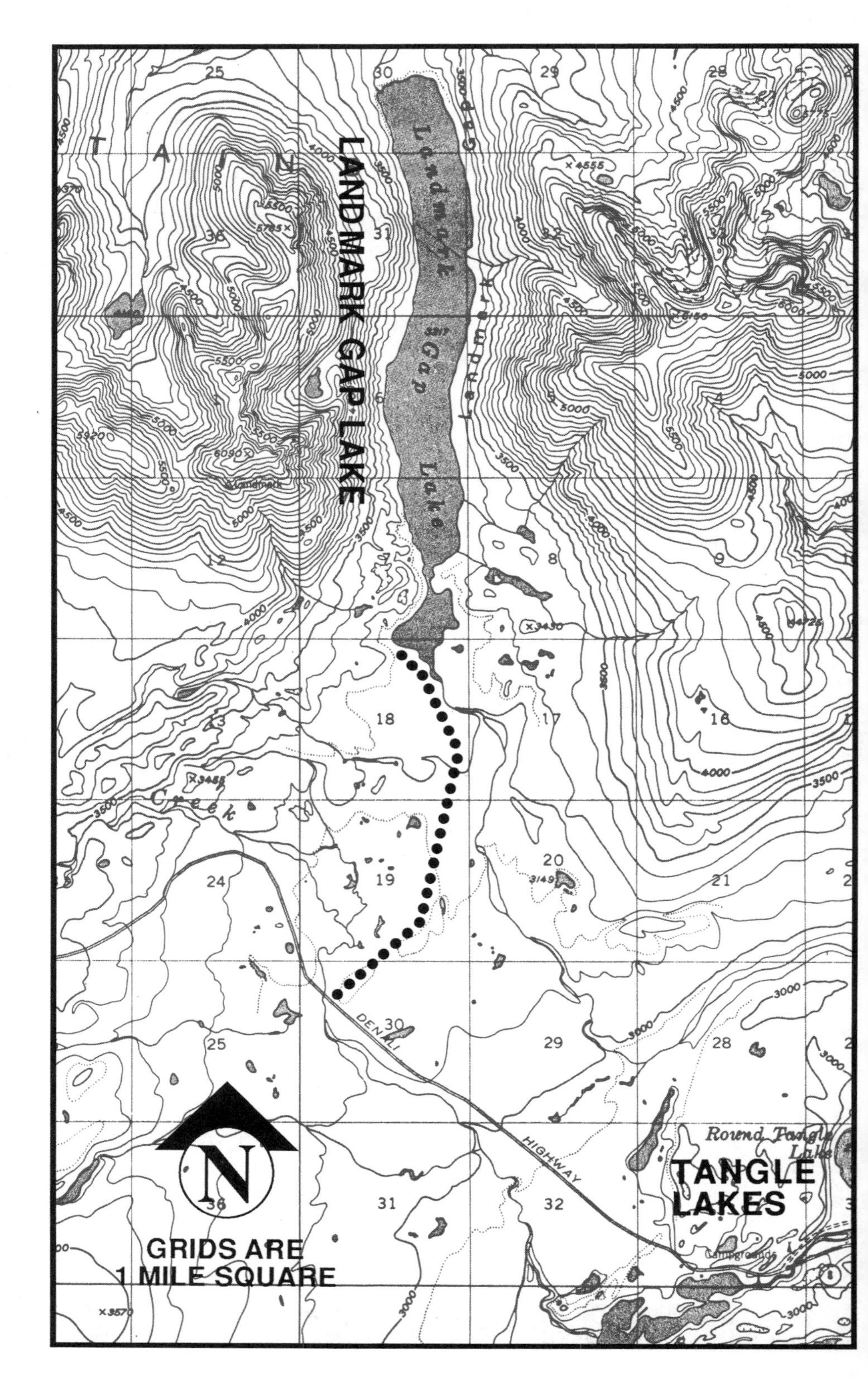

LANDMARK GAP LAKE
Landmark Gap Lake
Landmark Gap
Creek
DENALI
HIGHWAY
Round Tangle Lake
TANGLE
LAKES
N
GRIDS ARE
1 MILE SQUARE

trail 39 LANDMARK GAP

Northwest of the Tangle Lakes lies Landmark Gap Lake, tucked into the Amphitheater Mountains — foothills to the Alaska Range. Advancing glaciers 10,000 years ago carved out this interesting geological formation and this trail provides access to it. Through the gap and in the distance, towers Mt. Moffit (13,020 ft.) and McGinnis Peak (11,400 ft.). The Nelchina caribou herd uses this gap as a migration route. Look for beaver, bear, moose and a variety of migratory birds. Fishermen may wish to try their luck for grayling in the lake and in the mouth of its river. Ancient people also knew of the natural riches of the area. Their remains have been found throughout the immediate area. Because prehistoric artifacts have been discovered here the area is considered sensitive and has been placed within the protective Tangle Lakes Archaeological District. This trail, as any trail in the archaeological district, may be closed temporarily to all traffic, allowing archaeologists to recover data and artifacts. Call the BLM in Glennallen to check for closures. (see Agency Information)

AT - A - GLANCE

TRAILHEAD: ....mile 24.6 Denali Hwy.

FROM ANCHORAGE: ....284.1 miles

LENGTH OF TRAIL: .....5 miles round trip

RIDING TIME: ....2 to 4 hours

DIFFICULTY: ....2.5 to 3

LOW POINT: ....3,150 ft.

HIGH POINT: ....3,250 ft.

ELEVATION GAIN: ....100 ft.

U.S.G.S. MAPS: ....Mt. Hayes A-5, Mt. Hayes 1 : 250,000

Although this trail is only 5 miles long (round trip) it offers access to a beautiful spot in the Alaska Range. Several great camp sites around the lake beckon the cycling enthusiast to load up the bike with gear and spend several days exploring the wonders of this area.

A BLM signpost at mile 24.6 (Denali Hwy.) marks the trailhead for the Landmark Gap Trail (north). An earthen trail winds north toward an obvious gap between mountains and to the long shores of a sparkling blue lake. Skirt around muddy low spots and ruts made by ORVs. After a mile, trail conditions improve considerably as you pass a "No Motorized Vehicles" sign erected to protect archaeological sites in the immediate area. Soon you're biking parallel to a clear-running river as you make your way to Landmark Gap Lake. Those camping should consider one of several sites already established along the lake's edge. Leave your bike behind and follow a game trail around the west, or left, side of the lake to the area where land pinches the lake into two pieces. Hike up the west shoulder for a fantastic view down the length of Landmark Gap Lake and southeast to the shining Tangle Lakes.

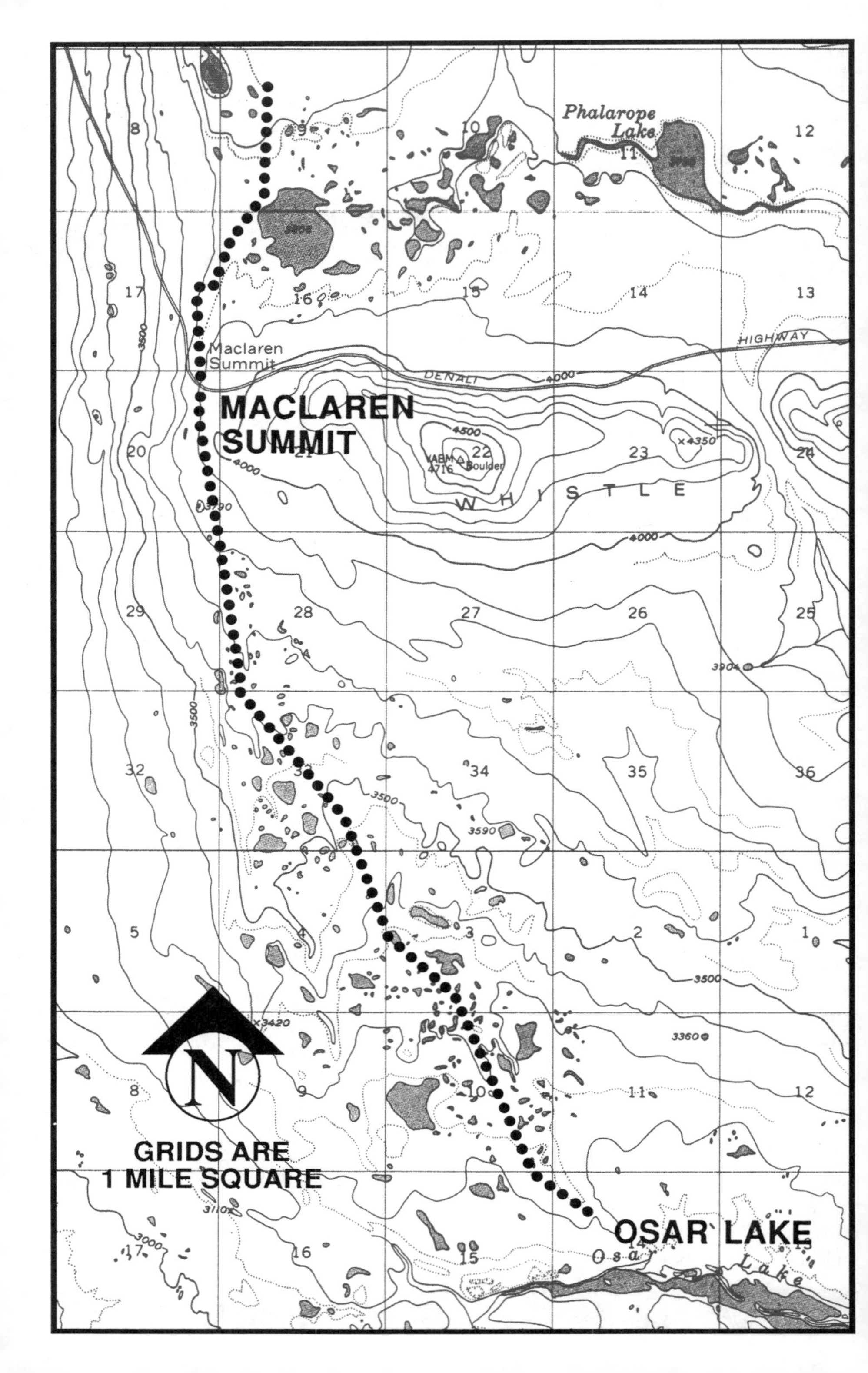
Phalarope Lake
MACLAREN SUMMIT
Maclaren Summit
DENALI HIGHWAY
WHISTLE
Boulder
OSAR LAKE
Osar Lake
GRIDS ARE 1 MILE SQUARE
N

trail 40

MACLAREN SUMMIT

AT - A - GLANCE	
TRAILHEAD:	mile 37 Denali Hwy.
FROM ANCHORAGE:	296.5 miles
LENGTH OF TRAIL:	10 miles round trip
RIDING TIME:	3 to 5 hours
DIFFICULTY:	3 or 4
LOW POINT:	3,200 ft.
HIGH POINT:	4,086 ft.
ELEVATION GAIN:	886 ft.
U.S.G.S. MAPS:	Mt. Hayes A-5, Mt. Hayes 1 : 250,000

Stand high above the rich and wild Maclaren River drainage, commanding a view of the rugged glaciated mountains that give this waterway life. A broad river basin, lined lush green and spotted with dozens of lakes, flows south to the Susitna River. Maclaren Summit (4,086 ft.) is the second highest highway pass in Alaska, after Atigun Pass (4,800 ft.) in the Brooks Range. Bring your binoculars. Birding opportunities abound. The Maclaren River drainage is summer habitat for a wide variety of migratory birds that include sandhill cranes and trumpeter swans. Bald eagles, moose, bear and caribou also live in this fertile wilderness.

Cyclists will find a hard-pack trail with little erosion. A few low spots may be filled with water, forcing the rider to scramble through tall brush in order to keep dry feet. A long downhill roller coaster glide drops the rider almost 1,000 ft. in a little more than 5 miles. This means a 5-mile climb back up to the trail head.

Two BLM trailheads are located at mile 37 of the Denali Highway. To the north, the short Maclaren Summit Trail crosses several miles of tundra on a soft, earthen path high above the Maclaren River. To the south is the Osar Lake Trail. At the south end of a long parking area, pick up an obvious ORV trail. This trail starts out rocky but soon turns into a hard, earthen path as it drops down in a series of rolling steps providing access to the vicinity of Osar Lake. You're soon winding and twisting on a well-defined trail through dense waist-high brush and skirting around a multitude of small kettle lakes. These lakes were formed when retreating glaciers left behind large, broken pieces of ice. Sediment, which covered these chunks of melting ice, fell into bowl shaped depressions or kettles. A less used trail branches off to the right (mile 3) and climbs a few small hills before fading out. The main trail continues to lose elevation, dropping and winding around lakes and climbing small hills for several more miles. Consider taking a lunch break halfway up on the return ride at a spot that caught your fancy when coming down. This will provide a pleasant break in the long climb back to the trail head. Nearby Maclaren River Lodge (mile 42 Denali Hwy.) provides full services.

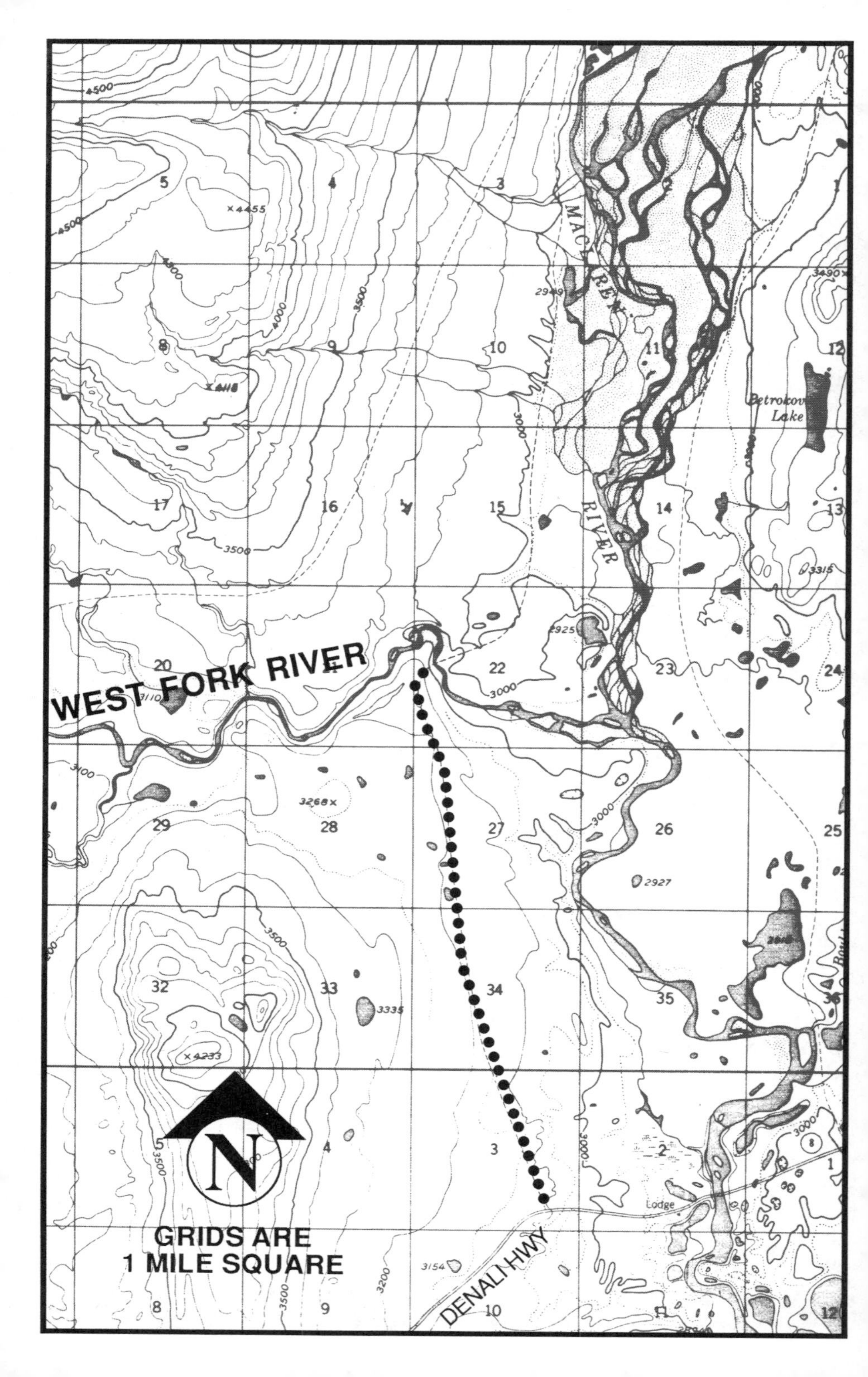

WEST FORK RIVER
MACLAREN RIVER
Petrokov Lake
DENALI HWY
Lodge
GRIDS ARE
1 MILE SQUARE
N

MACLAREN RIVER RD.

This short, easy ride on a flat gravel road takes the rider into the beautiful Maclaren River valley on the south side of the Alaska Range and provides recreational access to the area. The scenery along this trail is both impressive and expansive. Flanked by mountains on three sides, you ride north toward the Maclaren Glacier in the Alaska Range, while the Clearwater Mountains rise to the west. Across the Maclaren River to the east are the Amphitheater Mountains. The Maclaren River is a large glacial watercourse which eventually combines with the Susitna River and flows through the Talkeetna Mountains to Cook Inlet. Look for a variety of animals including moose, bear, beaver and caribou, along with a mix of birds that use the area as their summer habitat.

AT - A - GLANCE

TRAILHEAD: ....mile 43.5 Denali Hwy.

FROM ANCHORAGE: ....303 miles

LENGTH OF TRAIL: .....9 miles round trip

RIDING TIME: ....3 to 5 hours

DIFFICULTY: ....2.5 to 3

LOW POINT: ....3,000 ft.

HIGH POINT: ....3,100 ft.

ELEVATION GAIN: ....100 ft.

U.S.G.S. MAPS: ....Mt. Hayes A-6, Mt. Hayes 1 : 250,000

A smooth, gravel road rolls over small hills, dropping into small creeks as you travel north. Heavy rains have eroded parts of this roadway, stopping 4-wheel drive rigs. So be alert.

The trailhead, at milepost 43.5 of the Denali Highway, is well-marked with a BLM sign, complete with map and visitor's log. Park your vehicle off the roadway and out of traffic's way before beginning your outing. Approximately 4 miles in, the trail splits. The left trail goes a short distance around a knob hill, giving the cyclist a bird's-eye view of the clear-running West Fork River. This is a great vantage point for surveying the terrain for signs of moose, bear and other wildlife. A lake below has several active beavers and a number of resident water birds. Circle back around the hill on the same trail and take the right fork, which drops the cyclist down to the river bank. This is a great place to stop for lunch. Watch the beavers, listen to the river and explore the area. The West Fork River generally runs swift and deep, but during dry times and low water it may be possible to cross. Use good judgment and always exercise caution crossing moving water. The trail continues for approximately 8 miles, brushy in sections but obvious and in relatively good shape, toward Maclaren Glacier. The BLM-maintained Tangle Lakes Campground (mile 21.5 Denali Hwy.) provides camping needs and fishing. Maclaren River Lodge (mile 42 Denali Hwy.) has full services.

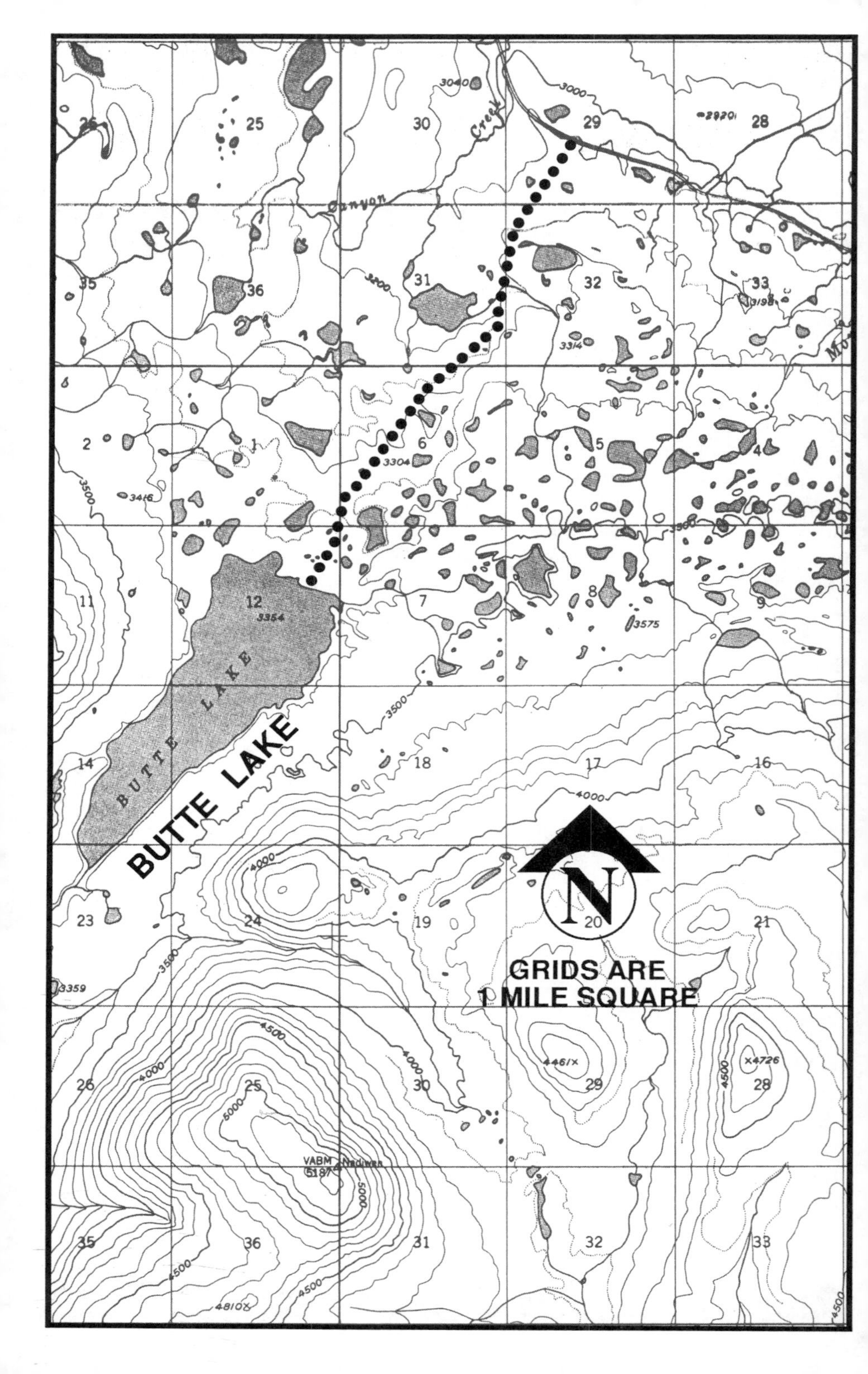

BUTTE LAKE
BUTTE LAKE
Canyon
Creek
N
GRIDS ARE
1 MILE SQUARE

trail 42 BUTTE LAKE

Visit spacious high country studded with lakes, with the towering peaks of the Alaska Range in the background. Look north across Monahan Flats to the glaciers that become the headwaters to the Nenana and Susitna rivers. Rising above all is Mt. Deborah (12,339 ft.) and Mt. Nenana (11,940 ft.). Butte Lake, known throughout the state for great fishing, offers the cycling angler a chance to catch 25-pound lake trout, 10-pound burbot and 20-inch grayling. This is a known route for migrating caribou, which graze upon the rolling hills. Also look for bear, fox, wolverines, wolves, moose and a variety of birds.

AT - A - GLANCE

TRAILHEAD: ....93.6 Denali Hwy.

FROM ANCHORAGE: ....253.9 miles

LENGTH OF TRAIL: ...7.5 miles round trip

RIDING TIME: ....2 to 4 hours

DIFFICULTY: 3

LOW POINT: ....3,100 ft.

HIGH POINT: ....3,400 ft.

ELEVATION GAIN: ....300 ft.

U.S.G.S. MAPS: ....Healy A-2, Healy 1 : 250,000

This soft, earthen trail guides the rider through a land of many lakes, with rolling hills carpeted in spongy tundra. When conditions are dry, only a few low spots may have mud. When conditions are wet the length of this route will likely turn to mud. The terrain is quite sensitive and recovers slowly, please tread lightly. Multiple user groups enjoy this trail including ORVs, horses, bicycles and hikers.

Butte Lake trailhead is located on the south side of the Denali Highway at about mile 93.6. At the south end of a small gravel pit pick up an obvious trail as it makes its way up and over a small hill. On occasion, the trail will split around muddy sections, forcing the rider to choose the driest route that day. Take the time to observe the surroundings as you crest small hills, affording the cyclist views of the inspiring panorama. The lake's edge is reached after cycling nearly 4 miles. Please respect private property and cabins in the area. Don't forget the camera, binoculars or mosquito repellant. The Brushkana River Campground (mile 104.3 Denali Hwy.) is 10.5 miles west of this trailhead and offers wonderful camping along the banks of the Brushkana River. More than a dozen camp sites, with tables, fire pits and drinking water makes this BLM campground an excellent staging area for Butte Lake trail. The Brushkana River also is a noted fishing spot. Start cycling here or drive the 10.7 miles east to the trailhead. (See this chapter for additional trails along the Denali Highway.)

chapter 7

EDGERTON HWY.

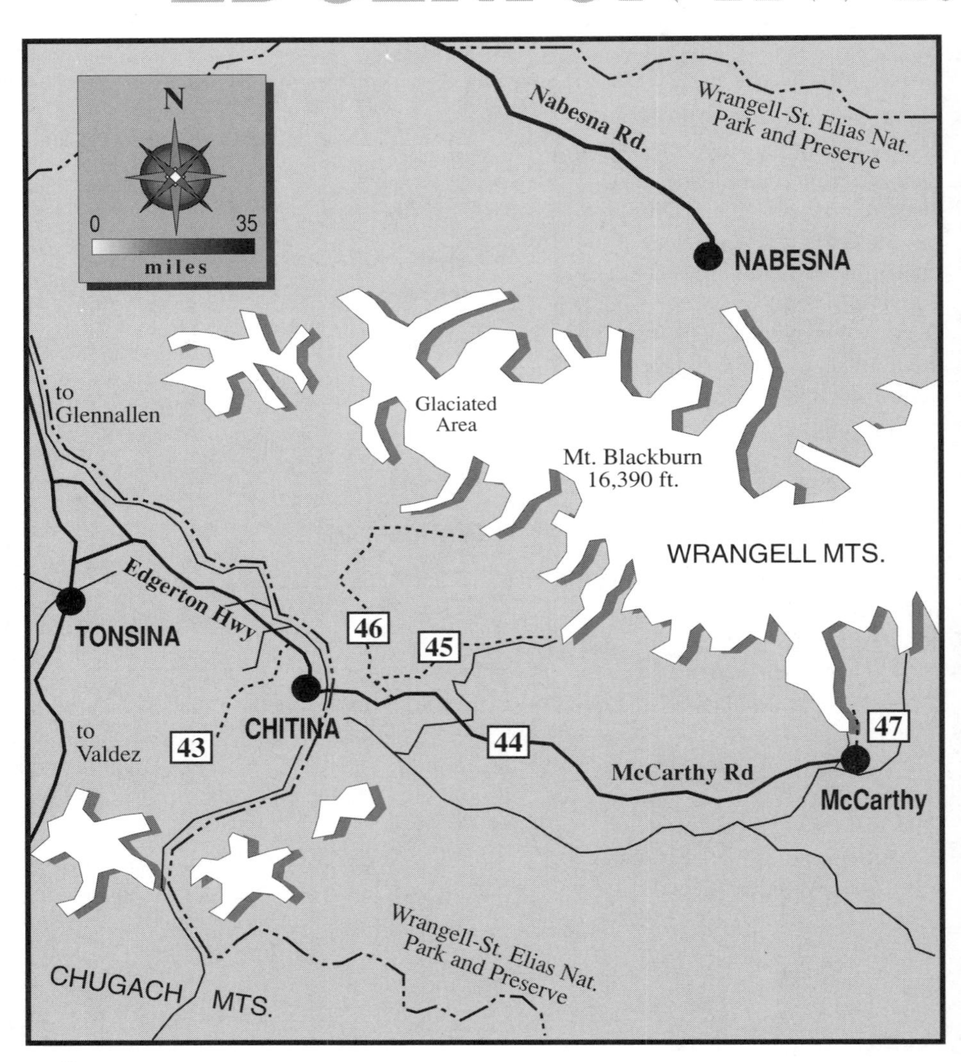

The Edgerton Highway is a 35-mile scenic corridor to the Wrangell-St. Elias National Park and Preserve, a park rich in wildlife and rugged beauty. The road travels from the Richardson Hwy. to Chitina. The remains of a once-flourishing mining industry are fun to visit and explore.

All of the rides listed in this chapter, except trail 43, take the rider into the Wrangell Mountains. Trail 43 instead climbs high into the Chugach Mountains, offering superb vistas of the nearby Wrangell's. The easiest ride is trail 47 and the hardest trails are 43 and 46. Trail 45 is possibly the most scenic.

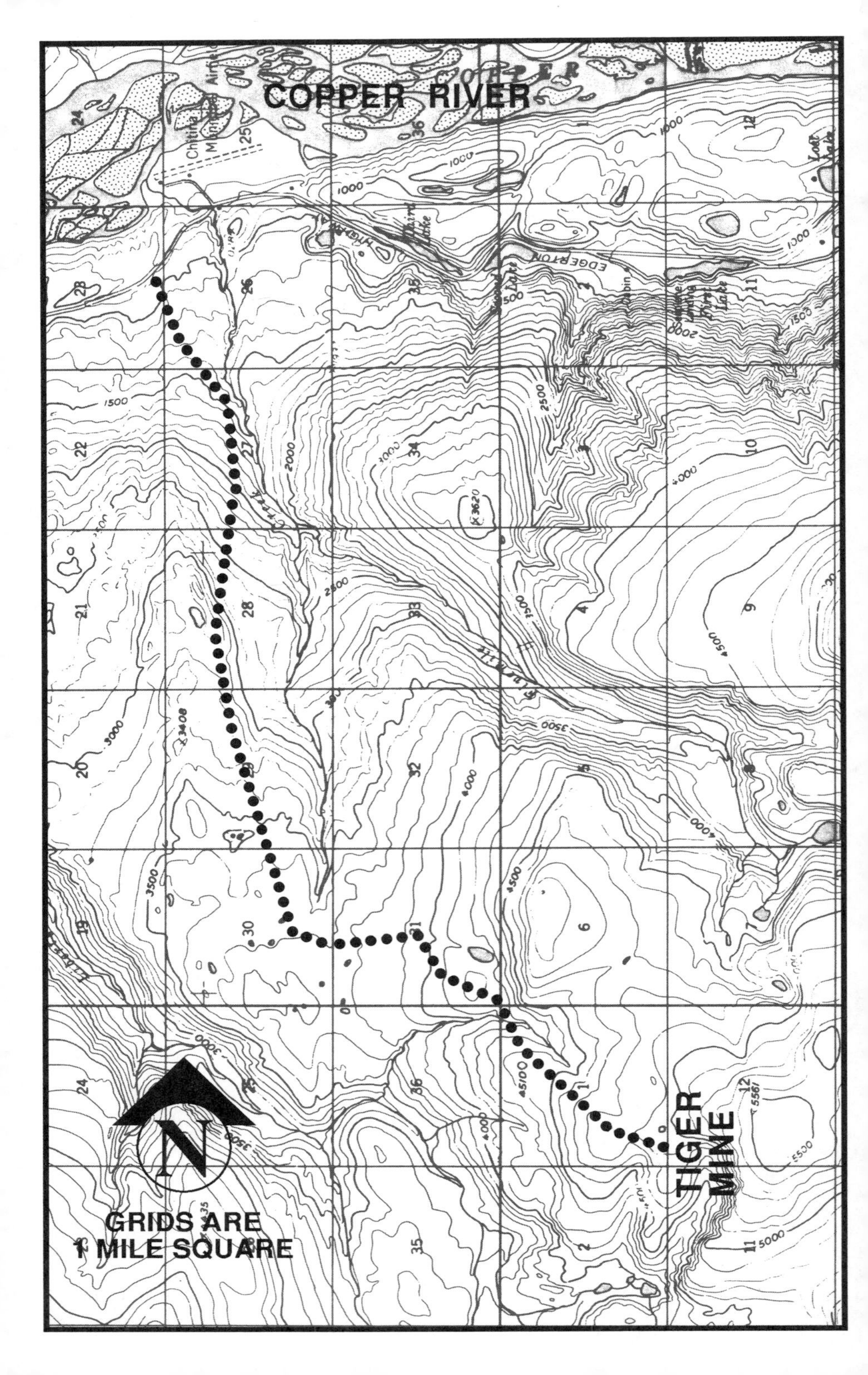

COPPER RIVER
TIGER MINE
N
GRIDS ARE
1 MILE SQUARE

trail 43

TIGER MINE

Pump up your legs with this 4,000-foot climb out of the Copper River Valley, cycling high above tree line into the Chugach Mountains. Be rewarded with spectacular views across the valley to the Wrangell Mountains as Mt. Blackburn (16,390 ft.) and Mt. Wrangell (14,163 ft.) tower above all. This is country that is dominated by glaciated mountain peaks and the thousands of rivers and streams that flow from them. Eagles, bear, fox and moose, among others, call this land home. Watch the flora change as you surmount a series of steep uphill steps that take the rider slowly skyward through dense forest and high alpine tundra.

AT - A - GLANCE

TRAILHEAD: .....mile 27.9 Edgerton Hwy.

FROM ANCHORAGE: ....249.3 miles

LENGTH OF TRAIL: ....15 miles round trip

RIDING TIME: ....5 to 7 hours

DIFFICULTY: ....5 (hill climb)

LOW POINT: ....850 ft.

HIGH POINT:..................4,850 ft.

ELEVATION GAIN: ....4,000 ft.

U.S.G.S. MAPS: ....Valdez C-2, Valdez 1 : 250,000

Mineral rich ground lured the present day miners who built this precipitous road. The road surface is hard-pack gravel with occasional rocky and sandy sections. Water erosion is minor and limited to a few places. Traction, in general, is very good and the few obstacles encountered on this 7.5 mile climb can be negotiated. Although there are a number of level sections, this is mostly a long uphill climb, which, conversely, means a long downhill ride. Properly functioning brakes and a helmet are required gear. Nearby Liberty Falls State Recreation Site (mile 23.7 Edgerton Hwy.) offers camping at established sites.

The Tiger Mine Road can be reached by driving 189 miles east from Anchorage to Glennallen. Take a right onto the Richardson Highway and drive 32.4 miles south. Turn left onto the Edgerton Highway. At mile 27.9, a "TONSINA CONTROLLED USE AREA" sign indicates the trailhead. Ample parking and camping can be found by driving in a short distance to a gravel pit. The trail immediately starts with an uphill climb as it winds its way up from the valley floor. After 4 miles of climbing, the trail flattens out above tree line, revealing a high plain with rolling hills and several lakes. In the distance you can observe the trail continuing to gain higher ground as it advances toward the highest point in the area. The trail progresses up a steep pitch before ending on a high ridge, where there has been recent mining activity. Fantastic hiking and exploring abound. Please respect private property.

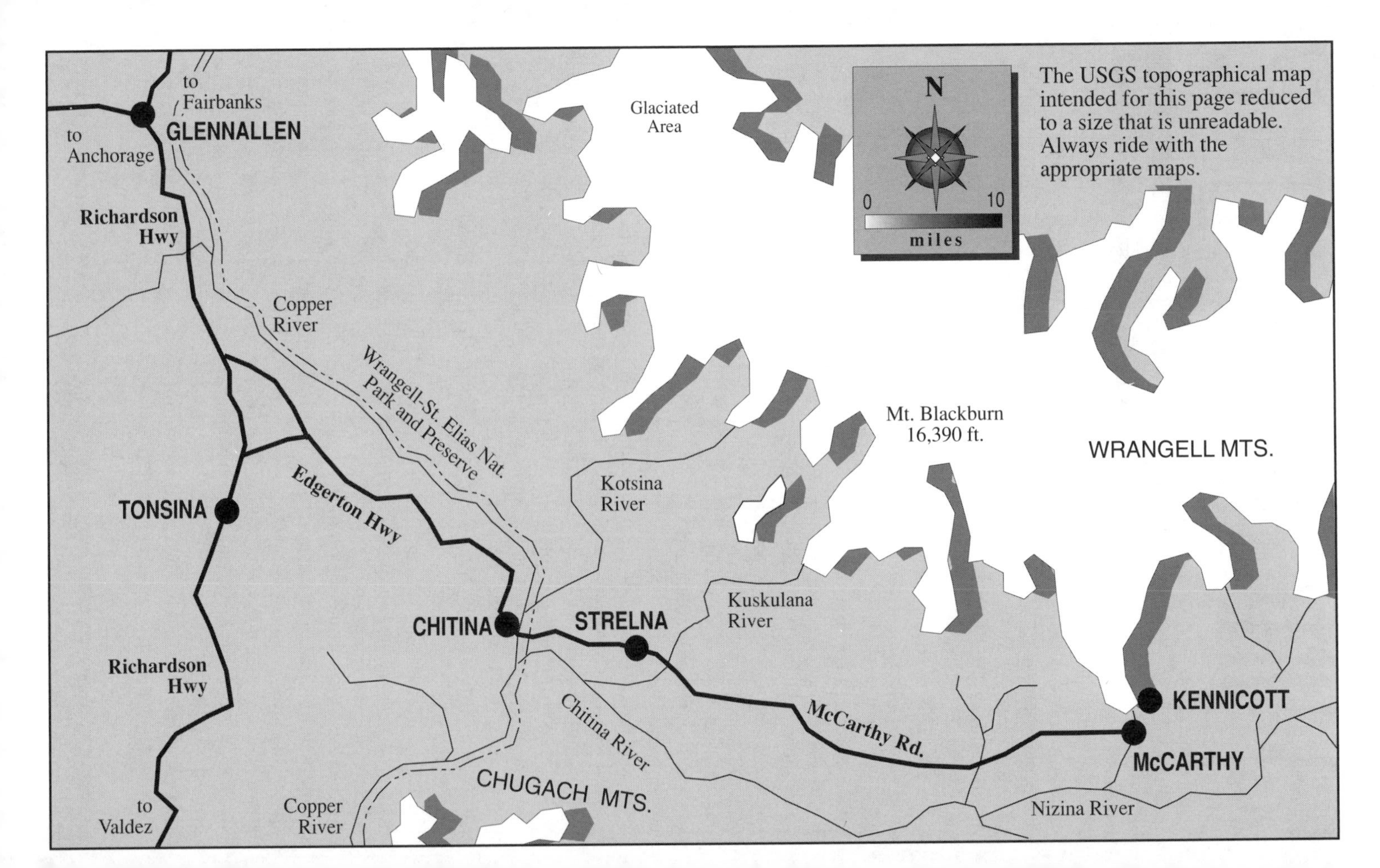
The USGS topographical map intended for this page reduced to a size that is unreadable. Always ride with the appropriate maps.
N
0
10
miles
to Fairbanks
GLENNALLEN
to Anchorage
Richardson Hwy
Glaciated Area
Copper River
Wrangell-St. Elias Nat. Park and Preserve
Edgerton Hwy
TONSINA
Kotsina River
Mt. Blackburn 16,390 ft.
WRANGELL MTS.
Kuskulana River
CHITINA
STRELNA
Richardson Hwy
Chitina River
McCarthy Rd.
KENNICOTT
McCARTHY
CHUGACH MTS.
Copper River
Nizina River
to Valdez

trail 44

McCARTHY RD.

Traverse miles of rugged and wild Alaska as you cycle deep within the Wrangell-St. Elias National Park and Preserve. This route, an old railroad grade, once carried ore from many of the 4,000 gold and copper claims in the area to Cordova, where ocean-going ships carried huge fortunes south to the Lower 48. The first trainload of copper ore, which averaged 70 percent pure, was so rich that it was shoveled into sacks and shipped without the need for milling. In 1980, more than 13 million acres were set aside, creating this unique park and preserve.

AT - A - GLANCE

TRAILHEAD: ......mile 35 Edgerton Hwy..

FROM ANCHORAGE: ....256.4 miles

LENGTH OF TRAIL: ....60 miles one way

RIDING TIME: ....4 to 8 hours

DIFFICULTY: ....3 to 4 (because of length)

LOW POINT: ....900 ft.

HIGH POINT: ....1,800 ft.

ELEVATION GAIN: ....900 ft.

U.S.G.S. MAPS: ....Valdez 1 : 250,000

Cycle past reminders of mining history on this gravel road that leads you 60 miles from Chitina to McCarthy, a popular ride with many visitors. An Anchorage bicycle club holds an annual race across this road in August, drawing as many as 60 contestants of all experience levels. Outstanding scenery make this long, bumpy, dusty road worth the effort. Expect those things generally associated with gravel roads: washboard, potholes, car traffic and a few hills.

The McCarthy Road can be reached by driving east from Anchorage to Glennallen (mile 189.5 Glenn Highway). Take a right onto the Richardson Highway and drive south. Turn left onto the Edgerton Highway (mile 82.6 Richardson Hwy.) and drive down this paved road 35 miles to Chitina. The dirt road to McCarthy starts just beyond Chitina after crossing the Copper River Bridge. Begin cycling here. Climb out of the Copper River Valley, stopping occasionally to view the Chitina River flood plains far below. A side road to the left, at the small community of Strelna (mile 13.5), is the trail head for the Kotsina and Nugget Creek trails (see Kotsina River, Nugget Creek). Cross the Kuskulana bridge nearly 300 feet above the river. When the trees part, watch for views of the spectacular Wrangell Mountains. Cycle through the Long Lake Wildlife Refuge (mile 44). A picturesque homestead sits on the lake's shore, complete with a beautiful garden, grass airstrip, wildflowers and spawning salmon (in season). At the trail's end, park in the upper lot to avoid summer flooding. To reach the historic town of McCarthy, cross the Kennicott River on hand-pulled trams (see Kennicott Mine).

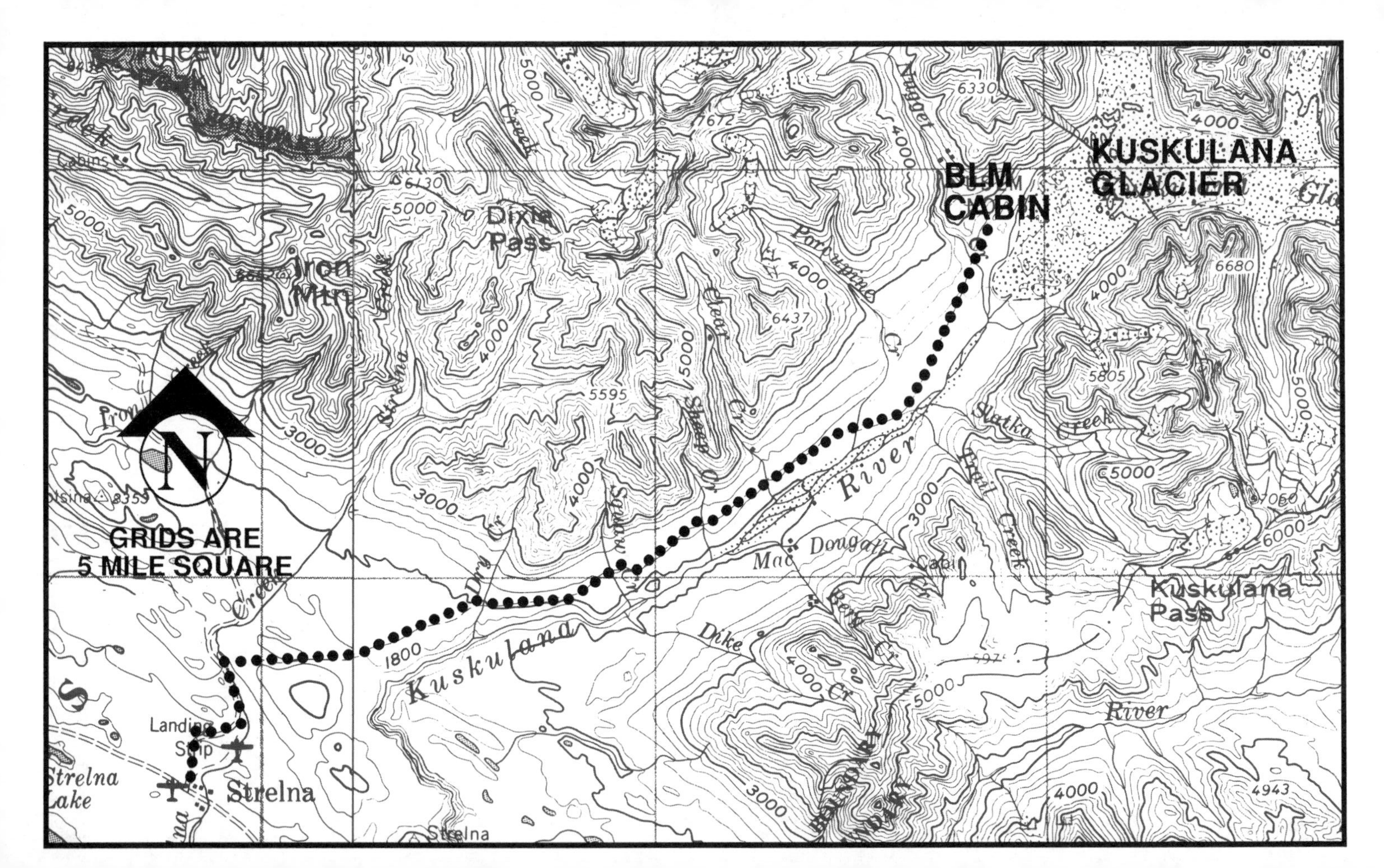
KUSKULANA
GLACIER
BLM
CABIN
Kuskulana
Pass
Dixie
Pass
Iron
Mtn
GRIDS ARE
5 MILE SQUARE
N
Strelna
Strelna
Lake
Landing
Strip
Kuskulana
River
Nugget
Porcupine
Cr
Clear
Sheep
Squaw
Dry
Cr
Slatka
Creek
Trail
Mac
Dougall
Cabin
Berg
Dike
Cabins
6330
4000
6680
5805
5000
6437
5595
7672
6130
3000
1800
4943
6000
7060

trail 45

NUGGET CREEK

Parallel the Kuskulana River as you cycle to the base of glaciers that flow south off Mt. Blackburn (16,390 ft.), deep in the Wrangell Mountains. Glaciated mountain peaks, clear-running streams, and a thriving animal population gives the visitor to Wrangell-St. Elias National Park and Preserve a real sense of wilderness. A fully equipped BLM cabin at trail's end beckons visitors to spend several days exploring Alaska's mountain kingdom. Around the turn-of-the-century, miners searched this countryside for hidden minerals and this trail is testimony to their efforts. In 1916 alone, 18 working mines from Chitina to McCarthy produced copper ore worth $32.4 million.

AT - A - GLANCE

TRAILHEAD: .....mile 13.5 McCarthy Rd.

FROM ANCHORAGE: ....270 miles

LENGTH OF TRAIL: ..34.4 miles round trip

RIDING TIME: ....5 to 7 hours

DIFFICULTY: ....3 to 4

LOW POINT: ....1,300 ft.

HIGH POINT: ....2,500 ft.

ELEVATION GAIN: ....1,200 ft.

U.S.G.S. MAPS: ....Valdez C-1, C-8, Valdez 1 : 250,000

This well-defined trail is generally quite dry with the exception of a low, wet section 3 miles into the ride. Soon the trail gains elevation as the rider travels effortlessly through rolling timberland on a country road. The hills that are encountered are relatively short in length and few in number. Several creeks must be forded, starting with Strelna Creek and ending with Nugget Creek. They are usually only knee deep, but sudden changes in volume and velocity can occur because of heavy precipitation or rapid snow-melt at higher elevations. Exercise caution on all water crossings.

Travel about 13.5 miles east of Chitina on the McCarthy Road to the small community of Strelna. The Nugget Creek/Kotsina Road leads in a northerly direction (to the left). Park here, off the road and out of traffic's way. Cycle on this dirt road, passing by several fenced homes. A public right-of-way allows access to the trail head. Please respect private property. In 2.5 miles a trail to the right crosses Strelna Creek and becomes the Nugget Creek Trail. Skirt muddy sections in this next area. Squaw Creek (mile 9.1) and Sheep Creek (mile 10.8) have camp sites that are well established on the banks of clear-running creeks. Cross the silty, glacial braids of shallow Nugget Creek (mile 17.2) before reaching the BLM cabin built near the base of Kuskulana Glacier. Consult BLM rangers in Chitina for availability of the cabin.

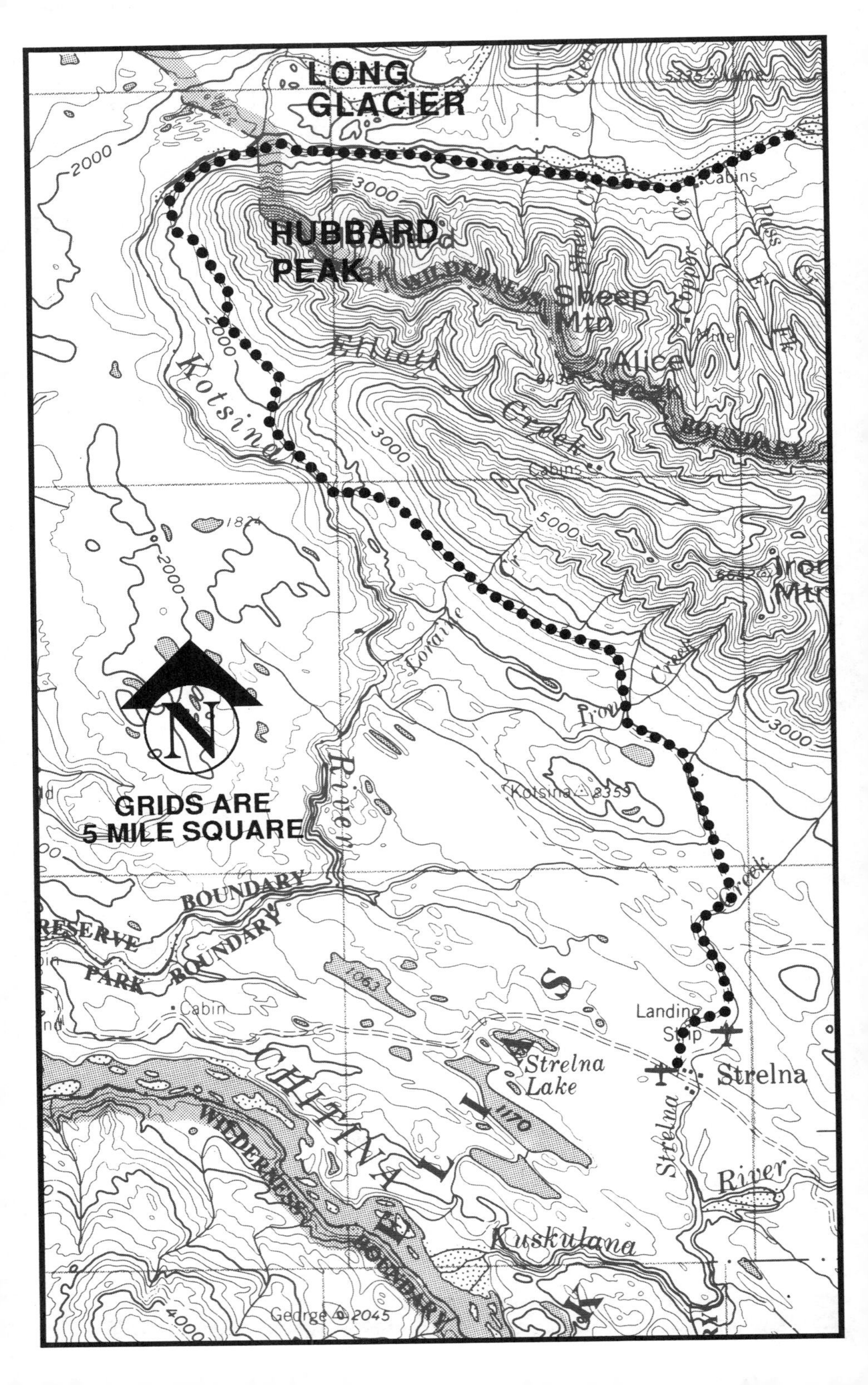

LONG GLACIER
HUBBARD PEAK
Sheep Mtn
Alice Peak
Elliott Creek
Kotsina
Cabins
Cabins
Iron Mtn
Loraine
Iron Creek
Kotsina 8359
River
GRIDS ARE 5 MILE SQUARE
BOUNDARY
RESERVE
PARK BOUNDARY
Cabin
Landing Strip
Strelna
Strelna Lake
Strelna
River
CHITINA
Kuskulana
WILDERNESS
George 2045
2000
3000
5000
3000
4000

trail 46

KOTSINA RIVER

AT - A - GLANCE

TRAILHEAD:	mile 13.5 McCarthy Rd.
FROM ANCHORAGE:	270 miles
LENGTH OF TRAIL:	67 miles round trip
RIDING TIME:	14 hours to several days
DIFFICULTY:	4 to 4.5
LOW POINT:	1,300 ft.
HIGH POINT:	2,200 ft.
ELEVATION GAIN:	900 ft.
U.S.G.S. MAPS:	Valdez C-1, C-8, Valdez 1 : 250,000

For the adventurer, this rolling mountain road offers 67 miles (round trip) of cycling into the remote and beautiful Wrangell-St. Elias National Park and Preserve. Rugged mountains, remote valleys and wild rivers combined with a healthy wildlife population, are a few of the reasons why this park has been placed on the internationally recognized World Heritage List for outstanding natural areas. The park's Dall sheep population is considered world-class. Bears also are abundant and may be present anywhere along this route. Precautions should be taken to avoid bear encounters. Park rules allow visitors to carry firearms for personal protection and it is suggested you leave a "backcountry trip itinerary" with the park service at its Chitina station.

Follow this old mine road, conquer numerous big hills and cross several creeks, just as miners had done during the rush of the 1900s. Cycle past Long Glacier, which flows south from the slopes of Mt. Wrangell (14,163 ft.), an active volcano. The trail, more of a road at times, is well-defined and easy to follow. Creek crossings are generally knee deep or less, except for the Kotsina River which is very swift and more than waist deep. Watch out for loose gravel on some of the long downhills. Because of the overall length of this trail, strength and endurance will be needed.

Travel about 13.5 miles east of Chitina on the McCarthy Road to the small community of Strelna, where the Nugget Creek/Kotsina Road heads out to the left. Park here, off the road and out of traffic's way. A public right-of-way winds through several homesteads. Please respect private property. In 2.5 miles a trail to the right crosses Strelna Creek and becomes the Nugget Creek Trail (see Nugget Creek). Do not turn, but continue, in a northwesterly direction. This trail travels across open country, dropping steeply into creeks, then climbing out of them, only to do it again. Several established camp sites can be found along the way. After almost 20 miles the trail rounds Hubbard Peak and begins to parallel the Kotsina River in an easterly direction up river. A bridge crossing the Kotsina River (mile 33.5) is out, preventing further travel.

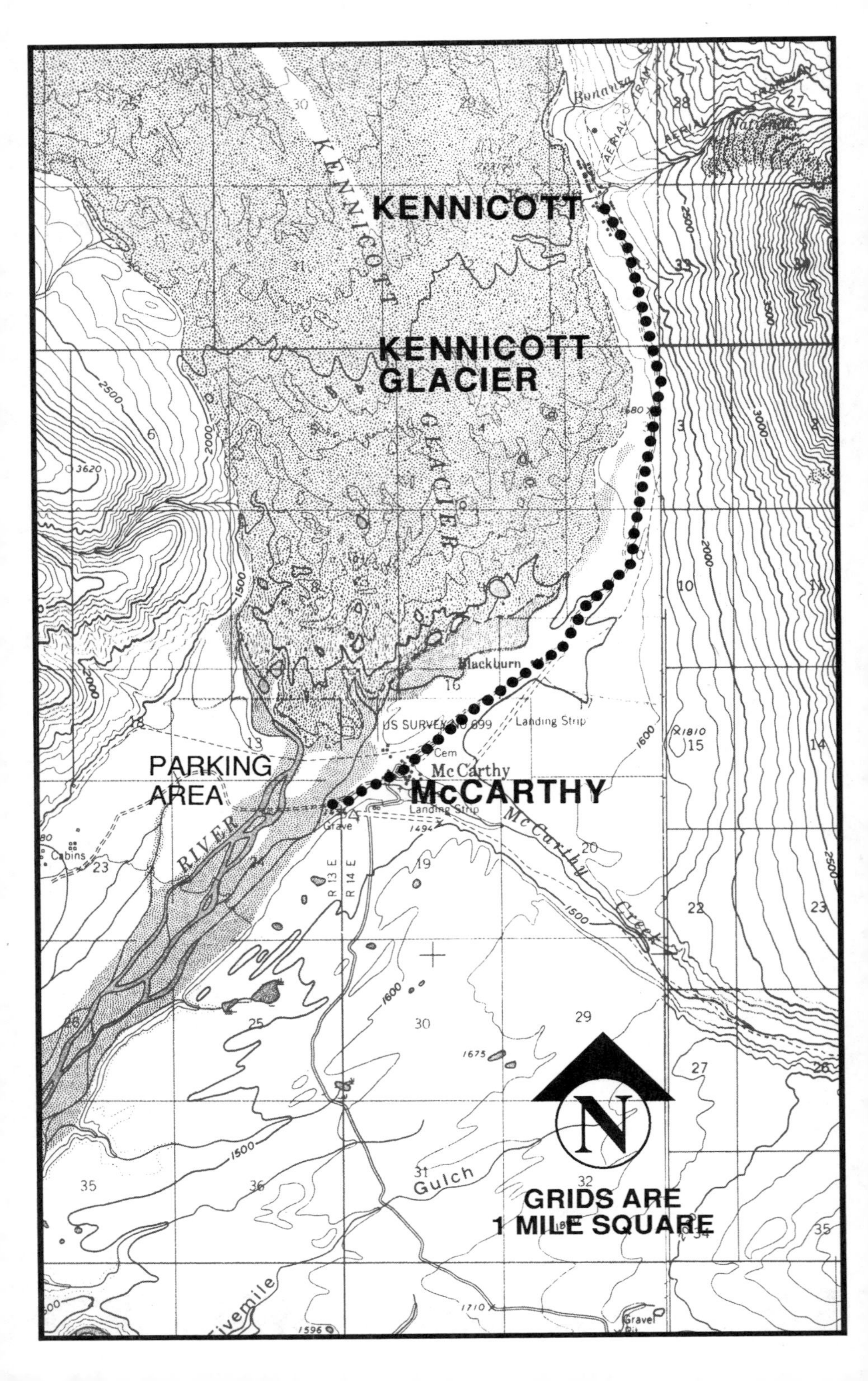
KENNICOTT
KENNICOTT GLACIER
PARKING AREA
McCARTHY
GRIDS ARE 1 MILE SQUARE
N
KENNICOTT
GLACIER
Blackburn
US SURVEY NO 699
Landing Strip
Cem
McCarthy
Landing Strip
Grave
McCarthy Creek
RIVER
Cabins
R 13 E
R 14 E
Gulch
Fivemile
Gravel Pit
Bonanza
AERIAL TRAM
AERIAL TRAM
National

trail 47

KENNICOTT MINE

An easy ride awaits the cyclist who wishes to explore the natural and historical beauty of McCarthy and Kennicott. Nestled deep within the 13-million acre Wrangell-St. Elias National Park and Preserve, this old mining district of the 1900s processed the world's richest find in copper ore. Above Kennicott are Jumbo and Bonanza mines, which can be reached by hikers, affording the visitor a sense of the rugged remoteness that faced the turn-of-the-century miners.

AT - A - GLANCE

TRAILHEAD: ....mile 60 McCarthy Rd.

FROM ANCHORAGE: ....316.5 miles

LENGTH OF TRAIL: .....9 miles round trip

RIDING TIME: ....2 to 4 hours

DIFFICULTY: 2.5

LOW POINT: ....1,400 ft.

HIGH POINT: ....2,000 ft.

ELEVATION GAIN: ....400 ft.

U.S.G.S. MAPS: ....McCarthy B-6, McCarthy 1 : 250,000

An abandoned railroad bed is the current route to the Kennicott Mine. It has a wide, maintained gravel surface with a 3 percent uphill grade. Cyclists visiting Kennicott will enjoy the benefits of having a bicycle. A long 8-mile walk (round trip) is transformed into a short, enjoyable ride, leaving more time to explore the magnificent surroundings. Please respect the private property of those in the area, including all the mine buildings.

Travel 60 miles east from Chitina to the end of the McCarthy Road (see McCarthy Road). Park in the upper parking lot. The lower one is known to flood during summer months, when a lake within the Kennicott Glacier breaks its natural dam. The Kennicott Mine Road is reached by crossing two hand-pulled cable trams across the glacial braids of the Kennicott River. Hooks on the down river side of the tram will accept bicycles but will scrape paint if not protected with some sort of padding. Finger gloves are recommended for pulling the tram. From the second tram, go left and then right, cycling a short distance to the McCarthy Museum — home to numerous historical photographs and artifacts of the region's mining past. Just south of here lies the community of McCarthy and the famous McCarthy Lodge. From the museum, bicycle north (left) 4 miles to the ghost town of town of Kennicott and the quaint Kennicott Glacier Lodge. A single-track trail continues for an additional 4 miles, taking the rider north along the rocky moraine of Root Glacier. Consider strapping on a pair of ice crampons with local guide Bob Jacobs (St. Elias Alpine Guides). For a fee he will take you on a guided tour of the mine ruins and trekking on an ancient river of ice.

chapter 8

WINTER TRAILS

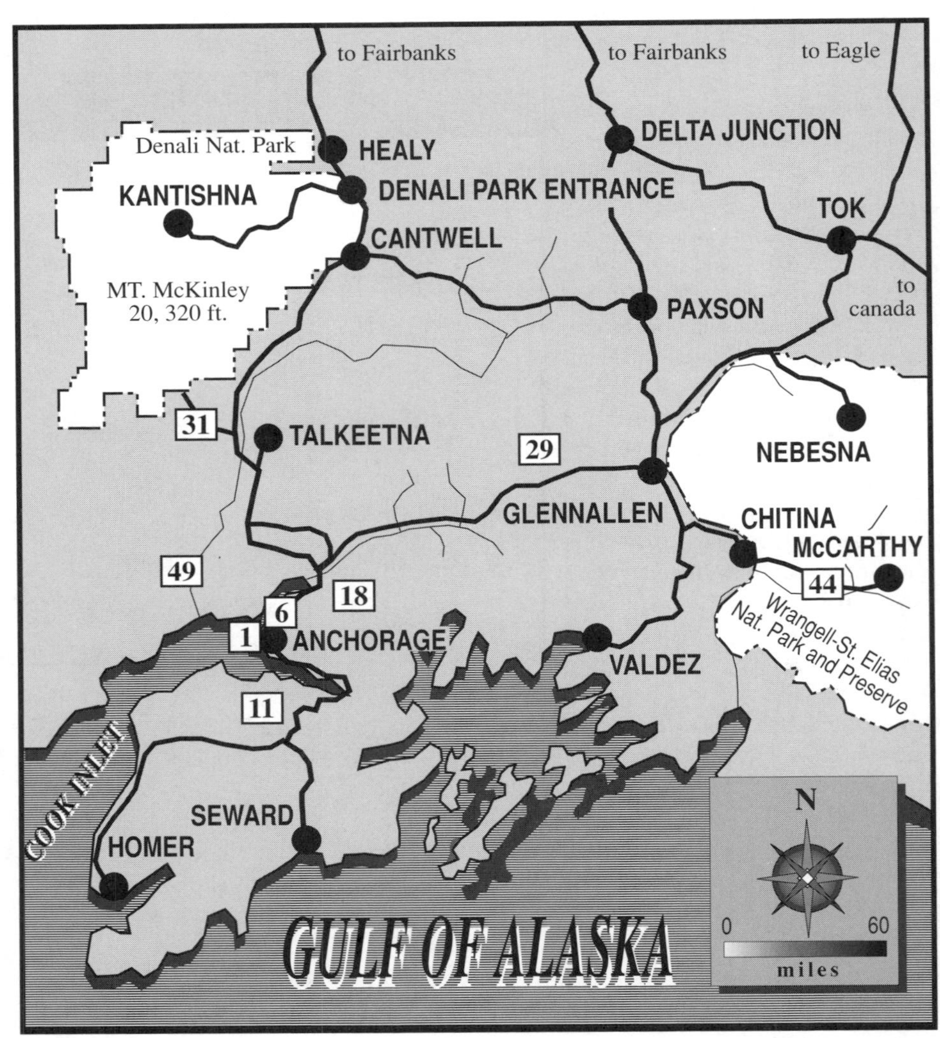

Snow machines travel is extensive in Alaska. These motorized machines are able to go almost anywhere when the ice and snow pack is deep enough to support their weight. Winter trails often go for great distances following major river systems. When the trails "set up" and become firm that's the time to haul out the bike and go backcountry winter riding.

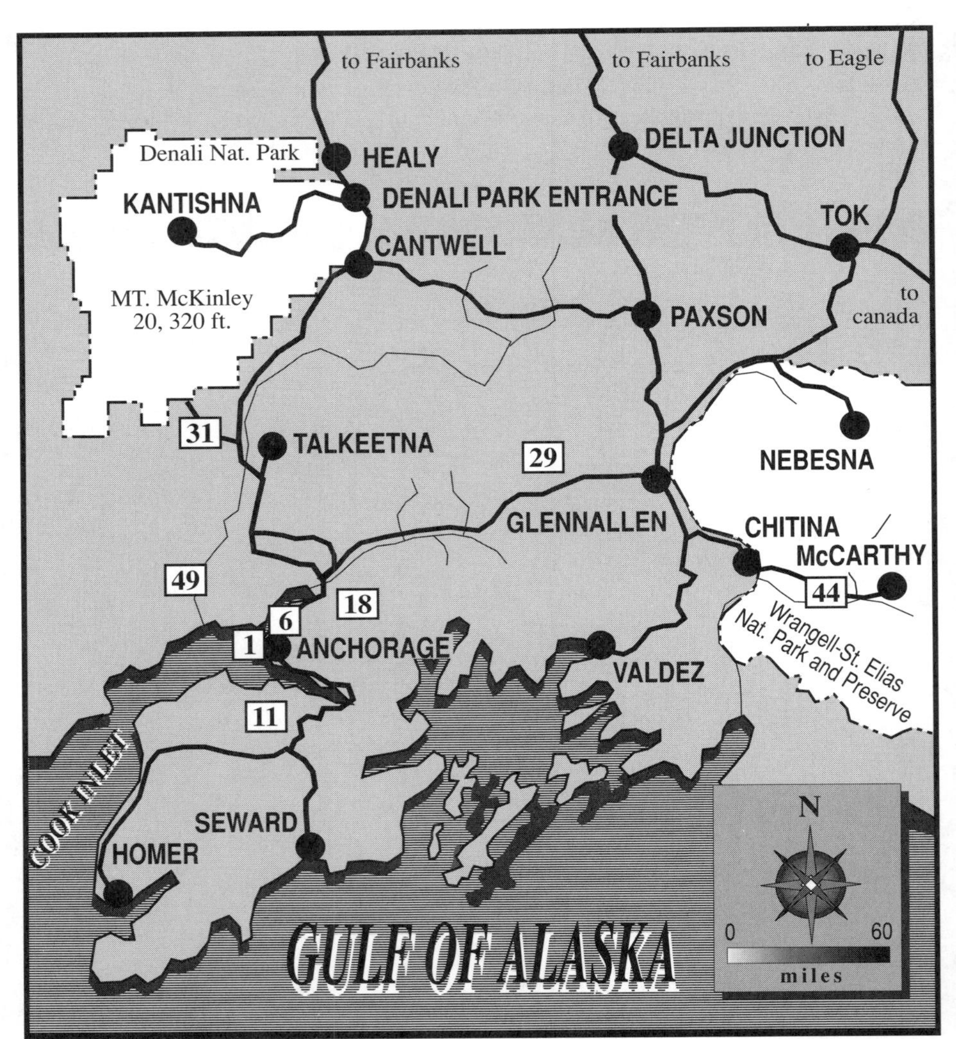
to Fairbanks
to Fairbanks
to Eagle
Denali Nat. Park
HEALY
DELTA JUNCTION
KANTISHNA
DENALI PARK ENTRANCE
TOK
CANTWELL
MT. McKinley
20, 320 ft.
PAXSON
to
canada
31
TALKEETNA
29
NEBESNA
GLENNALLEN
CHITINA
McCARTHY
49
44
18
6
1
ANCHORAGE
Wrangell-St. Elias
Nat. Park and Preserve
VALDEZ
11
COOK INLET
SEWARD
HOMER
N
0
60
miles
GULF OF ALASKA

trail 48

WINTER TRAILS

Blazing sunlight sparkles on ice crystals as the crunch of fat tires rolling on frozen trails penetrate the earmuffs. A musher and his team of trotters comes alongside. You exchange greetings and comment on the fine weather and firm trail. Cross frozen lakes and cycle up rivers of snow-covered ice. When conditions are right, backcountry winter cycling is a fantastic experience: fast, smooth and, at times, wonderfully eerie. Ice fog, wind drifts, snow-laden trees, long shadows and the northern lights paint the canvas before you. Consider loading the camping gear and donning head lamps for a fun-filled night ride and camp out.

AT - A - GLANCE

see each individual trail for this information

TRAILHEAD: .... varies, see text

FROM ANCHORAGE: .... varies

LENGTH OF TRAIL: .... varies

RIDING TIME: .... varies

DIFFICULTY: .... requires winter skills

LOW POINT: .... varies

HIGH POINT: .... varies.

ELEVATION GAIN: .... varies

U.S.G.S. MAPS: .... varies

Many times during the winter a combination of factors allow snow machine trails to "set up" and become hard-packed enough to allow winter mountain biking. Weather can change trail conditions quickly. You must be prepared for the worst at all times. Temperatures can fluctuate from 40 above to 40 below in less than 24 hours. High winds, breakable crust, and new snowfall are a few of the potential hazards that await those visiting the frozen backcountry. Begin with short rides, experimenting with different equipment and clothes. Standard bicycle water bottles freeze quickly, try using a "Camelback," which is worn on your back, where body heat keeps it from freezing. On long rides, carry extra clothes, a container of hot fluids, tools for field repairs and maps of the area. For those prepared, an enjoyable experience awaits.

The places to ride are where snowmobilers make tracks. Several of the summer trails featured in this book have snow machine use in winter. For example, Eklutna Lake, Petersville, Powerline Pass and Old Man Creek all are major snow machine routes. Other places to try include Big Lake (mile 52.3 Parks Hwy.) and Nancy Lake (mile 67.2 Parks Hwy.), where dozens of trails radiate in all directions, and the Iditarod Trail (see IditaSport). Many of the National Forest trails on the Kenai Peninsula allow snow machine use when snow cover permits. In addition, city bicycle paths are often ridable, particularly the Chester Creek Trail and the Tony Knowles Coastal Trail. Bicycles are not allowed on groomed ski trails or the Tudor Dog Tracks.

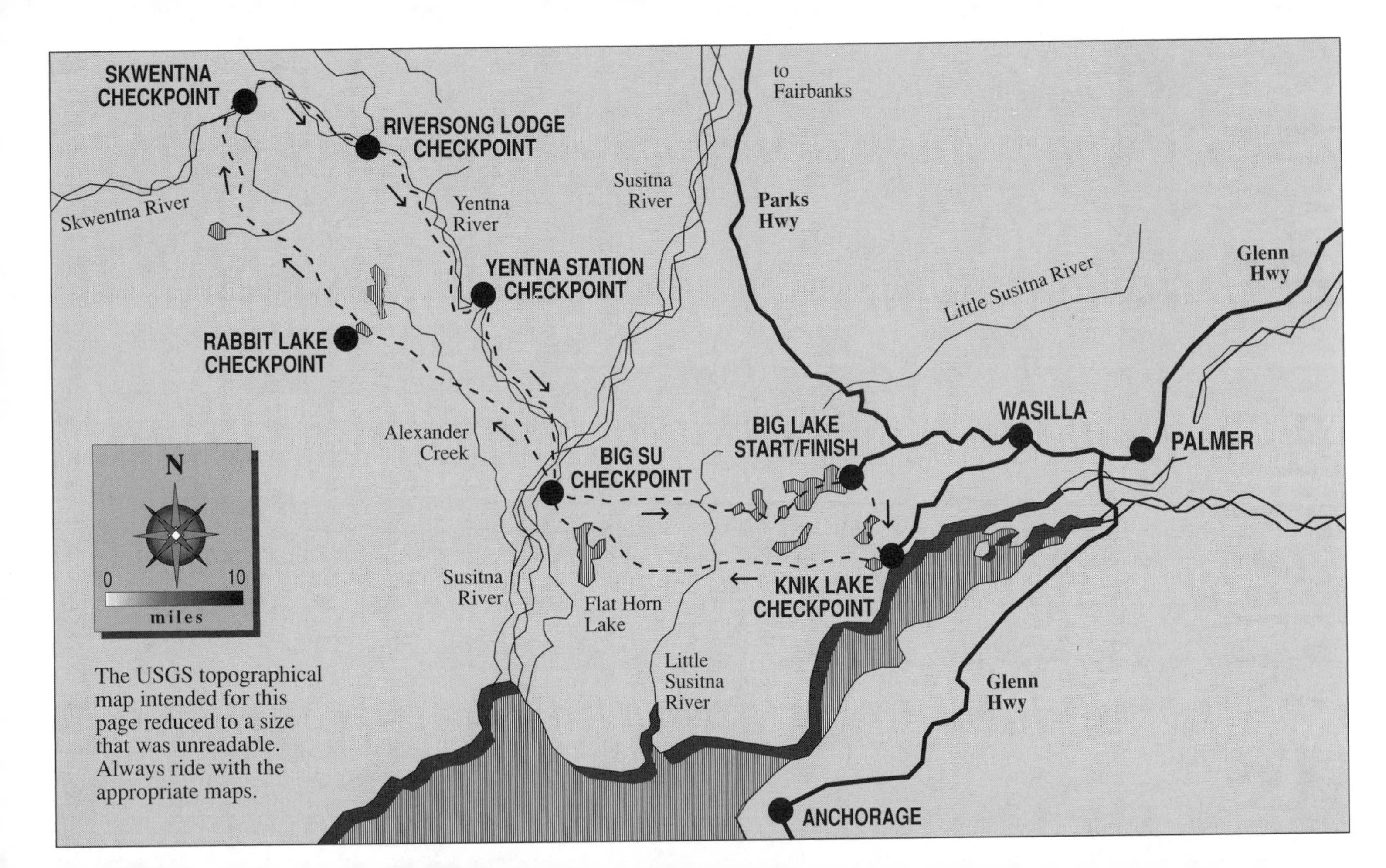
SKWENTNA CHECKPOINT
RIVERSONG LODGE CHECKPOINT
to Fairbanks
Susitna River
Parks Hwy
Skwentna River
Yentna River
YENTNA STATION CHECKPOINT
Glenn Hwy
Little Susitna River
RABBIT LAKE CHECKPOINT
WASILLA
BIG LAKE START/FINISH
PALMER
Alexander Creek
BIG SU CHECKPOINT
N
0
10
miles
Susitna River
Flat Horn Lake
KNIK LAKE CHECKPOINT
Little Susitna River
Glenn Hwy
ANCHORAGE
The USGS topographical map intended for this page reduced to a size that was unreadable. Always ride with the appropriate maps.

IDITASPORT

AT - A - GLANCE

TRAILHEAD: ....mile 13.3 Knik Rd.
FROM ANCHORAGE: ....55.5 miles
LENGTH OF TRAIL: ...200 miles round trip
RIDING TIME: ....1 to 4 days
DIFFICULTY: .....5 (winter skills required)
LOW POINT: ....50 ft.
HIGH POINT: ....250 ft.
ELEVATION GAIN: ....200 ft.
U.S.G.S. MAPS: ....Tyonek and Anchorage 1 : 250,000

Each year more than 60 athletes gather on frozen Big Lake, Alaska to await the start of IditaSport, a human powered ultra-marathon. This 200-mile winter wilderness race is the combination of the Iditaski, Iditashoe and Iditabike. An international cast of top athletes, curious Lower 48ers and adventure-seeking locals assemble to test themselves and their winter skills. New and interesting innovations are unveiled each year. Four and six-wheeled bicycles, home-made drinking systems and bicycles with skis on the front wheel have been tried.

It is the hard-pack snow machine trails that allow mountain bikers to traverse a snow-covered region that is more home to moose than man. When conditions are right, cross lakes, swamps and ride up and down river. The visitor to this country should be self-sufficient in temperatures as cold as -50. High winds, new snowfall, soft conditions, moose holes, steep hills, blazing northern lights, moonbeams and other distractions challenge the cyclist.

Drive north of Anchorage to mile 42.2 of the Parks Highway, turn left at a traffic light onto Knik Road. Drive down 13.3 miles to Knik Lake. Start here, eliminating an often-confusing trail from Big Lake, the official start. Although the exact route changes yearly, this description follows the 1991 race course, starting with Knik Lake, the first of seven checkpoints. Numerous side trails depart from the main. Talk with locals about trail conditions and directions, which change each year. Cycle across Knik Lake and enter rolling woods on the original Iditarod race trail. This well-used route meanders, crossing Burma Road, the Little Susitna River, Flat Horn Lake and the "Dismal Swamps," as it makes its way to the second checkpoint, Big Susitna River (mile 40). Cross the Big Susitna river and begin the "back section" to Rabbit Lake (mile 60). Joe and Norma Delia's Cabin at Skwentna is the finish for the snowshoe division and halfway point for all others. Cycle down the Yentna River, stopping at checkpoints Riversong Lodge (mile 120) and Yentna Station (mile 140). Revisit the Big Susitna checkpoint before cycling down the Irondog Trail (an 1,100-mile Snow machine race course) to Big Lake Lodge, the official finish.

AGENCY INFORMATION

STATE

ALASKA PUBLIC LANDS INFORMATION CENTER: 605 West 4th Ave., Suite 105 Anch., Ak. 99501 (907) 271-2737

ALASKA DEPT. OF FISH AND GAME: Main Office (907) 344-0541, SPORTS FISHING DIVISION 333 Raspberry Rd. Anch., Ak. 99518 (907) 276-2219

ALASKA STATE PARKS: Pouch 10-7001 Anch., Ak. 99510-7001 Main Office (907) 762-2617, Chugach Office (907) 345-5014, Kenai Office (907) 262-5581, Mat Su-Valdez-Copper River Office (907) 745-3975

CHUGACH STATE PARKS: HC 52, Box 899 Indian, Ak. 99504 Glacier Station (907) 345-5014, Recorded trail conditions (907) 694-6391

PORT GRAHAM CORPORATION: (907) 248-2212

FEDERAL

CHUGACH NATIONAL FOREST: 201 E. 9th Ave., Suite 206 Anch., Ak. 99501 Rangers Station (907)783-3242, Cabin Reservations (907) 271-2500

DENALI NATIONAL PARK AND PRESERVE: P.O. Box 9, Denali National Park. Alaska 99755 (907) 683-2294, Recorded Message (907) 683-2686

U.S. BUREAU OF LAND MANAGEMENT (BLM) Public Affairs Office (907) 271-5555, Glennallen Office (907) 822-3217

U.S. FISH AND WILDLIFE SERVICE: Anchorage Office (907) 786-3487

U.S. GEOLOGICAL SURVEY (U.S.G.S.): TOPOGRAPHICAL MAPS 4230 University Dr., Room 101 Anch., Ak. 99508-4664 (907) 786-7011

WRANGELL-St.ELIAS NATIONAL PARK AND PRESERVE: PARK HEAD-QUARTERS Mile 105, Old Richardson Hwy. P.O. Box 29 Glennallen, Ak. 99588 (907) 822-5234, Chitina Ranger Station (907) 823-2205

AGENCY INFORMATION

ANCHORAGE

MUNICIPALITY OF ANCHORAGE: PARKS AND RECREATION P.O. Box 196650 Anch., Ak. 99519 (907) 343-4474 or (907) 248-4346

ALASKA WILDERNESS STUDIES PROGRAM: University of Alaska. Anchorage 2533 Providence Dr. Anch., Ak. 99508 (907) 786-1468

ARCTIC BICYCLE CLUB OF ALASKA: RACING, TOURS, SAFETY AND EDUCATION, P.O. Box 140269 Anch., Ak. 99514, Mountain Bike Hotline (907) 694-0900

BICYCLE STORES: Arirang Bicycles (907) 522-1451, The Bicycle Shop (907) 272-5219, Breakaway Sports (907) 561-2453, Gary Kings (907) 272-5401, The Bicycle Dept. of the Motor Cycle Shop (907) 561-1311, REI (907) 272-4565, R&R Bicycle Fitness Store (907) 276-8536

CYCLES NORTH: BICYCLE SKILLS, SAFETY AND TOURS, 1102 W. 30th Anch., Ak. 99503 (907) 561-0799

LTR TRAINING SYSTEMS: Survival Training Consultants (Learn To Return), 3748 Chaffee Circle Anch., Ak. 99503 (907) 248-5010

FRAME BUILDERS: ICICYLE CYCLES (907) 243-0049, WELD SPECIALTIES (907)333-5255

USEFUL BOOKS

FEILD GUIDES

A FIELD GUIDE TO ALASKAN WILDFLOWERS by Verna E. Pratt, Alaskakrafts Publishing, Anch., Ak. 1989

A GUIDE TO THE BIRDS OF ALASKA by Robert H. Armstrong, Alaska Northwest Publishing Company, Anch., Ak. 1973

BACKPACKER'S DIGEST by Cheri Elliot, DBI Books, Northfield 1981

SOFT PATHS: HOW TO ENJOY THE WILDERNESS WITHOUT HARMING IT by Bruce Hampton and Dave Cole, Stackpole Books, Harrisburg, Pa. 1988

WILDLIFE IDENTIFICATION POCKET GUIDE Outdoor Empire Publishing, Inc. Seattle, Washington 1986

TRAVEL GUIDES

ALASKA WILDERNESS TRAILS by James Riley and Ted Schachle, S&R Publishing, Anch., Ak. 1989

EXPLORING McKINLEY NATIONAL PARK by Richard W. Montague, Alaska Travel Publications, Anch., Ak. 1973

55 WAYS TO THE WILDERNESS IN SOUTHCENTRAL ALASKA by Helen Nienhueser and Nancy Simmerman, The Mountaineers, Seattle, Washington 1985

MATANUSKA-SUSITNA BOROUGH TRAILS INVENTORY by the Matanuska-Susitna Borough, September 1987

THE DENALI ROADSIDE GUIDE, by Kim Haeacox, Lorraine Press, Salt Lake City 1986

THE MILEPOST, Alaska Northwest Publishing Company, Anch., Ak. 1991

USEFUL BOOKS

FIRST AID • SURVIVAL

A SERIOUS GUIDE TO SURVIVAL AND CAMPING by Richard H. Graves, Schocken Books, New York 1972

FIRST AID FOR BACKPACKERS by Lowell J. Thomas and Joy L. Sanderson, Holt, Rinehart and Wilson, New York 1978

HYPOTHERMIA: KILLER OF THE UNPREPARED by Thedore Lathrop, M.D., Mazamas, Portland, OR. 1972

THE POCKET DOCTOR by Stephen Bezruchka, MD., The Mountaineers, Seattle, Washington 1988

TOM BROWNS FIELD GUIDE TO WILDERNESS SURVIVAL by Tom Brown Jr. and B. Morgan, Berkley Books, New York 1983

HISTORICAL

A HISTORY OF MINING ON THE KENAI PENINSULA by Mary J. Barry, Alaska Northwest Publishing Company, Anch., Ak. 1 973

THE COPPER SPIKE by Lone E. Jason, Alaska Northwest Publishing Company, Anch., Ak. 1984

WHEELS ON ICE: BICYCLING IN ALASKA 1898-1908 by Terrence Cole, Alaska Northwest Publishing Company, Anch., Ak. 1985

WRANGELL-ST ELIAS: INTERNATIONAL MOUNTAIN WILDERNESS by Gill Mull and George Herben, Alaska Geographic Society, Vol. 8, No. 1, 1988

ABOUT THE AUTHOR

Richard Larson, a resident of Anchorage since 1966, grew up hiking and camping throughout southcentral Alaska. His love for back country travel grew when he was introduced to mountain biking. Richard sees himself as "a speed hiker with expensive tennis shoes." He has worked as an professional mountain bike guide and is active with the Arctic Bicycle Club of Alaska (ABC). As Tour Director for the mountain bike division of the ABC, he has organized dozens of group rides for all skill levels. Over 100 trails were explored to provide the selection found in this trail guide. His efforts in exploring backcountry trails has earned him the title of "Mountain Bike Guru" by The Anchorage Times. Richard also is an avid winter cyclist. He competed in the Iditabike and was the assistant director of the first IditaSport, a human-powered ultra-marathon for bikers, skiers and snowshoers.